IN MEDUSA'S GAZE

STILL LIFE PAINTINGS FROM
UPSTATE NEW YORK MUSEUMS

ALBANY INSTITUTE OF HISTORY AND ART

ALBRIGHT-KNOX ART GALLERY, BUFFALO

EVERSON MUSEUM OF ART, SYRACUSE

HERBERT F. JOHNSON MUSEUM OF ART, CORNELL UNIVERSITY, ITHACA

MEMORIAL ART GALLERY OF THE UNIVERSITY OF ROCHESTER

MUNSON-WILLIAMS-PROCTOR INSTITUTE MUSEUM OF ART, UTICA

Essay by Norman Bryson, Harvard University

Catalogue by Bernard Barryte, Memorial Art Gallery

ORGANIZED BY MEMORIAL ART GALLERY OF THE UNIVERSITY OF ROCHESTER

Editor: Andrea P. A. Belloli
Design: Dunn and Rice Design, Inc.
Printing: Upstate Litho, Inc.
Production Coordinator: Deborah Rothman

This book was published on the occasion of the exhibition
In Medusa's Gaze: Still Life Paintings from Upstate New York Museums,
organized by Bernard Barryte. This exhibition is supported in part
by a grant from the New York State Council on the Arts.

Schedule of the Exhibition:

Memorial Art Gallery of the University of Rochester,
December 7, 1991 - February 2, 1992

Munson-Williams-Proctor Institute Museum of Art, Utica,
February 22 - April 19, 1992

Everson Museum of Art, Syracuse,
May 15 - August 30, 1992

Herbert F. Johnson Museum of Art,
Cornell University, Ithaca,
October 2 - November 29, 1992

Albany Institute of History and Art,
December 18, 1992 - February 14, 1993

Albright-Knox Art Gallery, Buffalo,
March 19 - May 2, 1993

Library of Congress Cataloging-in-Publication Data

In Medusa's Gaze: still life paintings from upstate New York museums/
    essay by Norman Bryson; catalogue by Bernard Barryte.
        p. cm.
    "Organized by Memorial Art Gallery of the University of
Rochester, 1991."
    Exhibition held at various institutions between Dec. 7, 1991
and May 2, 1993.
    Includes bibliographical references and index.
    ISBN 0-918098-05-X:
    1. Still-life painting—Exhibitions. 2. Art museums—New York
(State)—Exhibitions. I. Bryson, Norman, 1949-. II. Barryte,
Bernard, 1949- . III. University of Rochester. Memorial Art Gallery.
ND1390.I5 1991
758'.4'074747—dc20   91-26148
                                                    CIP

Negra la natura morta e un confessare che non

si capisce la pittura, giacche e nella natura morta che la pittura si

manifesta in cho che la costituisce che afferma la sua essenza.

To deny the existence of the still life is to confess

that you know nothing about painting. It is through the still life that

painting can establish its true nature and affirm its being.

HENRY DES PRURAUX
"Della natura morta"

CONTENTS

PREFACE 4

ACKNOWLEDGMENTS 5

IN MEDUSA'S GAZE 6
Norman Bryson

COLOR PLATES 31

CATALOGUE 43
Bernard Barryte

CATALOGUE NOTES 128

INDEX 136

PREFACE

olatile art markets, political controversies, and severe financial cutbacks are but a few of the dilemmas facing art museums today. As budgets tighten, it is becoming apparent that museums must develop new strategies in order to meet these new demands. The Albany Institute of History and Art, the Albright-Knox Art Gallery, the Everson Museum of Art, the Herbert F. Johnson Museum of Art, the Memorial Art Gallery, and the Munson-Williams-Proctor Institute Museum of Art have been in the forefront, establishing collaborative programs that address the escalating costs of temporary exhibitions.

In Medusa's Gaze: Still Life Paintings from Upstate New York Museums is the fifth in a remarkable series of collaborative exhibitions that began in 1974. The current exhibition explores the development of still life painting from its inception in the seventeenth century through modern manifestations in the twentieth century. Selected from the permanent collections of the six upstate museums, the exhibition reveals the scope, diversity, and quality of these institutions' holdings.

While we salute the original vision of the museum directors, I want to thank my consortium colleagues for their continued commitment to this significant collaboration: Christine M. Miles (Albany Institute of History and Art); Douglas G. Schultz (Albright-Knox Art Gallery); Thomas W. Leavitt (Herbert F. Johnson Museum of Art); Ronald A. Kuchta (Everson Museum of Art); and Paul D. Schweizer (Munson-Williams-Proctor Institute Museum of Art). In addition, the scholarly efforts of Bernard Barryte, Curator of European Art, Memorial Art Gallery; Norman Bryson, Professor of Art History, Harvard University; and the curatorial staffs at the participating museums have resulted in a splendid exhibition and important catalogue. Finally, I want to thank Deborah Rothman, Public Relations Manager, Memorial Art Gallery, for her key role in the publication of this catalogue.

Grant Holcomb
Director
Memorial Art Gallery

ACKNOWLEDGMENTS

his exhibition would not have been possible without the cooperation and generosity of the trustees, directors, curators, and registrars of our consortium partners. The exhibition was enriched by the collaboration of Norman Bryson, who generously contributed advice and insight as well as the essay that binds the paintings drawn from the consortium collections into a cohesive whole.

Colleagues and friends without whom the catalogue entries would have been considerably poorer include Janet Abromowitz, Joan Baden, Marcia Blacklin (who generously offered translations from Dutch), Marlene Hamann, Kari E. Horowicz, Sona Johnston, William Johnston, Barbara Krulik, Judith O'Toole, Ruth Pasquine, Grace Seiberling, Scott Sullivan, Carol Forman Tabler, Patricia Tice, Thayer C. Tolles, José G. Moya Valgañón, Judy Colleschan van Wagner, Bruce Weber, John Wilmerding, Eric Zafran, and Federico Zeri. I am indebted as well to Judith Throm and the staff of the Archives of American Art, Washington, D.C.; Burton Fredericksen and the staff of the Provenance Index, Getty Art History Information Program, Santa Monica; and the staffs of the Frick Art Reference Library and the library of the Museum of Modern Art, New York. The entries could not have been written without the assistance of Stephanie Frontz, Katherine Kinsky, and Cynthia van Ness at the Art Library, University of Rochester. Gratitude is due as well to the university's interlibrary loan librarians and their colleagues throughout the United States. Their efficiency and forbearance were equally admirable. Even more than the authors, readers must be grateful to our thoughtful and exacting editor, Andrea P. A. Belloli.

At the Memorial Art Gallery, Marie Via, Curatorial Assistant; Lee Moulton, Registrar; Daniel Knerr, Assistant Registrar; Kathy Ertsgaard, Curatorial Department Secretary; and Lu Harper, Librarian, deserve special thanks for their support and good humor. Thanks are also due Christine Garland, Assistant Director for Development, and Joan Yanni, Public Relations Secretary. Deborah Rothman and the heroic Shirley Wersinger oversaw the publication—can martyrs be thanked?

Throughout this project, my wife's patience and encouragement have been of inestimable value.

Bernard Barryte
Curator of European Art
Memorial Art Gallery

Norman Bryson

I

o present an array of still life paintings produced in several differ-
ent countries (the Netherlands, the United States, France) over a
considerable span of time (from the seventeenth to the twentieth
century) is to raise immediately the question of *genre*. What do
these images have in common that enables one to say—without
feeling that a definition is being unduly strained—that they are all
part of a single, coherent branch of painting? If each of the works shown here participates in a common tradition of still life, what can be said about the tradition as a
whole? What, generically, takes place in the encounter between a painter and a
collection of inanimate objects, *nature morte*? What can the genre accomplish that
is distinct from what may be accomplished by the other classical genres of Western
painting—history painting, portraiture, landscape?

To these questions various kinds of answer are possible, according to the particular
intellectual framework that is brought to bear on the discussion: anthropology, social
history, the histories of individual painters or motifs, economics, theology, gender
studies, psychoanalysis. There are a great many ideas that may usefully be invoked in
the analysis of still life. With the present exhibition, my colleague Bernard Barryte and
I have been guided by a concern with still life's particular ways of portraying the visual
field, its unique style of managing attention (both the painter's and the viewer's), the
characteristic operations that still life performs on the facts of sight. Our focus has been
on still life's presentation both of the things of the world and of how those things are
seen within the genre, how the genre looks out at the world, how its mode of vision
differs from that of history painting or portraiture or landscape. The aspect we have
tried to place in the foreground, in a word, is still life's "gaze."

That the gaze of still life differs radically from the gaze, first of all, of history painting becomes clear when one considers the definitive importance to history painting of
narration. At the heart of history painting lie texts and stories: the events of the scrip-
tures, the legends of the gods, the deeds of heroes, the crises of history. As a genre,
history painting gravitates toward actions, to those momentous actions through which
what is human touches the divine, through which the destinies of nations and the fates
of individuals become manifest. Its narratives portray those times and places in which
the material world is crossed by forces that raise it to a level of intensity where the
narrative act becomes both possible and essential. In a sense, still life is just the opposite.
At its heart lies a vision of the world stripped of its narratives, the world minus its
capacity to generate narrative interest.

To narrate is to name that which is unique: the singular actions of exceptional
individuals, the critical moments of a personal or national history. But still life shows
the world as it persists below this threshold of the unique, the uneventful base of
ordinary life where things exist not as singularities but as repetitions and routines, the
daily round of mortal life summed up in the unassuming culture of the table. Narrative
works hard to explain why any particular story is worth telling—because the actions it
depicts are heroic or wonderful, frightening or ignoble, cautionary or instructive. The
whole principle of story-telling is in jeopardy if the hearer is able to object: "So what?"
But still life loves the "so what?" It shows the things it shows not because they are
associated with exceptional events; indeed, still life involves a wholesale eviction of
the Event. With history painting, the existence of the picture is always justified by the
prior importance of what is shown. But with still life, this permanent raison d'être or
alibi is absent.

By default, what still life shows is the gaze. Since most of the objects in still life
tend not to supply their own rationale for representation, what emerges when they are
depicted is the act of representation as *bestowed*, unearned, as *conferred*, gratuitously,

upon objects that exactly lack the power to summon representation. With history painting, the image is in a sense always secondary to its subject, like a client or a dependent who taps the primary wealth of intrinsic greatness. With still life, it is the objects that are cast in the dependent role. There is nothing inevitable or preordained about their being depicted at all. Perhaps one can say that, with history painting, representation is always already justified; with still life, representation is not justified *yet*. Something else must happen before the act of making these things the objects of representation becomes fully understandable. They have to be seen, and seen in such a way that a new dimension of value is made visible within them. It is precisely the humility, ordinariness, or abjectness of still life's objects that allows the gaze to represent itself and its own powers, as such.

The centrality of the gaze to still life is again confirmed if still life is compared with portraiture. The viewer who is able to respond to a portrait by asking, "Why paint *this* one?" threatens the genre at its foundations; portraits must be able to establish why the sitter is worthy of being painted, or they are nothing. That few portraits do in fact collapse in this way is testimony to portraiture's intimate involvement with idealization. The human figure is enhanced through association with whatever the cultural milieu proposes as the scale of values, whether authority, knowledge, prestige, virtue, wealth, or personal beauty. In so far as the sitter participates in such values, the portrait is justified; it may even be justified negatively, as in those portraits that explore the failures of idealization, where the sitter is measured against the values (of beauty, authority, virtue, and so forth) and is found variously wanting. Through its capacity to associate the human figure with cultural value, portraiture involves the viewer's gaze in responses of judgment and sympathy which supply the genre with all it might need by way of rationale.

The sitter's form is projected into a field which, in more complex forms of portraiture, multiplies the levels of the imagery in play. As Thomas Ruff (following Roland Barthes) has put it: "[Portraiture] is a closed field of force where four different images overlap, question each other, and distort each other. In front of [the canvas] people are what they think they are, what they pretend to be or want other people to believe, the person [whom the painter] thinks they are, and the person the artist uses to present his art—all at the same time."[1] If portraiture so rarely appears gratuitous, this is because its essential move is one in which the sitter enjoins the viewer to behold his or her likeness. To whatever extent and through whatever means, portraits are always prepared to meet the spectator. Essentially *advertent* in form, they show their sitters as turning a persona, decked out and waiting, toward the one who will come and view. Hence the amicability of the portrait, which opens in advance a path of entrance for the viewer to follow, in the manner of a social introduction.

Still life knows nothing of this; it is the genre in which (again, with exceptions) there appear no people, only things. If absence of the human figure is the fundamental condition of still life, one consequence is that its gaze is never socialized as it is in portraiture, is never channeled through a social field that manages or moderates its energies by subduing them to interpersonal exchange. In portraiture, the gaze is tempered by the fact that its object is always another person: this binds the force of the gaze to the conventions that a particular historical milieu establishes as appropriate forms of social looking. Still life is able to move in on the surfaces of its objects with unmitigated intensity, seeking out the minutest particulars, its avidity unchecked by the objects it scrutinizes. In portraiture, where the gaze enters a social circuit of exchange, such scrutiny would appear as intrusive or violent, but the possibility is held at bay by the mutual social presence of sitter, painter, and viewer. In the more complex forms of portraiture which Ruff describes—where in addition to the actual image of the sitter, further "imaginary" images are in play—the gaze is absorbed even more deeply into the ego's social theater. What structures it now are phantasmatic alongside actual images, images that "overlap, question, and distort" one another. Passing through this interface, the movement of the gaze becomes a matter of intricate deflections and reflections. But still life rarely generates this kind of complexity. Existing outside the social theater, it directly hones in on the objects it paints, without inhibition or detention by another social creature's power to capture and manipulate its force. In still life, the gaze appears openly, nakedly, without reservation.

The same might, perhaps, be said of landscape painting. Though elements of narrative and the presence of figures may be combined with landscape, that the figures are presented as *contained* within the landscape, and that visual description is typically raised above narration, enables landscape, like still life, to thematize and dramatize its own particular mode of vision as such. What particularly distinguishes its gaze from that of still life are factors of scale, depth of field, and aperture or frame.

Landscape is concerned with a gaze that opens, still life with a gaze that closes. With nearly all still life, a convention is observed that ensures that we stop asking questions of what might lie "beyond" the far edge of the surface (table, desk, shelf) on which the objects are displayed. A blank vertical plane rises up behind the furthermost surface, blocking the scene's potential depths. Sometimes the plane is actual, a wall or curtain; sometimes it is only virtual, a monochrome screen standing in the way of all recession, like the "edge of the world" in medieval maps: beyond, space simply ceases to exist. The convention that brackets out spatial recession creates an enclosure, a bounded arena, within which the gaze can concentrate its energies. With landscape painting, the spatial conventions work in quite the opposite direction. There, the gaze is lured away from the subject, out into greater and greater distances; if landscape is a camera, the lens tends to be set at infinity. Curiously, the space may come toward the viewer, but it never arrives; a convention cuts it off at the edges of the frame, especially the lower edge. In the real world, the landscape comes right up to us; there is, of course, no edge or boundary that slices it off. What the convention enables is landscape's representation of a gaze that moves through an indefinitely large number of planes and great depth of field. Its gaze is expansive, encompassing, long-sighted. As the vistas open out, there is a progressive loss of detail; vision finally reaches the limits of the particulars that may be seen, and represented, in the middle and far distance.

The opposite convention in still life—blocking distance—enables the possibility of progressive *recovery* of detail. Even the furthest object in still life is still close enough for its surfaces (if the painter chooses) to be recorded with minute attention to its specificity. With landscape, details drain out of the image with each recession in the depth of field. With still life, it becomes possible to prevent this leakage of detail from the visual field, to enclose and gather all of that field without loss. If in landscape painting, vision disperses into the world, dissipating as it travels out from the center of sight, in still life, vision concentrates and gathers the world into itself, through a gaze that stills and distills, a medusal gaze able, perhaps, to capture and possess the visual in its entirety.

art of the fascination of the earliest still life paintings is their discovery that, under the conditions of enclosure and concentration which the genre permits, it is possible for visual information to be poured into an image to the point of *saturation*.[2] Recording the findings of the gaze can be pushed to a pitch of intensity unavailable to the other branches of visual art. Still life enables images to be made that portray vision's work upon the things of the world without distraction or dilution.

In the early decades of the seventeenth century, there appeared—almost simultaneously, and in different countries—a historically new form of the image, marked by an unprecedentedly high concentration of visual data. In Spain, the *bodegones* of Juan Sánchez Cotán (1561-1627; fig. 1) took the humble contents of a larder (quince, cabbage, melon, and cucumber) and articulated their forms with such superabundance of detail that the simple forms became increasingly complex and intricate, to the point where the viewer recognizes the objects without difficulty yet cannot truthfully say he or she had ever seen them fully before rediscovering them in Cotán's paintings.[3] In Italy, Caravaggio (1573-1610) approached still life as a species of trompe l'oeil, deceiving the eye into accepting his *Basket of Fruit* (ca. 1598; Milan, Ambrosiana) as "real."[4] And in the Netherlands, still life painting acquired almost at once the look of hyperreality which remained central to it throughout the seventeenth and into the eighteenth century.

Yet with Dutch still life, visual saturation is only one aspect of the image. Equally important to the development of the genre was saturation of the image by the word.[5] For instance, in the *Still Life* by Jan Davidsz. de Heem (fig. 2; pl. 1), each surface is depicted with microscopic clarity.[6] Shells are portrayed, not as solid or "sculpted" forms, but as if constructed out of individual sedimented layers, tiers of colored *laminae*; a citrus is analyzed, not as a rounded volumetric shape, but as a waxy, translucent skin, complicated by pores, indentations, and blemishes. All of the objects are handled with the same exhaustive attention to detail (though much of this intensity is lost in reproduction). Yet at the same time, each of the objects takes part in a complex allegory. The oysters stand for gluttony and concupiscence; the smoldering wick and sulphur stick are reminders of the brevity of life and its sensual pleasures; the orange may represent the fruit of the Tree of Knowledge and the Fall from Eden. The knife symbolizes the virtue of moral discrimination; its black and white handle refers to the choice between good and evil; along its blade crawls a reptile, a further reference to Eden and the Fall. The loaf of bread and the *roemer* of wine point toward the Eucharist and promise of redemption; the pansies placed against the laurel branch connote the need for meditation in overcoming carnal desire and attaining spiritual victory.[7]

Or consider the emblematic meanings in David Bailly's *Vanitas with Negro Boy* (fig. 3; pl. 2). Each object adds cumulative weight to the picture's central idea of the nullity of pleasure: the hourglass, sundial, and candle invoke the fleeting passage of time; the dice and cards describe pleasure's baseness and vulgarity; the emblems of knowledge (books) and of the arts—sculpture (the putto), painting (the palette), and music (lute, guitar, recorder)—place the supposedly higher branches of human culture on a par with the other symbols of transience (tulips, the burning wick) and illusion (the bubbles). The convention is clear: the objects in the still life are depicted with extraordinary visual accuracy and acuity, yet they have been chosen not for their appearance but for the emblematic properties they possess.[8]

There can be no doubt that the discovery of the allegorical aspects of Dutch still life painting has been one of the major achievements of modern art history. Twentieth-century scholarship has alerted the educated viewer to a whole lexicon of emblems

Figure 1.
Juan Sánchez Cotán, *Quince, Cabbage, Melon, and Cucumber*, ca. 1602. Oil on canvas, 27 1/8 x 33 1/4 in. (69 x 84.5 cm). San Diego Museum of Art, Gift of Anne R. and Amy Putnam. Photo courtesy San Diego Museum of Art.

Figure 2.
Jan Davidsz. de Heem, *Still Life*, 1640s (cat. no. 3).

Figure 3.
David Bailly, *Vanitas with Negro Boy*, ca. 1650 (cat. no. 4).

that were once, for the original viewers of these works, a familiar repertoire of visual forms. For the modern viewer, however, there remains a crucial difficulty, which one might call that of the dual response. Looking at such still lifes seems to involve two quite different stages of reception: a "naive" stage, when the eye explores the images for their breathtaking realism and their dazzling visual design, and a "learned" stage, in which—with the help of art historical commentary—the forms appearing in the still life are correlated with their emblematic meanings (the dragonfly signifies the Resurrection, the pomegranate signifies *Ecclesia*, the melon signifies temperance, and so on). The problem is that between these two stages of the dual response, there seems to be no connection at all: they occur almost in different dimensions, different lobes of the brain. Under these circumstances, exploring the actual interconnectedness between the two registers at work in Dutch still life (realism and allegory) may be an urgent task.

It is important, first of all, to realize how heavily the symbolism of Dutch still life depends upon *arbitrariness* in its construction of the allegorical. In this it is very different from other kinds of symbolic language, both classical and Christian. When the figure of Hercules, for example, is recognized as an emblem of heroic prowess, the association is made easy by the fact that the bearer of the emblematic meaning actually possesses the designated qualities of heroism and strength: Hercules physically instantiates the meaning his figure represents. Aphrodite not only represents love; her appearance is itself erotic. In medieval representations of the Vices and Virtues, the figures directly embody their allegorical qualities: Envy is shriveled and destructive, Greed is obese, Charity is generous, Humility is humble. What enables the symbolism to seem natural and unforced is, of course, its reliance on the human body as an expressive matrix able to communicate an unlimited variety of abstract qualities through physical and gestural means. The symbolism in Dutch still life works quite differently. Instead of creating smooth liaisons between what is abstract and what is concrete, it installs distance and interval between them. Guesswork is impossible: there is nothing about the dragonfly that immediately suggests the Resurrection, nothing about pomegranates that makes *Ecclesia* readily spring to mind. *Only* a visual lexicon could reveal the connections between them.

The links between the physical objects and the ideas they are meant to represent is thus strangely oblique, or broken. Contemplation of still life allows contact with spiritual concepts, but the contact is far from direct. Looking at the pomegranate enables the viewer to entertain, mentally, the idea of *Ecclesia*, but the object that carries this meaning precisely does not participate in the idea (as Hercules participates in the idea of heroic strength). The objects in the still lifes by de Heem and Bailly make available to their viewer a number of transcendental ideas—the brevity of life, the snares of the flesh, the promise of redemption—but those ideas do not appear *in* the objects themselves, which remain inert, opaque, untransfigured. The allegorical object enables transcendence to enter the mind, yet that transcendence does not enter the objects themselves *qua* objects. In their *in*ability to participate in what they represent, they reveal the entire domain of objects as cut off from transcendence, as a fallen world that specifically cannot be galvanized or redeemed from the transcendental sphere the objects may point to but cannot join.[9]

Divorced from transcendence, the objects in allegorical still life remain desolately material. It is this persistence of the object as sheer materiality that is explored in Dutch still life's other register, in the cult of surfaces and textures. With every added quantum of detail, with every increase in saturation of the image by visual information, the object figures forth its fallen condition more strongly. Instead of opening on to transcendence, the object shows itself as a material cul-de-sac, a barrier of surfaces screening the viewer from the transcendental. *Vanitas* pictures, in particular, supply intimations of infinity, yet their purview cannot get beyond the nearest objects; these gather around the viewer like walls around a prisoner, with a force of inertia and gravity nothing can escape. The transcendental can be sensed only in the inability to reach it and, worst of all, in the grim downward slide of spiritual vision as it is drawn, by the still life, further and further into the trammeling surfaces of the world.

Think of the surfaces in de Heem and Bailly: the rainbow colors in the shell of an oyster, the beads of condensation on a cool *roemer* of wine, the translucent rind of a lemon, the sheen on a laurel leaf. They are surfaces the eye cannot fail to be drawn toward. Detail, and saturation by detail, create a magnetic field that draws vision into the canvas and holds it there. Still life does not, then, simply illustrate a "theme" of Vanity; it *enacts* Vanity, with each new viewer, through its own schism between transcendental meanings that are known but cannot be seen and a visual fascination that captivates the gaze and proves on the flesh of the eye the weakness of the flesh of the body.

Dutch still life of the seventeenth century obviously conceived of its function as moral and illustrative, yet what is perhaps hardest to grasp are the seriousness and consistency of its didactic enterprise. There are perhaps three chief ways in which it is possible for modern viewers to underestimate the moral aspect of this genre.

The first takes place in the modern dual response. Here, the viewer acknowledges that the painting has its didactic side, known through the emblematic meanings said to inhabit the image, but that moral aspect of the painting seems simply disconnected from what is actually presented on the picture's surface. One probable result is that the viewer will conclude that the emblematic dimension exists but is negligible; it belongs to a realm of art historical footnotes and pedantry; it does not intersect with the facts of vision.

The second underestimation occurs in art historical scholarship, whenever commentary announces the emblematic "equals sign": that the pomegranate equals *Ecclesia*, the melon equals temperance, the artichoke equals heavenly majesty, and so forth. The risk here is that of reducing the emblematic dimension of still life to a mere iconography, of missing the point that the signifier (dragonfly) exactly does not "equal" the signified (Resurrection), that it is the inadequacy of the symbol to what it symbolizes which counts as much as the lexical connection, that the "equations" are also *blocked*.

A third mode of underestimation is to conclude that still life's high moral purpose cannot have been meant altogether seriously, since although the sentiment that "all is vanity" may be respected in a sermon or tract, it is hard to be persuaded by a denunciation of worldly vanity when the denunciation takes the form of a luxury commodity obviously embroiled in worldliness hook, line, and sinker. Here the *vanitas* is likely to be thought of as an egregious example of bad faith or hypocrisy: it does not, and cannot, practice what it preaches. Its emblematic dimension is only a pretense—what proves the hollowness of the "moral" aspect is that the paintings lavish an attention on the surfaces of the world that is clearly at odds with the Jeremiah-like tone of world rejection through which Dutch viewers of the seventeenth century evidently eased their consciences about their taste for worldliness, and for worldly painting.

An alternative to these points of view is to consider Dutch still life as fundamentally structured by a gaze split between worldliness and transcendence. The visual field is presented in detail yet is also traversed by a system of spiritual meanings whose disconnection from what still life actually shows—the surfaces and textures of the object world—is tense and agonized (rather than simply odd or self-contradictory). That the relation between the objects and the meanings they carry is so arbitrary and oblique may be the essential feature of still life's symbolism. If this is so, critical commentary could do worse than attend to this broken or inadequate aspect of the paintings' symbolic work rather than deploy the (now heavily overused) "equals sign" as a panacea. As to the suspicion that still life cannot practice what it preaches—that its ability to denounce sensuality and luxury is fatally compromised by its own status as *objet de luxe*— the charge loses much of its force if we start from the hypothesis that the idea of *vanitas* is *deliberately* built on paradox and that the conflict between worldly ensnarement (embodied in its cult of visible surfaces) and spiritual meditation (embodied in its "invisible" emblems) is in fact the governing principle of the genre.

Still life does not state the theme of Vanity through some device of official and hypocritical allegory while secretly indulging in all the vices it criticizes. Rather, it *performs* Vanity through its seduction of the viewer's gaze; it proves worldliness's power through its own immersion in the world's textures and surfaces. By placing the transcendental beyond the reach of its own vision, it acts out the conflict between spiritual aspiration and material entrapment.[10] In the paintings by de Heem and Bailly, though the objects are sensually beguiling and opulent, there emerges nevertheless a kind of claustrophobia. Saturation with visual information gives the image a drilling quality, a *glare*; the endlessly detailed surfaces captivate, but also fatigue, the beholder's gaze. There is no relief from the sensation that vision is an appetite, a drive, with an avidity that nothing can satisfy, except another image and another after that, without end.

Dutch still life does not, then, conceive of its work in moral instruction as delivered from "on high," from an elevated vantage point, a pulpit, from which it condescends to speak of human carnality and sensuality as though these were the vices of others. Whatever moral authority it possesses derives from the way in which it proves its ideas of transcendence and fallenness in the first place upon itself: its primary testing ground of moral truth is its own activity. While the eventual goal is to influence and instruct the viewer, in order to earn the status of moral *exemplum* the image deals first with its own case, its own agonistic situation at a moral crossroad between spirit and worldliness or transcendence and visual desire.

Dutch still life's interest in including itself at the center of its own spiritual meditation is felt in a number of ways. The genre does not, for example, propose that the still life belongs in some space other than the space where the painter stands. In Leon Battista Alberti's theory of the image, the ruling idea had been that the painting opens on to another scene, a different world, seen as it were through a viewfinder or a proscenium arch; what goes on in that other, fictive space does not bear directly on the viewer's own situation. But here, no frame or threshold separates the painter from the representation.[11] Instead, painter and represented scene are shown as adjacent and continuous. Hence the motif of the artist's studio reflected back from the scene's inner depths: in Bailly's *Vanitas with Negro Boy*, the windows of the room where the still life was painted are reflected back by the bubbles, the studs of the chair, the polished metal of the candlestick; the artist's face is mirrored in the upper half of the hourglass. Self-reflectively, the still life portrays within itself the means—palette, brush—by which it has come into being, as well as an inset, quoted picture, the portrait miniature held in the boy's hand. The miniature seems to form curious internal rhymes with the bubbles and the hourglass, emblems of illusion and transience, and also with the picture as a whole, as though Bailly's painting were constantly working to implicate itself in its own moral injunctions, constantly applying the homily to its own situation.[12]

With Dutch still life, such self-reflexivity is not incidental but essential: it is because the pictures reflect in the first instance on their own moral perplexities that they are able to speak authentically, at first hand, about sensuality and transcendence in general. It is a profoundly self-conscious genre, able to operate at the same time on a primary and on a "meta" level—to depict a scene and also to comment on its own involvement and investment in depicting that scene. Interestingly, this tendency toward self-consciousness and self-analysis does not seem to diminish in the later phases of the tradition; it may even increase in intensity and sophistication.

What does seem to weaken is still life's reliance on emblematics as the principal means to reach the goal of moral self-scrutiny. It is still possible, with the *Still Life with Thistle* by Otto Marseus van Schriek (fig. 4; pl. 3), to recognize the familiar repertoire of emblems: the thistle, emblem of earthly sorrow and of Christ's Passion (the crown of thorns); the butterfly, emblem of the Resurrection; the lizard, emblem of the quest for salvation.[13] But the relation between the emblems and the image as a whole seems tenuous and muted when compared with the relation one finds in the works by de Heem and Bailly. With the earlier still lifes, the objects seem more closely and directly tied to their emblematic meanings: each of the dozen or so objects in the Bailly *vanitas* plays an equal part in elaborating the emblematic sentence, and it is clear that they have all been gathered there on the table precisely in order to produce the *vanitas* message (which comes across loud and clear). With the work by Marseus, however, it is as though the emblematic meanings were becoming faded and remote. Whereas the objects in the Bailly could *only* be encountered in their present configuration in the context of a *vanitas* picture, the thistle is something one might come across in nature: it has a reality independent of its allegorical function. The emblematic meaning no longer *explains* the object with the same direct force, and the image as a whole seems less stabilized by the allegory, which comes through muted, obliquely: a botany lesson that somehow mysteriously conveys an atmosphere of Golgotha.

The result of this shaking or uncoupling of signifier and signified is a tremendous *excess* of the visual over the emblematic. The thistle becomes towering in scale, with an architecture of thorns and spikes dazzling in its complexity. One could, of course, attribute this simply to "naturalism" and say that Marseus is just more interested in the thistle as a *Wunderkammer* spectacle than as an emblem. But that would not fully account for the extraordinary impact the thistle has in this painting. An alternative would be to suggest that the image is interested in loosening the hold of emblematics over itself precisely in order to analyze in greater detail what it is that the gaze "wants"— what the nature of its appetites and desires might be. By generating this new level of excessive visibility, Marseus was able to isolate and to explore more deeply the negativity already associated with visual appetite by such painters as Bailly and de Heem. In those earlier paintings, the eye's hunger for appearances, and its seduction by the picture's appearances, were described as a robust, uncomplicated kind of hedonism: pleasure in looking was presented as the same as the pleasure taken in any of the world's other delights—tobacco, music, reading. With the work by Marseus, the eye's hunger for appearances goes beyond this simple pleasure principle. The thistle that so captivates and fascinates the gaze has a quality of the monstrous: the lighting in the picture (phosphorescent, crepuscular) makes it seem lurid and sinister; the nature of the habitat is disturbingly uncertain (we may be in nature, we may be in a *Wunderkammer*); and, above all, these forms that so stimulate and excite the sense of sight are

Figure 4.
Otto Marseus van Schriek, *Still Life with Thistle*, ca. 1670
(cat. no. 5).

repellant to the sense of touch. Evidently, the fact that the object of the fascinated gaze is, in certain ways, frightening or alarming in no way interferes with the eye's desire to explore in infinite detail the forms that are also experienced as negative and menacing. The quest for visual pleasure is found to lead into dangerous or disturbing terrain: Marseus's picture locates in the eye's avidity or appetite a strain of perversity of which the earlier pictures by Bailly and de Heem seem unaware.

Rachel Ruysch's *Floral Still Life* (fig. 5; cover) analyzes the gaze in similar terms. Ruysch's subject is the same as that of the first generations of flower painters: prize blooms, flowers of the kind that Dutch collectors, during the great horticultural manias of the seventeenth century, were prepared to spend fortunes to acquire.[14] But her interest also extended beyond the flowers to the conditions of their display, from horticulture itself to the diorama and the vivarium.[15] Her work is as much about the peculiar conditions of visibility which obtain inside the cabinet of the amateur as it is about the flowers themselves.

Figure 5.
Rachel Ruysch, *Floral Still Life*, 1686 (cat. no. 7).

The basic structure of *Floral Still Life* could be said to involve two moves. First, Ruysch has shifted attention away from the *object* of spectacle to the *conditions* of spectacle by translating flower painting into the language of the diorama. Then, the diorama has been projected back into nature through the pretence or conceit that the artificial display actually takes place in a natural woodland setting. One might perhaps expect that this reprojection of the diorama back into the landscape would naturalize it and make its aspect of artifice disappear. In fact, the opposite occurs: what emerges are the ways in which the diorama exactly does *not* correspond to the natural world. The return to a woodland scene only highlights the spectacle's sheer impossibility (flowers simply cannot grow together in this way), and this enables Ruysch to explore directly what it is that such visual devices as the diorama, the vivarium, and taxidermy want—what kinds of instruction and pleasure their gaze pursues.

What *Floral Still Life* examines is the strange mixture, in *Wunderkammer* visuality, of the normative and the bizarre.[16] One might perhaps think of Ruysch's picture as spanning a spectrum from the Specimen to the Curiosity. The Specimen is a normative category; it is concerned with species that, under the conditions of the display, express their full species-being or essence—the definitive tulip, or lily, or butterfly. The Curiosity is a transgressive category. It is concerned with aberration and irregularity: the unpredictable variations horticulture is able to obtain through cross-breeding; objects that seem to blur taxonomic categories—as shells or coral blur the distinction between nature and artifice;[17] exotic species of insects and reptiles; the singularities of nature which can be immortalized through taxidermy. In its portrayal of the decaying elder stump, the rearing snail, and the fire-spitting salamander, it is this transgressive aspect of vision that Ruysch's painting particularly explores.

Though emblematic meanings may still be active in her still life, essentially Ruysch's work belongs to a later stage of the still life tradition, in which the original, theological polarities (matter/spirit, carnality/transcendence) were transformed into terms more concerned with the operations of the gaze as such (Curiosity/Specimen, sinister/luxuriant, repellant/beautiful). In ways similar to Marseus's still life, Ruysch's floral scenes in sylvan settings explore the gaze's capacity to derive pleasure not only from what is agreed to possess beauty (flowers) but also from the phantasmatic and the grotesque. It is the latter aspect that is, of course, disquieting: one can easily imagine why vision should be drawn toward beauty, but the eye's compulsion to seek out monstrosity and aberration is harder to explain. Ruysch's still lifes not only pinpoint this negativity at work in sight; like earlier still life, they perform negativity, and in such a way that the viewer is forced to experience the dark or nightmare side of vision directly.

The still life tradition that extends—in terms of the present exhibition—from de Heem to Ruysch is, in a sense, a confessional genre, akin to such cultural forms as religious confession, the spiritual diary, and prayer. The scene of *stilleven* opens onto questions of the soul's place in the world, its conflicted position between a transcendental realm that is sensed but cannot be experienced or represented and a fallen materiality that may be resisted but cannot be escaped. The painting of simple objects entails a meditation on what exactly goes on in human vision, on the ways vision itself is shot through with both spiritual and carnal yearnings, and on the perversity and negativity that are found to inhabit visual desire. It lies beyond the scope of this essay to trace Northern still life's gradual loss of this sense of its own profundity during the eighteenth century. But by the time of Cornelis van Spaendonck's *Still Life of Flowers* (fig. 6; pl. 4), the loss is fairly complete. Cornelis has nothing to confess except the brilliance of his technique. And, technically, there are passages in his painting that hold their own against de Heem or Ruysch. But the technique does not open out beyond itself. Awareness of the emblematic language of flowers has gone, and since, accordingly, there can be no sense of conflict between the poles of transcendence and carnality—of vision as stretched out between these extremes—the image has no way to articulate its own formal tensions with the larger and deeper tensions that give to seventeenth-century flower paintings their feeling of moral urgency and spiritual drama. Leading to nothing beyond themselves, the flowers become what they remain for us today: attractive decoration.

Figure 6.
Cornelis van Spaendonck,
Still Life of Flowers, 1793
(cat. no. 9).

III

iewing the development of Dutch still life from the seventeenth to the eighteenth century, it is hard to avoid thinking in terms of attenuation or decline. A technique of representation which in its beginnings had opened onto the intensity and drama of spiritual meditation seems to have lost the momentum of its moral urgency and self-scrutiny, gradually becoming an end in itself, a display of the painter's professional virtuosity.

At its most compelling, Dutch still life had been able to address the central questions and problems of the culture at large. As Simon Schama has shown, Dutch society in the period of its greatest economic success faced the enormous difficulty of harmonizing its officially ruling "puritan" values—industriousness, probity, self-denial—with the tide of affluence which made the Netherlands in the seventeenth century the richest nation in Europe.[18] Dutch still life goes to the heart of this contradiction between worldliness and world-rejection. It, too, is a refusal of the world (a subjugation of the things of the world to higher allegorical meanings) which is nevertheless wholly immersed in worldliness (in textures and surfaces that irresistibly seduce the senses). In countries outside the Netherlands, it was maintained by the academies that history painting alone could represent the largest questions of national history and social value, but in the Netherlands this function was carried out by still life; there was perhaps less need for Dutch painters to cultivate history painting as a separate category, since still life was able to touch on the deepest questions of the culture from its own resources. Interestingly, this capacity to reach out toward the central issues of national culture and identity emerged in another golden age of still life, this time in the United States.[19] American still life painting of the nineteenth century resembles Dutch still life of the seventeenth century in the profundity of the questions it addresses: how the objects of the New World differed from those of

Europe; what objects and material life in general were now like, in a country transformed by economic and industrial forces unprecedented in their magnitude and accelerated development.

Perhaps the most important difference between American and European still life painting of the nineteenth century is that whereas in the European countries, an unbroken tradition of academies and academic training guaranteed that all those who completed their professional training would attain a secure level of technical accomplishment, in America, the question of fluency remained a persistent structural problem. In Europe, the neophyte still life painter was initiated into a centuries-old accumulation of technical expertise; even those without exceptional talent could be sure that, eventually, their work would be able to hold its own against the professional standards preserved within the academy. In the United States, still life painters had to work from scratch. Compared with the Europeans, this constituted their disadvantage and, at the same time, their edge.

Their disadvantage, in that until the end of the nineteenth century, it was difficult for still life painters to reach the collective momentum the European academies guaranteed. American painters had to devise, individually, their own repertoire of skills and forms; often working in isolation, they were obliged to spend far longer than their counterparts in Europe securing the basic formats and routines that yielded still life's particularly demanding realistic effects. Yet it is precisely this prolonged involvement with the basic language of high-fidelity realism that gives American still life its distinctive take on the objects of the world. The act of transcribing the appearance of things onto canvas is never taken for granted; the sheer technical difficulty of the task establishes the act of transcription as a central and inevitable preoccupation. Where the technical repertoire comes to painters ready-made, as in Europe, the process of transcription tends to become transparent and effortless; the awkwardness—the strangeness of the primary encounter among object, eye, and hand—disappears within proficiency. But in the American case, this sense of the uncanniness of the basic confrontation between painting and its object stays in the foreground. American still life never entirely loses touch with its own first stages of technical growth. This remains true whether one looks at the very beginnings of American still life, at the "naive" style represented, in this exhibition, by Rubens Peale (cat. no. 12) and Elizabeth Pitkin's "theorem" painting (cat. no. 10), or at the ultra-veristic work from the end of the century, by Harnett, Haberle, or Peto (cat. nos. 15, 19, 20). Even when the painters were at last able to command the rhetoric of illusionism, their own ability to produce the illusionistic continued to fascinate them. Having achieved fluency in the still life idiom, they did not move past questions of lifelikeness into some other artistic game; they did not behave as if high-fidelity realism were ever fully naturalized or an idiom in which one could go on to speak of other things. It is as though with each new painting, still life were encountering *mimesis* for the first time.

It would be wrong, though, to think of this wonderment before *mimesis* as the condition of a perpetually innocent eye or as always involving Eden, seen through the eyes of the American Adam.[20] Even at the beginning, the *mimesis* is complex and double-edged. Consider, for example, Peale's *Still Life Number 26: Silver Basket of Fruit* (fig. 7; pl. 6).[21] Clearly, it is a work that builds up the image with extreme difficulty. Hence its need constantly to simplify the task at hand. To mitigate the difficulties of thinking in three dimensions, all the forms have been handled frontally. Though the basket is curved, the pears manage to avoid tilting toward or away from the viewer (this would require foreshortening) and instead present themselves in silhouette, almost ideographically. One knows that the basket must be oval or circular, but this is indicated

Figure 7.
Rubens Peale, *Still Life Number 26: Silver Basket of Fruit*, 1857-58 (cat. no. 12).

16

only by the changing curves of the silver loops that make the basket's sides, as if imagining the basket as a truly rounded form involved mental calculations too strenuous to carry out (the basket does not "turn" in the sense that teachers of drawing give the word). Through simplifications such as these, and the difficulties they point to, the image creates its feeling of sincerity and freshness: it is as though the historical slate had been wiped clean, and painting, returning to first principles, could discard those stale recipes that might have enabled a more competent likeness but would also have interfered with what is represented here, a primal encounter between object and eye. The difficulty of transcribing the scene establishes its truth: the objects were there and the eye saw them, not through the mediation of tradition but directly.

Yet this innocence of the eye is only one side of the coin of "naivety." Equally present in the image is the opposite: that the picture is composed only of mediations. This is a painter who, faced with a representational problem, hit upon a single solution and repeated it endlessly (one recalls the title, *Still Life Number 26*): repeat this stroke from one side of the canvas to the other, and it will make the edge of a shelf; having found the satisfactory template for a cherry or a leaf or a loop of silver, apply it again and again. The same awkwardness that underwrites the sincerity of the image's attempt to approximate the object also makes for a dependence on the formulaic that negates that sincerity and its value. Original and copy change places: what produces the image is not the object but the schema. The image accordingly circulates between two opposite poles: directness and mediation, sincerity and deception, reality and unreality. The image is veridical: precisely in its stammerings, its inadequacy to the task it sets itself, it speaks its truth. And at the same time the image countermands its realism: the objects are mere projections of the technical means; they may never have been originally there. Since the painter has within his range none of the fluency that gives substance (or plausibility) to represented objects, the image is stretched between presence (truth, pure-heartedness, an original out there in the world) and absence (artifice, simulation, perception's takeover by technology). The duality present in Rubens Peale can be found in American still life as a whole: the painter's gaze finds reality directly but, in the process, the reality it finds is, in varying degrees, irrealized.

Figure 8.
Elizabeth Pitkin, *Still Life on Velvet*, 1825 (cat. no. 10).

What is interesting is that this play between sincerity and deception, built into its technical foundations, provided American still life with a principle of outward expansion: by assimilating what it encountered in other domains of culture through analogy with its own central structure of presence/absence, it was able to move out of a purely technical sphere toward larger questions of culture and modernity. Take, for example, the "theorem" painting by Elizabeth Pitkin (fig. 8). No account of this kind of work can avoid mentioning the theorem procedure: the artist traced a design on paper, cut its edges to make a stencil, and painted through the stencil on fabric (often velvet). Clearly, this sort of imagery is close to the "naivety" of Rubens Peale: the pleasure of the technique lies in the way it enables those who do not know how to paint nevertheless to produce a kind of painting—highly simplified, to be sure, yet evocative of high art. The idea itself is charming, and one can see why it became a craze in the early nineteenth century. Where embroidery had demanded long and painstaking labor, theorem painting was quick: one produced in minutes what would have taken months to embroider or to learn how to draw or paint.

The technique touches quite deeply changing perceptions concerning the relations between duty and pleasure in domestic life; it marks one of the points at which the modernization of domestic life was becoming apparent. Theorem painting required little discipline; although to make one involved production, it moved production much closer to consumption. And in fact, the patterns could be bought ready-made. The regime in which female virtue was supposed to express itself, Roman fashion, through the dutiful working of textiles, was beginning to give way to a later dispensation in which domestic life would cut down on labor in order to free time for a historically new category, leisure. What freed (or constructed) leisure time was, of course, mechanization: a complex manual process (embroidery, drawing, painting) was replaced by an accelerated and streamlined version of itself, based on repetition (the stencil). Work and play in the household began to be inflected by the rhythms of mechanical reproduction, which were destined to transform all manufacturing processes. This modern aspect of theorem painting stands out all the more clearly against the archaic background of artisanal labor in the old style. The slowness and laboriousness of making a still life painting were linked, metaphorically, to the old regime of labor in the household (the loom, the sampler); against this, the speed and instant gratification of theorem painting stood for a new order in which time, now stripped of labor, could be spent or wasted by those who possessed the surplus that mechanization produced.

Though Pitkin's still life is modest and unexceptional, in its own way it points to a key aspect of American still life painting: the way technique is able to contact, and give visual organization to, large-scale changes in the surrounding social milieu. If Pitkin's velvet painting expresses in a restrained fashion some of the repercussions of modernization as these were felt by women of genteel middle-class households, the still lifes of Severin Roesen express the impact of modernization on domestic space without inhibition and on a grand scale (fig. 9; pl. 7). At midcentury, still life in the United States entered its first boom phase: national wealth had reached a level at which households could now highlight their prosperity by acquiring a still life to decorate the family dining room. Roesen's imagery was the perfect response to this new situation: representations of the plenty of the household and the nation, full of allusions to the old master tradition but apparently without any of that tradition's misgivings about gluttony and sensuous indulgence. The aim of Roesen's pictures was to sum up the idea of an object world awash in material plenty for viewers who enjoyed their new-found wealth and, far from wanting to conceal it, wished to see it celebrated in as spectacular a form as possible.[22]

However well Roesen may have satisfied the needs of the timber millionaires of Williamsport, Pennsylvania, where he settled in 1862, it is doubtful that his pictures often find so sympathetic a response from the modern viewer. One of the lessons of Roesen, perhaps, is the extent to which notions of prosperity and its display are circumscribed by their time and place. What is striking is how much his scenes of plenty differ from the Dutch still lifes of luxury, *pronkstilleven*, which they invoke. Quite new ideas are at work, concerning quantity, massing, and repetition. Roesen is not content with one bunch of grapes; there must be five. Fruit comes by the dozen, wine by the magnum. Roesen was being required by his patrons to figure, through a part for the whole, the general wealth of the material world. But by the mid-nineteenth century, that world was being generated and structured according to principles unknown in the seventeenth century. In the advanced agricultural economy of the United States, farming itself now followed the principles of rationalized manufacture: the natural abundance of the country had been cut across by the logic of mechanization. This completely altered the sense of the still life object's outline and position. It is no longer the specific, singular entity of Dutch still life: *this* lemon, *this* glass, *this* peach. Abundance, with Roesen, is essentially plural or multiple: the idea of prosperity emerges fully only when objects are seen to replicate identically and in great numbers. It is as though the midcentury's sense of the industrial object, based on mechanical repetition and seriality, had been ingrained so deeply that nature itself could seem abundant only if it exhibited the same scale and rhythmic pattern.

One perplexing consequence of this internalization of the mass-manufactured form is that, paradoxically, Roesen's vision of prosperity seems somehow hollow or vacuous.

Figure 9.
Severin Roesen, *Still Life with Fruit*, ca. 1860-65 (cat. no. 14).

Quantity, as a sheer force in the world, pushes each individual object aside to move on to the next one, and the next, until the point of saturation is attained. Only then will any of the objects have securely arrived; until then, their existence, individually, is provisional and incomplete. But this feeling of the lack within the individual object disturbs the entire scene, since if all of the objects, taken severally, are truly incomplete, then aggregation and accumulation will never, in fact, eliminate their insufficiency. What such perpetual postponement of plenitude may figure is, of course, appetite itself: desire goes on forever, because its fulfillment lies always ahead, never in the present. This aspect, the insatiability of appetite, may supply the one note of qualification or reservation in Roesen's otherwise straightforwardly gluttonous paintings, lending them a residual flavor of *vanitas* morality. But one notes, again, the momentous shift from the traditional *vanitas*. There appetite is insatiable because of the soul's fallen condition. Here, if appetite appears insatiable, it is because it has become externalized as the new economic machine: it is the productive sphere itself that cannot be stopped or slowed. "Individual" consumption is now about as impossible, and archaic, as the singular object (*this* lemon, *this* peach): consumption is on as massive a scale as production. It involves huge markets, distribution networks, and populations. Both production and consumption have begun to be governed by economic abstraction.

With Roesen, the historical change in the nature of consumption is felt in two principal ways. First of all, the picture itself has lost something of its former specificity. When Roesen's patrons bought a Roesen, they had enough to fit out a dining room: the painting became part of a room's furnishings. Particularly revealing in this regard are the frames given to his works, which transmit or relay the paintings' abundance-through-repetition into the room where they are destined to hang. Instead of portraying some other, fictive space, the picture is absorbed into the viewing (or dining) space: it disperses into decor. This leaves it curiously drained or depleted-looking. Secondly, the objects in the image seem to lose sensuous charge. Since the picture as a whole seems unable to stay with any single fruit, but has—as it were—to mass-manufacture them, it seems that the senses are only able to respond to quantity, as though the force of repetition had dulled the sharpness of appetite. This is especially true of vision: Roesen's fruits lack *acuity*; none of them is sharply visualized in individual terms. Again, one could take this blunting of sensuous immediacy as a moralizing comment, in the manner of a *vanitas*: that greed is self-defeating, because it finally numbs the senses it intends to serve. But it seems more likely that what Roesen was portraying was a historically new aspect of the object world in the nineteenth century: an environment of objects whose overabundance was accompanied by something like anesthesia, a gradual loss of the senses' ability to discriminate, to isolate, to compare; where the object itself was losing its individual outline, and pleasure its precision.

With Roesen, the sense that the inherited language of still life has been disturbed by new conditions of the object world is still, perhaps, only emergent. But with American still life of the later nineteenth century, the upheaval wrought in the world of objects by the conditions of modernity becomes a central preoccupation. It was not only still life painters, of course, who perceived in the advent of the industrially or mass-produced object a radical break with the past; for John Ruskin, Karl Marx, William Morris, the reorganization of production by the factory and industry represented a new historical epoch in man's relation to the material world. Yet still life painters were particularly sensitive to the changes occurring in their lifetimes within the ecology of objects. In a sense, industrialization challenged their whole enterprise.

Consider the material environment, for example, in the work of Jean-Baptiste-Siméon Chardin (1699-1779). The objects depicted in *Kitchen Table* (fig. 10) are individually crafted; Chardin took particular care in describing the joins of a table or

Figure 10.
Jean-Baptiste-Siméon Chardin, *Kitchen Table*, 1755. Oil on canvas, 15 5/8 x 18 3/4 in. (39.8 x 47.5 cm). Boston, Museum of Fine Arts, Gift of Mrs. Peter Chardon Brooks. Photo courtesy Museum of Fine Arts.

chair or the marks left by the potter's hand. In his genre scenes, the objects were worked on once more by human touch: laying a table, drawing water from a well, preparing a meal. All of Chardin's objects are consecrated by human use. Finally, they have been taken up into paintings that seem to consummate this general thematic of craft and labor. Chardin's own work as a painter is presented as similar in kind to the work that had crafted the objects and to the work of the household that used them. Continuous with these, it absorbs them into itself and raises them to a higher power. What unifies Chardin's interiors and gives them their atmosphere of harmony and ease is the uninterrupted activity of vision and touch working upon objects that respond by forming around their users a companionable dwelling place (a home, a still life).[23]

Figure 11.
William Michael Harnett, *Music and Literature*, 1878
(cat. no. 15).

Classical still life aestheticizes the ordinary, routine spaces of daily life by drawing from their objects and patterns of use and intimacy a quality of touch which the painter subsumes and elaborates through the touch of brush on canvas, returning to the objects their own value of harmony, now enhanced. The industrial object threatens the whole classical order of still life by blocking the artisanal harmonies that circulated between the scene of still life and the canvas. The industrial object comes into being by a fundamental *withdrawal* of craft and touch from the object world. It entails a deep severance of the body from the world. On its surface the new form of the object bears no traces of its making, and as industrial objects proliferate and gradually fill the environment to saturation, a milieu is created in which the human subject can no longer find itself *reflected* in the surrounding world. Disconnected from the binding force of touch, objects by the same token lose their connectedness one with another; they appear atomized, without syntax, absurd.

The thoroughness with which members of the so-called "Harnett School" explored the collision between the genre of still life, rooted in craft and the celebration of craft, and the new order of object generated by mass production is what distinguishes their work from earlier still life. In the *Still Life* attributed to J. M. Schmidt (cat. no. 16), all the principal objects—bank note, ink label, coins, the spines and pages of the books, the envelope with its stamp and cancellation mark—have been produced by mechanical action, specifically the impress of metal dies. The image as a whole works hard to absorb these objects back into an old master idiom, but in some ways this only highlights the difficulty; the ink bottle, in particular, looks like a time-traveler from the future.

Figure 12.
John Frederick Peto, *Fish House Door with Eel Basket*, 1890s
(cat. no. 20).

With William Michael Harnett's *Music and Literature* (fig. 11; pl. 8), the sense of a crisis of the object is more oblique (though elsewhere in his work it can be extreme, for instance in his bank-note pieces).[24] On the one hand, the old master manner is managed with real conviction. Harnett versed himself in the European academic techniques of still life, and in terms of technical sophistication a work such as this represents a quite new level of accomplishment on the American scene. What Harnett's now fluent illusionism enables is a feeling of enhanced and undeniable presence in the objects depicted. But other aspects of the image work in precisely the opposite direction. The assortment of objects on the table lacks an effective rationale. Is the inhabitant of the scene reading, writing, or playing music? It is hard to connect the album leaf for flute with the rolled score of *La Traviata*, or to imagine what sort of gestures could have led to the individual placement of the books. Through inconsistencies of this kind, the image begins to imply that the objects are not in fact real but are *props*, standard pieces of studio equipment. This quickly raises the question of the *point* of Harnett's display of illusionism. If, as seems likely, the reason for the incoherence of the assembled objects is that the contents of the scene are only a vehicle for the demonstration of painterly skill, the picture as a whole seems curiously perverse or self-canceling: the very technique that is supposed to render the objects' presence evacuates that presence.[25]

John Frederick Peto's *Fish House Door with Eel Basket* (fig. 12) is similarly split between extremes of presentation and evacuation, or presence and absence.[26] The objects themselves—eel basket, lantern, slicker, and pike—hover between the actual incongruity they present to the eye and some fiction (of an old fisherman and stormy seas) in which, somehow, they would all fall into place (as trusty equipment). The structure is much the same as in Harnett's *After the Hunt* (fig. 13), which similarly pits the visual against the narrative order.[27] If the viewer of *After the Hunt* supplies the missing narrative center (the hunter to whom all the objects in the picture must belong), then the hat and horn and pouch—all the paraphernalia and trophies of the hunt—cohere around the imagined protagonist. Yet the image supplies everything *but* this unifying figure, and, as a result, the syntax of the objects breaks up into stranded individual elements. To this idea of the absent protagonist Peto added further complications. Unlike the robust and vigorous huntsman implicit in Harnett's picture, Peto's implied fisherman seems a ghost. Assuming that the objects in the picture stand for a character, the many signs of decrepitude (the dark and dust-covered lantern, the broken hinge) imply that the fisherman is ancient and worn out; he may even be dead. This attenuation of the implied protagonist's existence means that the objects cannot quite consolidate around the missing narrative center— they have lost their center of gravity.

Peto's response to the prospect of an object world atomized and robbed of syntax is nostalgic, conservative, and somewhat maudlin. It is to create a homespun poetics of the object, laid out between extremes of vitality and extinction. To reunify the object world, Peto employed the glue of masculinity: an old man of the sea, completely at home in one place, with a salty accent and lines of experience in his face (in his "bachelor's drawer" pictures, Peto "imagined" a man-about-town, a *flaneur* and ladies' man, as much at home in the city as the fisherman was at sea). But these vigorous biographical subjects are known only through the trivia of personal effects; it is as if their red-bloodedness could not, after all, defeat death, leaving Peto to go through the dead men's clothes: painting as mourning.

John Haberle's response to the same prospect is buoyant, satirical, and extraordinarily perceptive about the changing ecology of the object world at the turn of the century.[28] *Torn in Transit* (fig. 14; pl. 9) is a work that has given up the attempt to translate the new conditions of material life into the language of the old masters, perhaps because Haberle perceived the conditions of modernity as too far gone for recollections of the older regime of the object to have much purchase on the present. Looking back to "Schmidt's" *Still Life* and Harnett's *Music and Literature* from *Torn in Transit*, it is clear that one problem with the old master approach was its structural inability to describe the objects of modernity in ways that acknowledged their radically new deployment of space and time. In classical still life, space is always proximal and enclosed; screening out the middle and far distance, it gathers objects around the body and pens them in. But in the era of mechanization, since objects exist only in the plural, they do not settle singly in any one place. *Torn in Transit* describes the ubiquity or multiple positionality of the new order of the object in terms of a permanent dislocation or unfixing of the object in space: permanently "in transit," the object never fully arrives at any destination. Again, in classical still life, time is represented against a background of permanence: what is fleeting or ephemeral (flowers, pleasure, mortality) tends to be seen *sub specie aeternitatis*. But in the era of industrialization, the

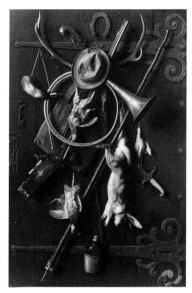

Figure 13.
William Harnett, *After the Hunt*, 1885. Oil on canvas, 71 1/2 x 48 1/2 in. (181.6 x 123.2 cm). Fine Arts Museums of San Francisco, Mildred Anna Williams Collection. Photo courtesy Fine Arts Museums of San Francisco.

Figure 14.
John Haberle, *Torn in Transit*, ca. 1888-89 (cat. no. 19).

framework of the eternal becomes generally unavailable. Ephemerality is all there is, and in the new conditions, the ephemerality of objects intensifies. A postcard or an express label exists to be looked at only briefly; it releases its charge and is instantly spent.

Haberle's exploration of ephemerality is particularly sharp. An early explorer of industrial ecology, he seems single-handedly to have identified the class of objects—long before it entered general awareness—which we describe today as "disposable." What is more, he seems to have recognized in the disposable object an odd kind of lyricism or pathos. In a world where commodities proliferate exponentially, while the amount of attention that can be invested in them remains the same, the time spent with individual objects must inevitably diminish. Haberle detected in this situation—the diminishing half-life of objects—an unexpected problem within modernity, the predicament of *memory* in a world whose objects seem to be disappearing: how to appropriate or salvage from the accelerated flux of ephemera those items that seem of special value? Haberle saw modernity's solution to the problem as *bricolage*, or hoarding: the best that could be done was to snatch from the flux those few odds and ends that resonated with feeling or desire, tuck them away, and return to them at some future date. The irony is that the modern object, geared to ever-accelerating consumption, was never built for prolonged inspection, cannot sustain it, and can only appear the more degraded when looked at for longer or more intensely than its producers had in mind. Haberle presents the subject of modernity as trying to rescue, from the flux of commodities, memory-objects pitifully unsuited to the job, objects too ephemeral to preserve anything, hardly able to preserve themselves.

Torn in Transit takes on board the degraded state of objects under modernity, and especially modernity's images (Haberle seems to have anticipated almost all the points concerning the loss of "aura" that Walter Benjamin later developed in his essay, "The Work of Art in the Era of Mechanical Reproduction" [1936]). But perhaps the most suggestive aspect of the picture is that its theme is not simply the degraded objects themselves but the ways in which these were assimilated by the subject through processes of consciousness that are historically new, perhaps barely emergent. Haberle seems to have been sketching such processes in two rather different ways. The first is optimistic and satirical. The subject who is implied as hoarding these absurd ephemera is not regarded as particularly involved with them; the lurid cigarette-card pin-up and the awful amateur Impressionist view are tangential and unimportant: "It just so happens that these images, degraded though they are, appealed to a particular individual at some point; one finds such odds and ends in any bachelor's drawer; they do not reflect much about the individual, except quite comically bad taste." The second is somewhat darker, the serious side to Haberle's visual joke: "In the modern world, the sheer quantity of objects, and their accelerating production and consumption, produce something rather like monetary inflation—the value of each item becomes less and less; nevertheless, it is with these degraded materials that consciousness must now build its images of beauty (the Impressionist landscape) and desire (the pin-up); look inside any mind and you will find the same bric-a-brac, the same disjointed detritus; modernity is the internalization of junk."

ne of the strongest tendencies in American still life of the nine-teenth century is its insistence on giving the viewer access to the object that is to the highest possible degree unmediated and abrupt. In the words of Barbara Novak, "The presentation of the object is controlled by a knowledge of its properties that is tactile and intellectual, rather than optical or perceptual."[29] This emphasis on laying bare the sheer existence of the object "in itself"—rather than portraying the object as it unfolds within ordinary human perception, the object "for us"—is remark-ably constant in the American tradition.[30] In Raphaelle Peale's *After the Bath* (1823; Kansas City, Nelson-Atkins Museum), the human form is briefly glimpsed (taking a shower), then swallowed up by a blank linen towel that usurps the entire surface of the picture.[31] In much the same way, the "bachelor's drawer" paintings of Haberle imply the detailed biography of an individual yet evict the individual from the scene, leaving only the objects behind. Such "letter rack" paintings as Samuel Lewis's *A Deception* (ca. 1805-09; private collection) aim at recording the look of objects "away from us"—the appearance that things might have if there were no one there to per-ceive them.[32] It is the same with Haberle's *Torn in Transit*: the objects have separated from their owner, have literally turned up as lost property. Divorced from use and ownership, they are free to enter into their own independent objecthood.

In order to establish this metaphysical existence of the object, certain possibilities of representation are necessarily foreclosed. One is the handling of the image as the record of a perception. There must be no sense that the picture is based on someone else's prior view, coming between the object and the picture's actual viewer. For the encounter between viewer and object to be direct, it must seem as though no one else in the universe assists at this primal encounter; there must be no feeling that the image relays, at second hand, a perception belonging to another consciousness (the painter's). The metaphysics of the object are achieved at the expense of phenomenology. By the same token, the image cannot permit itself to display the traces of its own production. The independent visibility of brush strokes would break the direct line between object and viewer; in order to be *presentation*, the painting must sacrifice itself as *representation*.

It is precisely these latter possibilities that European still life of the nineteenth century pursued—the object as it exists "for us," through the filter of the painter's consciousness, and, as a condition of that, the foregrounding of the act of repres-entation. Consider, for example, the cult of blur and indistinctness which overtook French still life after midcentury. From Edouard Manet and Henri Fantin-Latour, the forms of still life progressively rid themselves of the precise and all-over focus, the glare of hyperreality, that had been established for them in the seventeenth century. The genre renounced its Medusa-like stare at the world, the drilling clarity that set out to capture and set down every last detail in the surfaces and textures of the world. One immediate result of this relaxation of vision's grip on the visible was that it now became possible to explore an entirely different range of relations between people and things. When vision is vigilant, and the brush extracts from the scene of still life every microscopic detail, it is impossible for the objects transcribed not to appear objectified by the gaze; clarity itself holds the objects at a distance. With Dutch still life of the seventeenth century, this estrangement was functionally justified by the genre's mor-alizing intent, which was precisely to problematize the object world and, in the *vanitas*, to imply its negation. But when such a program was no longer the central issue in still life, the legacy of the hyperreal made it almost impossible for still life to rejoin the world as a familiar inhabitant.

In fact, the familiar objects that still life deals in—glasses, bowls, pitchers, plates, flowers—involve visual conditions directly at odds with vigilance and clarity: they are things which, belonging to the mundane spaces of daily life, are taken so entirely for granted that familiarity itself pushes them far below the threshold of visual distinctness. Exactly because they are things we constantly use, they are things we no longer need to see. Habit and routine cast over them a mantle of invisibility. They are felt as presences; familiarity knows them as "there" but in a mode of erasure.

How to represent this blindness, this felt presence of the overlooked? In the later nineteenth century, one answer was abstraction. The term needs to be handled with care; it can refer to a number of very different processes. One can think of abstraction as, among other things, enabling exactly this kind of registration of objects to take place—to depict their presence but not their accurate optical surfaces. In Antoine Vollon's *Still Life* (1880-85; cat. no. 17), one finds a persistent avoidance of high focus; the brush has been dragged to obscure detail, or loaded to build an impasto that acts as a barrier preventing the viewer from looking too closely "inside" the scene. Foregrounding of brushwork and pigment causes the scene to cloud over, and in this way Vollon suggests an intimacy between the vessels and their user based on the secure home ground of the familiar. Though Pierre Bonnard's *Wild Flowers* (fig. 15) is utterly different in technique, the strategy is similar; the picture conveys the sense that the colors of the flowers exist as an energizing presence that cannot be adequately conveyed simply by repeating their natural hues. Bonnard was seeking "equivalents" to the actual colors of the flowers and of the other objects in his scene: the equivalents transmit the sense that the presence of the colors is powerful yet distinct from what the eye objectively sees. Or consider Jonas Lie's *The Black Teapot* (fig. 16; pl. 10). Imagine the same forms as they would appear to a camera: they would lie at a distance, separated by an optical interval from where the viewer stands. The shedding of detail and play of indistinctness build the opposite sense: the distance between self and world diminishes, and the forms pass into the viewer's consciousness as felt presences. Here indistinctness stands for an immersion in the world, a giving way to things, and equally for the passing of the world into the mind, so that it is there, within consciousness, that the forms fully express themselves, in a mutual *circulation* between objects and consciousness for which indistinctness seems the only adequate vehicle or sign. Optical precision would only interfere with this mutual opening of world and self (the "chiasmus" magnificently analyzed by Maurice Merleau-Ponty in *The Visible and the Invisible*).[33]

Abstraction, with pictures such as these, is not accurately described if the loss of distinctness in the forms is attributed too quickly to the pursuit of pictorial flatness or the wish to liberate painting from *mimesis*. It may be more accurate to say that the level of *mimesis* has shifted, enabling it to bypass the retina and reach a different relationship between people and things, a level where the world exists as internalization. The objects are objects-in-consciousness. Yet it would also be less than accurate to imagine that in these works by Bonnard and Lie, the act of painting exists neutrally to transcribe a preexisting referent—with the only difference from more obviously mimetic work being that the referent now lies somewhere below the optical threshold. Abstraction not only allows access to the (nonoptical) referent; it obviously permits the image to separate from the referent, to establish a parallel existence, to become a *further* object for consciousness to move in. Here the case of Paul Cézanne (1839-1906) is exemplary. In a picture such as *Still Life with Statuette* (fig. 17), Cézanne's hundredth stroke responds to the previous ninety-nine, and launches a further move, whose outcome is not yet known. The work acts recursively and reflexively upon itself in real time, through the consciousness of its embodied creator.[34] Abstraction brings into being a new object for consciousness, yet this new object is not abstract in the sense of breaking away from the consciousness of its creator or declaring its unilateral

Figure 15.
Pierre Bonnard, *Wild Flowers*, ca. 1915-20 (cat. no. 27).

Figure 16.
Jonas Lie, *The Black Teapot*, 1911 (cat. no. 24).

Figure 17.
Paul Cézanne, *Still Life with Statuette*, ca. 1895. Oil on canvas, 24 5/8 x 31 5/8 in. (63 x 81 cm). Stockholm, Nationalmuseum. Photo courtesy Statens Konstmuseer.

independence. This new object—the image as it separates from or exceeds *mimesis*— exists *only* through the decisions of its maker, who, in building the design, must minutely calculate the consequences of each new stroke as it unfolds into the design as a whole. This new or second object—the image as it cleaves from reference—is saturated with conscious activity; it forms a field within which consciousness is quickened to its fullest extent.

Two kinds of object, then: the objects of the world, as these pass into consciousness as internalized presences, and then the object that, of all objects, stands for the deepest internalization, the design on canvas. How do these two relate? There are many possibilities. With the Vollon, for example, the design stays close to the referent; it does not build up, as with Cézanne, a strongly independent field of force. With the Bonnard, the design cleaves from reference to a far greater degree, and as the objects in the still life pass into the field of quickened or vibrant attention defined by the canvas, they seem to light up, not with their actual colors but with heightened consciousness of their presence as color. *Abstraction* is the name still given to this process, but in many ways the word seems inappropriate. It inevitably suggests a shedding of lived experience, a stripping away of sensuous attachments, whereas here perhaps the opposite is true: as still life objects pass into abstraction, their originally experienced presence is enhanced and intensified. Whereas in the seventeenth century, objects might have been known only externally, now they enter consciousness on the inside. Their existence as design has less, then, to do with a two-dimensional form that can be spun out of them, taken away from them, and applied like a stencil to the canvas. It involves the deepening of their existence as objects-in-consciousness and, as part of that, the settling of consciousness itself more deeply inside the world.

One would not wish to insist too heavily on these "phenomenological" underpinnings of early still life abstraction; obviously, not every work that starts with the objects of the world and then moves on can be described in this way. It is perhaps only one possibility, built into the technical means of still life under abstraction, which some painters and some pictures are interested at certain moments in developing. It is hard, for example, with the still lifes by Raoul Dufy (cat. no. 21) and Charles Dufresne (fig. 18) to maintain that their goal was to make abstraction stand for the in-dwelling of objects in consciousness and consciousness in the world. They are too frankly decorative to support that kind of claim; their forms have too evidently been generated on the surface of the picture. This points to an element of precariousness within the phenomenological register of still life painting as a whole. At times, the work of abstraction is a way of deepening the liaisons among object, image, and consciousness. In Cézanne, the independent visibility of each stroke suggests a slow, grave concentration in which, between strokes, there has been a pause for the painter to reflect on what aspects of the object have just been revealed by the brush and on how these new aspects will affect the direction of the image as whole. Cézanne's brush, so to speak, shuttles between the image and the world, weaving them together, with each acting dialectically on the other, through the medium of the painter's consciousness. But clearly, Dufy (for one) did not work this way. Far more than with Cézanne or Bonnard or Lie, Dufy's image is built up on canvas, away from the world. It is abstract in the sense that the forms appearing on canvas are not necessarily backed by reference; the viewer is unlikely to feel an interpenetration of world and image which deepens with each separate stroke. At most, the exuberance of color and spontaneity of gesture in the Dufy can stand, metaphorically, for the sensuous enjoyment of the objects invoked.

Figure 18.
Charles Dufresne, *Still Life*, ca. 1928 (cat. no. 32).

But there is little feeling that the pictorial forms are actually linked, through dialectical involvement, to any actual object of experience. At this point, still life's use of abstraction as a way of binding together object, image, and consciousness collapses on the picture plane as decoration.

On the other hand, it is precisely this possibility of liberating the image from the categories of world, object, and experience that seems to have constituted still life's appeal to Cubism. For George Braque (in *Still Life with Pipe* [fig. 19] and *Glass, Grapes, and Pear* [cat. no. 33]) and Juan Gris (*Still Life* [cat. no. 29]), the advantage of still life's traditional objects—pipes, playing cards, glasses, fruit, tables, bottles—was that they could be rendered as legible forms while making the least possible commitment to describing their space. If Cubism was seeking ways to break with *mimesis*, such forms were ideal: the merest sketch of an *F*-curve is enough to suggest a violin, the simplest profile enough to establish a wine glass or a table or a newspaper. What is more, the violin remained recognizably a violin and the wine glass a wine glass through even the most drastic transformations. In the iconography of traditional still life, Cubism discovered a fundamental legibility that it could use, so to speak, as a trampoline.

Cubism's analysis of still life objects reveals the extent to which they may not, in fact, be *optical* forms at all. With things seen for the first time, detail is of the essence, but with the objects that most typically surround us, those which are in constant use day by day, detail is drained by familiarity: the hand takes over from the eye. The routines of hands around the objects on a table, or (to take Cubism's "higher" case) the routines of fingers around a musical instrument (violin, mandolin, guitar), are blind; they move through space, but it is not a space the eye follows. We do not ordinarily sit in rapt contemplation of cups and plates. These things generally disappear—or rather, they become abbreviated signs. By eliminating from them every aspect of retinal detail and by pushing the forms back toward the basic threshold of recognition, Cubism practiced a *glyphic reduction* that may not, in fact, be essentially different from the kind of semiotic reduction that takes place in ordinary perception. This is not to say that despite appearances Cubist still lifes are, after all, realistic. Rather, Cubism anchored its own transformations of space in a space of tactile cohesiveness strong enough to bind together even the impossible fragments and smithereens that Cubism invented; it *needed* that stable bonding of blind or gestural space as an operational base.

With Picasso, in particular, interest was less in abstraction per se than in the *pull* between the forces of abstraction and the gravity and inertia of still life's familiar shapes. In *Glass, Vase and Fruits* (cat. no. 36), the glyphic forms move farther and farther away from legibility; a first level of distortion supplies the starting point for a second and a third; the image as a whole pushes transformation toward the point at which reference to the original object is almost lost—but not quite. At the penultimate stage, beyond which the forms would become altogether unrecognizable, the work of transformation is interrupted. The image wants to see just how far transformation can go—which is never all the way. To move over the edge into nonrecognizability would be to destroy the act of transformation itself, which must always be the transformation of *something*—a glass, fruit, a vase. Through every stage of distressing and disfiguring forms, the process is governed by the minimal scheme of recognition, which is stretched to breaking point. But the scheme must not actually be broken, or all of the painting's tension—its tug-of-war between form and the *informe*—would escape.

With Braque and Picasso, still life opened the image to extremes of formal experimentation precisely because its objects, of all the objects in the world that painting might choose to work with, seemed to offer the least resistance to glyphic or semiotic reduction. They were the object at degree zero: unproblematic, infinitely accommodating and elastic, without connotations, free of historical and cultural weight. Still life was a genre particularly suited to those tendencies within modernism that sought to discard historicity and contextuality; its objects can without difficulty be presented as timeless, transcendent, beyond ideology. In the twentieth century, still life has accordingly served well the cause of depoliticized art. Its apparently unchanging object world offers the solace of escape from the contingencies of history, a consolation all the more effective when the fantasy of an escape from history is combined with the look of modernity, of the avant-garde, in such a way that the "timelessness" of still life's objects and forms seems to lie *deeper* than modernity—and so can appear to neutralize modernity itself. Still life as the rejection of modernity is always an option. When Giorgio de Chirico wished to turn his back on everything that had been disturbing in earlier "Metaphysical" paintings such as *The Regret* (cat. no. 28; pl. 11), still life, as can be seen in *Florentine Still Life* (cat. no. 30), provided the safest and most conservative of refuges.

Figure 19.
Georges Braque, *Still Life with Pipe*, 1913-14 (cat. no. 26).

Yet in other practices of twentieth-century still life, the historicity of the genre's supposedly timeless *mise-en-scène* is central. Fernand Léger's *Still Life with Glass* (fig. 20), for instance, refuses one of the genre's most enduring conventions, that of closing off the space behind the table in order to separate the still life scene from any larger social space that might disturb its proposal of intimacy. Instead, the traditional table surface has been integrated with a larger architecture of industrialization and mechanization, as though the privacy and perceptual solitude of still life's traditional space could no longer be sustained. Elements from the public and private spheres change places: the glass or goblet has migrated from the table onto the industrial scaffolding, becoming an architectural form, while on the table itself appear forms suggestive of the factory and technocracy. Léger takes one of the defining features of the genre—the absence of the human figure—and makes it stand for the obsolescence of individualism in a milieu now shaped and determined by the larger forces of modernization. If the rounded shape at the right edge is the human figure, it appears only as another cog in a greater machine.

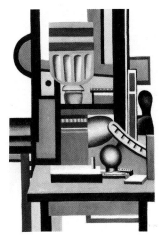

Figure 20.
Fernand Léger, *Still Life with Glass*, 1924 (cat. no. 31).

Léger's vision of the totalizing social machine is itself highly problematic: who, for instance, is imagined as running the machine, and at whose expense? The image seems to hover between description (this is actually how things already stand, the individual is already fully integrated into the general circuitry of social production and management) and prescription (this is the kind of totally functioning and planned society we should be aiming at), and its prescriptive (or conscriptive) tone has a distinct authoritarian edge. But Léger's totalism points, by contrast, toward some of the more disquieting political assumptions at work in even such "sweet" still lifes as those of Bonnard, Lie, or Dufresne. We have argued that, at their best, the hedonism of such paintings works toward overcoming the split between subject and object implied in seventeenth-century still life's medusal gaze by grounding objects in the internal life of the subject and settling consciousness more deeply inside the world. But it should also be said that, at its worst, this utopian project dwindles into a kind of luxurious complacency. Dufresne's *Still Life* is a case in point: in the end, what it celebrates is less some homecoming of the subject into the ground of Being than bourgeois comfort, *luxe, calme et volupté*. The echoes of Cézanne bring out how utterly different Cézanne's still lifes are, with their metaphysical seriousness, the strain of their exertion at the limits of pictorial convention. The Dufresne is much more about what it is like to be comfortably off. And the same could be said of the Bonnard and the Lie: alongside all of the other things the paintings communicate is an ideology of the home as the center of authentic being, domestic prosperity as the arena of personal fulfillment. Which is not necessarily to criticize these pictures, but rather to point out that they participate in an ideology of the private self that is, in its own quiet way, just as politically assertive as Léger's totalitarian humanism-bashing.

The Léger, from 1924, and the Dufresne, from ca. 1928, are close enough to each other in time for one to see them as taking part in the same quarrel of the private versus the public sphere. They polarize in ways that can be traced directly to political polarization in France in the 1920s: private sensuality and the discrete charm of the bourgeoisie versus conscription into public-mindedness or collectivism. In Andy Warhol's *Big Electric Chair* (fig. 21), it seems that the quarrel has already been superseded. A continuation of Warhol's disaster series from the earlier 1960s (car crashes, plane crashes, suicides), the image shows an electric chair, handled in such a way as to stand for the whole class of extreme images that constitute media violence. The cultural conditions Warhol used his image to pinpoint are those in which the classical opposition between what belongs to the private and what belongs to the public sphere has been generally undermined. The home, which in Bonnard and Lie (as in Monet or Matisse) appeared as idyllically secluded from the greater world, has in the interim been plugged into radio, magazines, and TV. Permanently tuned to mass media, what had been formerly known as the private domain is now bombarded by mass imagery to the point of numbness—that peculiar state of affectlessness or anesthesia which Warhol made his own ("I like boring things, but that doesn't mean I'm not bored with them"). What in Haberle's *Torn in Transit* remained only a glimpse of the future—the internalization of degraded imagery—is now the governing reality: images from the public sphere are the primary stuff of consciousness. In this sense, the classical division between private and public is senseless, since the principal form taken by the public sphere is that of imagery aimed at the private sector, while the private sector is permanently saturated by the mass-manufactured image stream.

Figure 21.
Andy Warhol, *Big Electric Chair*, 1967
(cat. no. 40).

Janet Fish's *After Leslie Left* (fig. 22; pl. 12) looks out on much the same cultural landscape as Warhol's *Big Electric Chair*. Here, too, the public and the private have collapsed in on one another: domestic space has been extensively colonized by the objects and imagery of mass culture (Windex bottle, *House and Garden*, coupons), to the point where Leslie, or Fish herself, are felt as biographical presences mostly through the inflections they have made in the field of industrial objects, the slight ripples their existence has caused in the general pool of commodities. That private space has been made rather deeply continuous with public is suggested by the picture's peculiar hyperrealism, and by its palette. It is as if painting could approach the visual field only in terms of photography—as though mass photography now constituted the typical or hegemonic case of vision, and painting had internalized the photographic form so thoroughly that its entire management of realism, its way with edges, reflections, and focus, conveyed the prior mediation of color photography. The luminosity that is so interesting in Fish's painting, with its acidic colors all keyed toward brilliant white, suggests photographic paper or a color transparency as the matrix from which the forms emerge, as though the retina itself were just another kind of photographic film. The difference from Warhol is perhaps that there are no particular signs of protest against the cultural processes the image implies. In *Big Electric Chair*, the outlook is almost that of a moralist or satirist. While it is never possible to define Warhol's exact tone in relation to popular culture (for instance, on a scale from tragedy to comedy), his famous deadpan constantly poses the effects of mass culture as a *problem*. With Fish's still life, the inability to separate public and private, the internalization of photography into painting or of the image stream into consciousness—these are no longer real issues; they are simply the way it is, conditions to be accepted more or less with pleasure (there is none of Warhol's negativity here). To paint a corner of a loft in SoHo is necessarily to paint the cultural terrain we all inhabit. Still life may, after all, be the history painting of our time.

Figure 22.
Janet Fish, *After Leslie Left*, 1983-84
(cat. no. 41).

Notes:

1. "Thomas Ruff," in J. Harten and D. A. Ross, *BiNationale: German Art of the Late 1980s*, exh. cat. (Städtische Kunsthalle [Düsseldorf]/Museum of Fine Arts [Boston], Cologne, 1988), p. 261.

2. On the emergence of still life painting, see C. Sterling, *Still Life Painting from Antiquity to the Twentieth Century*, 2d rev. ed. (New York, 1981), pp. 34-64.

3. On Cotán's still life, see J. G. Ricart, "Natures mortes de Sánchez Cotán (1561-1627)," *Pantheon* 35 (1977), pp. 314-17; M. S. Soria, "Sánchez Cotán's *Quince, Cabbage, Melon and Cucumber*," *Art Quarterly* 8 (1945), pp. 311-18; and N. Bryson, *Looking at the Overlooked: Four Essays on Still Life Painting* (Cambridge, Mass., 1990), pp. 63-70.

4. On Caravaggio's *Basket of Fruit*, see the remarkable essay by M. Butor, "La corbeille de l'Ambrosienne," in *Répertoires* 3 (Paris, 1968), pp. 43-58; S. Bann, *The True Vine: On Visual Representation and Western Tradition* (Cambridge, 1989), pp. 79-83.

5. On the allegorical dimension of Dutch still life, see I. Bergström, *Dutch Still-Life Painting in the Seventeenth Century*, trans. C. Hedström and G. Taylor (New York, 1983); E. de Jongh, *Still-Life in the Age of Rembrandt*, exh. cat. (Auckland City Art Gallery, 1982); S. Segal, *A Prosperous Past: The Sumptuous Still Life in the Netherlands 1600-1700*, exh. cat. (Kimbell Art Museum [Fort Worth], The Hague, 1988), pp. 29-38.

6. On de Heem, see "De Heem and His Circle," in Segal (note 5), pp. 141-64; Bryson (note 3), pp. 121-24.

7. See cat. no. 3.

8. On the emblematic meanings in Bailly's painting, see cat. no. 4.

9. On the melancholy or desolation of the allegorical object, see W. Benjamin, *The Origin of German Tragic Drama*, trans. J. Osborne (London, 1977).

10. On the "performative" aspect of Dutch allegorical painting, see Bryson (note 3), pp. 116-21.

11. On the differences between spatial representation in "Albertian" and Northern painting, see S. Alpers, *The Art of Describing: Dutch Art in the Seventeenth Century* (Chicago, 1983).

12. On the self-reflexivity of Dutch painting, see C. L. Virdis, *Il quadro e il suo doppio: Effeti di specularita narrativa nella pittura fiamminga e olandese* (Modena, 1981).

13. See the discussion of the emblems in Marseus's picture under cat. no. 5.

14. See N. W. Posthumus, "The Tulip Mania in Holland in the Years 1636 and 1637," *Journal of Economic and Business History* 1 (1929), pp. 434-66. On Dutch flower pictures, see N. Schneider, "Vom Klostergarten zur Tulpenmanie," in *Stilleben in Europa*, exh. cat. (Westfälisches Landesmuseum für Kunste und Kulturgeschichte, Munster, 1979), pp. 294-312; P. Pieper, "Das Blumenbukett," in ibid., pp. 314-49; C. Grimm, *Stilleben: Die niederländischen und deutschen Meister* (Stuttgart, 1988), pp. 78-84; Bryson (note 3), pp. 104-10.

15. See cat. no. 7.

16. On *Kunst-* and *Wunderkammern*, see T. DaC. Kaufmann, "Remarks on the Collections of Rudolf II: *The Kunstkammer* as a Form of *Representatio*," *Art Journal* 38 (1978), pp. 22-28; G. Luther, "Stilleben als Bilder der Sammelleidenschaft," in *Stilleben in Europa* (note 14), pp. 88-128.

17. See S. Alpers, *Rembrandt's Enterprise: The Studio and the Market* (London, 1988), p. 20.

18. S. Schama, *The Embarrassment of Riches: An Interpretation of Dutch Culture in the Golden Age* (Berkeley, 1988). See also idem, "The Unruly Realm: Appetite and Restraint in Holland in the Golden Age," *Daedalus* 108 (1979), pp. 103-23.

19. For general discussion of American still life, see A. Frankenstein, *After the Hunt: William Harnett and Other American Still Life Painters 1870-1900*, rev. ed. (Berkeley, 1969); W. H. Gerdts, *Painters of the Humble Truth: Masterpieces of American Still Life 1801-1939*, exh. cat. (Philbrook Art Center [Tulsa], Columbia, Mo., 1981).

20. For an excellent analysis of "naivety" and perception in the American context, see T. Tanner, *The Reign of Wonder: Naivety and Reality in American Literature* (Cambridge, 1965).

21. On Rubens Peale, see C. C. Sellers, "Rubens Peale: A Painter's Decade," *Art Quarterly* 23 (Summer 1960), pp. 139-51; Gerdts (note 19), pp. 64-65.

22. See L. G. Marcus, *Severin Roesen: A Chronology* (Williamsport, Pa., 1976); Gerdts (note 19), pp. 84-89.

23. On the relationship between Chardin's paintings and the material environments they represent, see N. Bryson, "Chardin and the Text of Still Life," *Critical Inquiry* 15 (Winter 1989), pp. 227-52.

24. On *Music and Literature*, see cat. no. 15. For an excellent discussion of Harnett's illusionism in general, see B. Novak, *American Painting of the Nineteenth Century* (New York, 1979), pp. 221-34.

25. For a discussion of Harnett's work in relation to the *vanitas* tradition, see B. S. Groseclose, "Vanity and the Artist: Some Still-life Paintings by William Michael Harnett," *American Art Journal* 19, no. 1 (1987), pp. 51-54.

26. See the essay on Peto by A. Frankenstein, in *John F. Peto*, exh. cat. (Smith College Museum of Art, Northampton, Mass., 1950); J. Wilmerding, *Important Information Inside: The Art of John F. Peto and the Idea of Still-Life Painting in Nineteenth Century America*, exh. cat. (National Gallery of Art, Washington, D.C., 1983).

27. On this painting, see pp. 80, 84 below. See also Frankenstein (note 19); L. Goodrich, "Harnett and Peto: A Note on Style," *Art Bulletin* 31 (March 1949), pp. 57-58; Gerdts (note 19), pp. 179-86.

28. See A. Frankenstein, "Haberle: Or the Illusion of the Real," *American Magazine of Art* 41 (October 1948), pp. 222-27; R. F. Chirico, "John Haberle and Trompe L'Oeil," *Marsyas* 19 (1977-78), pp. 37-43.

29. Novak (note 24), p. 223.

30. "Place a Harnett still life, of the middle 1870s…next to a Raphaelle Peale of 1815…and it is impossible to believe that they are separated by two generations, that the one belongs to the era of James Madison and the other to that of U.S. Grant" (Frankenstein [note 19], p. 31). See also Novak (note 24), p. 221.

31. See Gerdts (note 19), p. 53.

32. Among the earliest examples of this trompe l'oeil genre painted in America, Lewis's *A Deception* was formerly attributed to Raphaelle Peale; see W. H. Gerdts, "*A Deception* Unmasked; An Artist Uncovered," *American Art Journal* 23, no. 2 (1986), pp. 4-23. I am grateful to Bruce Weber for this reference. See also Gerdts (note 19), p. 50; D. Bolger, " 'Cards and Letters from His Friends': Mr. Huling's Rack Picture by William Michael Harnett," *American Art Journal* 22, no. 2 (1990), pp. 4-32.

33. M. Merleau-Ponty, *Le visible et l'invisible* (Paris, 1965).

34. See Bann (note 4), p. 103; N. Bryson, "Intertextuality and Visual Poetics," *Critical Texts* 4, no. 2 (1987), p. 5.

▲

Plate 1
Cat. no. 3
Jan Davidsz. de Heem
Still Life,
1640s
Oil on panel, 14 3/8 x 18 5/8 in. (36.4 x 47.9 cm)
Inscribed, u.r.: *Ja[ ] de heem*
Memorial Art Gallery of the University of Rochester,
Marion Stratton Gould Fund, 49.63

▲

Plate 2
Cat. no. 4
David Bailly
Vanitas with Negro Boy,
ca. 1650
Oil on canvas, 37 1/4 x 45 3/4 in. (94.6 x 116.2 cm)
Herbert F. Johnson Museum of Art, Cornell University,
Gift of Mr. and Mrs. Louis V. Keeler, by exchange, 86.6

Plate 3
Cat. no. 5
Otto Marseus van Schriek
Still Life with Thistle,
ca. 1670
Oil on canvas, 49 1/2 x 40 in.
(125.7 x 101.6 cm)
Herbert F. Johnson Museum of Art,
Cornell University, Gift of Mr. and
Mrs. H. A. Metzer, 60.195

◄

Plate 4
Cat. no. 9
Cornelis van Spaendonck
Still Life of Flowers,
1793
Oil on canvas, 31 1/4 x 25 in.
(79.4 x 63.5 cm)
Inscribed, l.r.: *Corneille / Van
Spaendonck.1793*
Herbert F. Johnson Museum of Art,
Cornell University, Gift of the Estate
of David B. Goodstein, 86.30.8

▲
Plate 5
Cat. no. 11
John Vanderlyn, Jr.
Still Life: Fruit in a Classical Setting,
1854-58
Oil on canvas, 30 x 42 in. (76.2 x 106.7 cm)
Albany Institute of History and Art, 1983.11

▲
Plate 6
Cat. no. 12
Rubens Peale
Still Life Number 26: Silver Basket of Fruit,
1857-58
Oil on tin, 13 x 19 in. (33 x 48.3 cm)
Inscribed, l.r.: *26*
Memorial Art Gallery of the University of Rochester,
Gift of Helen Ellwanger, 64.40

▲
Plate 7
Cat. no. 13
Severin Roesen
Still Life with Fruit and Champagne,
1853
Oil on canvas, 30 x 44 in. (76.2 x 111.8 cm)
Inscribed, l.r.: *S. Roesen / 1853*
Munson-Williams-Proctor Institute Museum
of Art, 82.53

▲

Plate 8
Cat. no. 15
William Harnett
Music and Literature,
1878
Oil on canvas, 24 x 32 1/8 in. (61 x 81.2 cm)
Inscribed, l.r.: *W Harnett / 1878*
Albright-Knox Art Gallery, Gift of Seymour H. Knox,
41.10

Plate 9
Cat. no. 19
John Haberle
Torn in Transit,
ca. 1888-89
Oil on canvas, 14 x 12 in.
(35.6 x 30.4 cm)
Inscribed, l.r.: *from Haberle-*
Memorial Art Gallery of the University
of Rochester, Marion Stratton Gould
Fund, 65.6

Plate 10
Cat. no. 24
Jonas Lie
The Black Teapot,
1911
Oil on canvas, 35 x 42 in. (87.9 x 106.7 cm)
Inscribed, l.l.: *Jonas Lie 1911*
Everson Museum of Art, 13.121

Plate 11
Cat. no. 28
Giorgio de Chirico
The Regret,
1916
Oil on canvas, 23 3/8 x 13 in.
(58.9 x 33 cm)
Inscribed, l.l.: G. *de Chirico / 1916*
Munson-Williams-Proctor Institute
Museum of Art, 54.150

▲

Plate 12
Cat. no. 41
Janet Fish
After Leslie Left,
1983-84
Oil on canvas, 48 x 62 in. (121.9 x 157.4 cm)
Inscribed, l.r.: *JANET FISH* ©
Albright-Knox Art Gallery, Norman E. Boasberg,
George Cary, and Charles W. Goodyear Funds, 1984.2

CATALOGUE

Bernard Barryte

Italy, seventeenth-early eighteenth century

he authorship of this painting is questioned. In 1964, Ferdinando Bologna attributed it to Tommaso Realfonso, called Massilo (ca. 1677-after 1743), citing similarities with signed paintings in its placement of objects, facture, and use of chiaroscuro.[1] The study of Italian still life painting has advanced considerably during the past thirty years, and on the basis of a photograph Federico Zeri has suggested Paolo Antonio Barbieri (1603-1649) as the author.[2]

Realfonso was considered the best student of Andrea Belvedere (ca. 1652-1732), a Neapolitan still life painter who specialized in flower pieces. According to Bernardo de Dominici, the painter's earliest biographer, Realfonso painted flower studies, game pieces, dried fruits, "and any number of other objects."[3] Working well into the eighteenth century, Realfonso continued the regional tradition in which the influence of Caravaggio (1560/65-1609) persisted. A still life specialist, Paolo Antonio was the younger brother of the famous Emilian artist Giovan Francesco Barbieri, called Guercino (1591-1666), with whom he occasionally collaborated and from whom he learned the dramatic use of chiaroscuro.[4]

Still life painting in Italy, which seems to have developed autonomously, experienced in the seventeenth century a golden age comparable to that in the Netherlands, Spain, and France. Although Northern influences filtered south, what were usually assimilated were compositional formulas and motifs rather than content, for the Italian paintings generally fulfilled a decorative function and lacked the moral imperative informing their Northern counterparts.[5] *Still Life with Quince* celebrates abundance by offering a variety of foodstuffs in a composition that recedes deeply into space. This Baroque formula is typical of Italian works throughout the seventeenth century, though it is more prevalent during the second half. The use of dramatic, form-defining chiaroscuro remained fashionable after its introduction by Caravaggio and popularization by a succession of influential followers, who perpetuated the tradition throughout the seventeenth century. That similar qualities are found in Italian paintings from different regions made when Caravaggio's influence was still fresh contributes to the difficulty of affirming the authorship of or specifying a date for this picture.

In *Still Life with Quince*, light enters sharply from the left, casting dense shadows that dramatize the volumetric solidity of the forms before fading into the tenebrous background (made even darker by the effect of time on the pigments). The artist took pains to achieve verisimilitude, manipulating the pigments and using light to imitate the variety of surfaces and render each object in a manner that suggests its unique tactile qualities. The waxy hardness of the cucumbers is differentiated from the tender smoothness of the olives; the glossy surface of the apples is smoothly painted in comparison to the impasto used to render the pulpy and porous rind of the lemons. A drier pigment and crisp brush work imitate the coarse surface of the wicker basket, whereas the brush work is invisible on the smoothly reflective body of the vase in the foreground.[6] That each undulation and flaw on the surface of each quince is the subject of detailed study, is indicative of the naturalistic impulse pervasive in seventeenth-century Italian still life paintings.

▲

Still Life with Quince,
seventeenth-early eighteenth century
Oil on canvas, 27 1/2 x 43 in. (69.9 x 109.2 cm)
Memorial Art Gallery of the University of Rochester,
Gift of Dr. and Mrs. Fred W. Geib, 64.110

PROVENANCE:
Mortimer Brandt, New York (dealer).

till Life with Two Partridges and a Teal was attributed to Rembrandt and described as "painted in the artist's most vigorous style" when it was first published by John Smith in 1836,[1] and it retained this attribution until quite recently. Today, the painting is generally believed to be a product of the master's workshop. Unfortunately, our knowledge of organization and production within Rembrandt's shop is fragmentary. His many students included some young apprentices as well as an unusually high proportion of more mature artists. Aert de Gelder, Govaert Flinck, Carel and Barent Fabritius, and Ferdinand Bol, for example, had already learned their craft from other masters. According to the seventeenth-century writer Arnold Houbraken, these older students came to Rembrandt specifically to assimilate his fashionable new style. Joachim von Sandrart, another contemporary painter and theoretician, reported with some displeasure that Rembrandt charged even his most advanced assistants an annual fee of a hundred guilders, although he earned between two thousand and twenty-five hundred each year from the sale of their paintings and etchings.[2]

The extent of Rembrandt's involvement in paintings by his students remains uncertain, but the commercial element of his enterprise may account for the signature on the Ithaca canvas. Moreover, despite the efforts of scholars during the past decades, the artistic personalities of Rembrandt's numerous students have not all been defined precisely, and attempts to assign paintings to these individuals are made with varying degrees of assurance. Attributions are especially difficult for works created during the poorly documented decade of the 1630s. Thus, while Two Partridges and a Teal can be dated with some precision, there is as yet no consensus regarding the identity of the author.[3]

Rembrandt's oeuvre contains works in all genres, but his production of still lifes is comparatively meager. An inventory made in 1656 mentions five *vanitas* still lifes, but the only surviving works to which this description may apply are *Dead Peacocks with a Girl* (1644; Amsterdam, Rijksmuseum) and *Dead Bittern Held by a Hunter* (1639; Dresden, Gemäldegalerie). Also belonging to this group is a third painting, *Dead Bittern and a Girl with a Dead Snipe* (163[7]; Zurich, E. G. Bührle collection), which was formerly attributed to Rembrandt but whose authorship is now questioned.[4] In each of these paintings, the game is accompanied by a prominent human figure. The pictures thus represent a transitional moment between the late sixteenth-century kitchen and market pieces of Pieter Aertsen (1508-1575) and Joachim Beuckelaer (ca. 1530-1573) and the independent game pieces (*jacht-stilleven*) produced by specialists such as Elias Vonck (1605-1652) and Cornelis Lelienbergh (1626-1676) during the 1640s and 1650s. Later in the century, opulent trophy pictures by such artists as Jan Weenix (1642[?]-1719) and Melchior d'Hondecoeter (1636-1695) marked the further elaboration of the genre.[5]

In composition, technique, and tonality, the Ithaca painting is closely related to the still life elements in the three paintings cited above. It features three game birds[6] suspended individually from nails, though only the nail supporting the central bird is clearly visible. The hunt motif is clarified by the broadly painted crossbow[7] and the game bag lying on the stone shelf beneath the birds. As is typical of this period in Dutch painting, *Two Partridges and a Teal* is almost monochromatic. The design is based on a harmonious blend of brown and golden hues highlighted by judicious strokes of red, green, and white. Individual brush strokes were used with great precision to define texture, differentiating the polished stock of the crossbow, for example, from the stiff wing feathers and downy breasts of the birds.

Light enters from the left, illuminating the round volumes of the bodies and accenting the white markings. The contrast between the birds and the dark shadows they cast, in combination with this internal modeling, affirms the trompe l'oeil intention of the artist, who painted the figures life-size. The light also silhouettes each shape against the subtly modulated surface of the wall, emphasizing the carefully balanced composition formed by the birds and their shadows. The wall, stone ledge, and crossbow are indicated in a comparatively summary fashion, focusing attention on the deftly executed birds. Viewed in its entirety, the golden tonality and rich chiaroscuro endow

Still Life with Two Partridges and a Teal,
ca. 1638-40
Oil on canvas, 28 1/2 x 22 in.
(72.4 x 55.9 cm)
Inscribed, u.r.: *Rembrandt*
Herbert F. Johnson Museum of Art,
Cornell University,
Bequest of David B. Goodstein,
Class of 1954, 86.30.7

PROVENANCE:
Thomas Emmerson, London, 1836;
David B. Goodstein (by 1967).

SELECTED BIBLIOGRAPHY:
J. Smith, *A Catalogue Raisonné of the Works of the Most Eminent Dutch, Flemish, and French Painters…*, 9 vols. (London, 1829-42), vol. 7 (1836), p. 76, no. 184; C. Hofstede de Groot, *A Catalogue Raisonné of the Works of the Most Eminent Dutch Painters of the Seventeenth Century*, trans. E. G. Hawke, 8 vols. (London, 1916), vol. 6, p. 445, no. 988 (as by Rembrandt, ca. 1638); K. Bauch, *Rembrandt: Gemälde* (Berlin, 1966), no. 560 (as by Rembrandt, ca. 1638); J. Bruyn et al., *A Corpus of Rembrandt Paintings, III (1635-1642)*, trans. D. Cook-Radmore (Dordrecht, 1989), p. 38 (as by Workshop, late 1630s); S. A. Sullivan, *The Dutch Gamepiece* (Totowa, N.J., 1984), p. 86, n. 16.

the painting with a rather meditative quality. What is in any case a morbid subject has been transformed by means of light and color into what may be a sober celebration of abundance.

During the seventeenth century, hunting was restricted in Holland to the nobility. It is believed, therefore, that game pieces are linked iconographically with notions of social prestige.[8] The partridge was an appropriate motif in this context. As an epigram by the popular author-physician Jan van Beverwijck suggests, its relative rarity made the partridge a delicacy: "You won't find partridge often on our poor table, / That meat is fare for lords, food for the epicure."[9] Although foodstuffs may serve an emblematic purpose in Dutch still lifes, we must be judicious in our interpretations. In this case, the absence of supporting motifs makes it unlikely that the Ithaca

painting was intended as a warning against luxury. Though partridges were considered to be the most libidinous of birds, it is equally doubtful that the partridges in this game piece were intended to fill their traditional role as symbols for lust.[10] On the other hand, it is difficult to avoid thinking of such paintings as reminders of the inevitability of death and therefore at least tenuously related to the *vanitas* theme that pervades much of Dutch still life painting (cat. no. 4).[11] Whatever its intended meaning, the Ithaca painting is both an important early example of the independent game piece and a notable example of the aesthetic that prevailed in Rembrandt's studio during the late 1630s.

Dutch/Flemish, 1606-1683/84

 e Heem lived in both Holland and Flanders, and his work encompasses the two regional styles. The synthesis he achieved influenced his contemporaries throughout the Lowlands. His many students and imitators extended this influence to succeeding generations. Famous for the immaculate realism of his still lifes, de Heem's most exquisitely fluid brushwork is frequently found in paintings produced when this tremendously prolific artist was in his seventies.[1]

De Heem was born in Utrecht. A misunderstanding of the documents gave rise to the traditional belief that he was taught by his father, David de Heem the Elder, though Jan's earliest paintings are most closely related to works by Balthasar van der Ast (1593/94-1657).[2] Around 1625, de Heem moved to Leiden, where he painted *vanitas* pictures in addition to monochrome breakfast pieces.[3] He may have lived briefly in Haarlem before traveling to Antwerp in 1635/36. This move may have been motivated by de Heem's religious convictions as well as his interest in the art produced in the southern Netherlands, but his contemporary Joachim von Sandrart reported that the still life painter was attracted by the variety of exotic fruit available in the great port city.[4] De Heem became a citizen of Antwerp and joined the local guild of Saint Luke. He remained there until 1669, when he left for Utrecht. The French invasion of 1672 caused the painter to return to Antwerp, where he remained until his death.

In Antwerp, the expressive simplicity of de Heem's Dutch style was enriched by contact with the grandiose still lifes of Frans Snyders (1579-1657) and other artists in the entourage of Rubens. For patrons who sought opulent celebrations of abundance, he painted *pronkstilleven*, large canvases in which billowing draperies and monumental architecture dramatize tables overflowing with rabelaisian quantities of foodstuffs, precious objects, and exotic creatures. He also painted flowers and fruits in garlands, baskets, and hanging bouquets that reflect the influence of the Flemish painter Daniel Seghers (1590-1661).[5] Paintings such as the present example satisfied the demand for richly nuanced but more intimately scaled compositions.

Transience and temperance were central themes in the seventeenth-century still life tradition. By virtue of their allusive content and arrangement, the objects in this meticulously crafted painting are intended to encourage the thoughtful viewer to consider alternative moral choices. The validity of the painting as a vehicle for moral truth is affirmed by the self-portrait reflected on the surface of the glass *roemer*, which assures the viewer that the painting is indeed a true mirror of the world. In addition, de Heem may have intended to locate the still life before a window opening onto a view of the world,

a motif he developed during the 1640s. The background paint has become translucent with age, and the outlines of a stone embrasure are now visible in the upper right quadrant.[6]

The painting's theme is established by the glass *roemer*, its central element, which defines the apex of the triangular composition. A peeled citron (a type of lemon) has been set in the *roemer* to temper the sweetness of the white wine in which the fruit floats.[7] In the foreground are a variety of objects painted with a mimetic clarity that emphasizes their distinct forms and textures. Set casually on the marble plinth that defines the base of the triangular composition, they function almost literally as footnotes, giving specific meaning to the general idea of temperance suggested by the lemon-in-wine motif.

Analysis of their symbolic connotations clarifies the significance of this apparently haphazard array of items. The burning wick and smoking sulfur stick remind the viewer of the transient nature of sensual pleasures, exemplified by smoking, and signify as well the general idea of the brevity of life. That human mortality is the consequence of the Fall in Eden is recalled by the seville orange, depicted with just the first signs of decay. During the seventeenth century, this citrus fruit was frequently used to represent the fruit of the Tree of Knowledge which afforded humanity knowledge of good and evil.[8] Oysters were common symbols of gluttony and concupiscence; de Heem has painted the opalescent sheen of these succulent delicacies with consummate skill. The combination of full and empty shells again recalls the idea of temporality and transience.[9] Knowledge of good and evil is given active significance by the knife, a common symbol for the power of discrimination. By reference to Proverbs 23:2 ("And put a knife to thy throat, if thou be a man given to appetite"), knives suggest the need for temperance, a point emphasized by the diagonal placement of the handle, which directs our attention toward the tempered wine. Sam Segal has suggested that knives with inlaid handles were especially popular among still life painters because the black and white pattern could represent good and evil, between which a choice must be made.[10] The nature of this choice is clarified by the reptilian creature that crawls along the blade, recalling the serpent in the Garden of Eden. Moreover, the knife separates symbols associated with the Fall from the bread and wine, which are obvious eucharistic symbols offering the hope of redemption. The pansies twined around the laurel branch invite meditation.

The Rochester *Still Life* is typical of the genre in that it functions perfectly as a decorative object containing an unobtrusive moral lesson. On one level, it is simply a beautiful

culinary display. When its contents are considered more carefully, however, the composition expresses the idea that rejecting the temptations of the senses enables mankind to overcome the consequences of the Fall and attain redemption. No element of the composition is extraneous to the content, and this restraint was considered admirable and characteristic of the artist. When Samuel van Hoogstraten warned young painters that "a multitude of images which have no function is loathsome," for example, he referred them to de Heem as a model of pictorial conciseness.[11] The nondenominational character of the message and the subtlety with which its didactic content is expressed insured the popularity of such paintings in both the Protestant north and Catholic south of the Netherlands.

▲
Still Life,
1640s
Oil on panel, 14 3/8 x 18 5/8 in. (36.4 x 47.9 cm)
Inscribed, u.r.: *Ja[ ] de heem*[12]
Memorial Art Gallery of the University of Rochester,
Marion Stratton Gould Fund, 49.63

Plate 1

SELECTED BIBLIOGRAPHY:
S. D. Peters, ed., *Memorial Art Gallery: An Introduction to the Collection* (Rochester, 1988), pp. 90-91.

DAVID BAILLY
4

Dutch, 1584-1657

ailly was born in Leiden, where he was taught by his father. Subsequently, during a six-year apprenticeship in Amsterdam, Bailly studied painting with Cornelis van der Voort (ca. 1576-1624). Beginning in 1608, he traveled through Italy and Germany before returning in 1613 to settle permanently in Leiden. He established a considerable reputation for his vivid portraits, which range in scale from life-size images to precious miniatures.[1]

It remains uncertain whether Bailly also studied with Jacques de Gheyn II (1565-1629), whose *Humana vana* (1603; New York, Metropolitan Museum of Art) is considered the earliest surviving *vanitas* still life.[2] Nevertheless, as a successful portrait painter whose clients included the professors and theologians of Leiden's university, Bailly moved in the same social and intellectual circles as de Gheyn II, and this may account for his virtuosity in manipulating *vanitas* imagery. Bailly was presumably familiar with attitudes engendered by Calvinism and the fashionable Neo-Stoic philosophy[3] that encouraged the development of this admonitory genre in an environment tainted by chronic war and recurring plague.

Bailly has been considered the father of *vanitas* still life painting in Leiden, but this reputation is now doubted, as only three *vanitas* subjects are unanimously accepted as autograph works: a drawing dated 1624 in the *Album amicorum Cornelius de Clarges* (The Hague, Koninklijke Bibliotheek), a *vanitas* still life that he added to his own portrait by Thomas de Keyser (ca. 1627; Paris, private collection),[4] and *Vanitas Still Life with a Portrait of a Young Painter* (1651; Leiden, Stedelijk Museum de Lakenhal).[5] On the basis of these works, however, several other *vanitas* paintings have been attributed to him.[6] Though the present example has been ascribed previously to Jan Davidsz. de Heem, Jacob Walscapelle, Hendrick Andriessen, P. van den Willigen, and Jacques de Gheyn III,[7] the current attribution to Bailly is supported by similarities of theme, facture, format, and iconography with Bailly's Leiden canvas.

Vanitas still lifes were austere when the genre first became prevalent during the 1620s and 1630s. Following the pattern of other still life genres, however, *vanitas* paintings became increasingly ornate and intricate by midcentury. During this same period of maturation, the theme spread from Leiden and Utrecht to other artistic centers in Holland and then throughout Europe, religious differences proving no obstacle to the rigorous *vanitas* message.[8] Initially reflecting Calvinist ideals, *vanitas* pictures assailed moral and ethical laxness. By depicting aspects of wealth, luxury, and pride in worldly success, they reminded viewers of the brevity of life and vanity of worldly things. Emerging initially from the *memento mori*

▲

Vanitas with Negro Boy,
ca. 1650
Oil on canvas, 37 1/4 x 45 3/4 in. (94.6 x 116.2 cm)
Herbert F. Johnson Museum of Art, Cornell University,
Gift of Mr. and Mrs. Louis V. Keeler, by exchange, 86.6

Plate 2

PROVENANCE:
Christie's, London, *Old Pictures and Drawings from Various Sources,*
June 19, 1953, lot 43 (as by Jan Davidsz. de Heem), bought Eastern
(Euston?); Malcolm R. Waddington Gallery, London (by 1961);
Prof. Dr. and Mrs. W. Muensterberger, London; P. and D. Colnaghi
and Co., Ltd., London.

SELECTED BIBLIOGRAPHY:
*Ijdelheid der Ijdelhaden: Hollandse Vanitas-voorstellingen uit de
Zeventiende Eeuw,* exh. cat. (Stedelijk Museum de Lakenhal,
Leiden, 1970), no. 13 (as by Jacques de Gheyn III, 1629[?]).

tradition, *vanitas* paintings affirm the commonplace "Death makes all things equal" (*Mors omnia aequat*), and they shared as their collective theme a refrain from Ecclesiastes I:2: "Vanity of vanities, all is vanity."

Whereas other still life genres frequently disguise their didactic content, in *vanitas* pictures the grim meaning is explicit. The images are composed of motifs that, individually and in combination, reinforce the moralizing intention. Their message is summarized in a poem by Johan Albert Ban:

> Everything that is of man hangs by a thin thread
> And collapses by an unexpected fall.
> What are world, pleasure, vain delight?
> Defection, pain, smoke and shadow: nought.
> Nor gold nor ivory, food, drink, music nor acclaim
> (Which quickly pass) together cause happiness.
> Time and eternity, these two are our true possession.
> This man must consider—the rest is for death.

Ban's verse is appended to Theodor Matham's 1622 still life engraving depicting musical instruments set below a cartouche inscribed *VANITAS*.[9]

In *Vanitas with Negro Boy*, Bailly offers a centralized composition painted in a mellow gray and brown monochrome appropriate to the sober subject. Highlights enliven the surface with patches of brilliant color which focus attention on the pyramidal table-top still life. Wealth and power, suggested by the richly attired black servant and by the authoritative columns that bracket the table, allude to the motto *Sic transit gloria mundi* (Thus passes the glory of the world). The servant displays an oval portrait miniature whose subject directs the gaze of the spectator toward the treasures piled on the table below.[10] Dominating the composition is an exquisitely painted skull, the prime symbol of mortality. Adjacent to it are a portable sundial, a guttering candle, and an hourglass—all common reminders of time's passage. In the literature of the period, too, the transient values of fame and earthly goods are often likened to reflected images, which are deceptive and fleeting. Artists were commonly known as makers of illusions, and so this complex of ideas could be referred to by the self-portrait reflected on the upper bulb of the hourglass.

Other objects on the table represent a comprehensive inventory of *vanitas* imagery. Today, their symbolic significance is often clarified by reference to the Bible or such contemporary texts as the moralizing poems of Jacob Cats and the edifying emblems of Roemer Visscher's *Sinnepoppen* (Amsterdam, 1614). For example, the cards and dice in the foreground of our painting appear in Visscher's book accompanied by the motto "The worst things please the most people."[11] Next to the gunpowder bottle and the open pocket watch—another reminder of time's passage—are a burning wick, a pipe, and a packet of tobacco. These smoker's requisites may allude to contemporary aphorisms such as "The glory of the world is naught but smoke," which paraphrases the lament in Psalm 102:3, "My days are consumed like smoke." Smoking was a new and popular vice deplored by seventeenth-century moralists as a harmful pleasure indulged in merely for sensual gratification. Visscher summarized this disapprobation when he illustrated the adage "There is often something new, but it is seldom good" with a picture of a man smoking.[12]

Above the skull, the budding, blooming, and decaying tulips offer a less than subtle reference to the transitory nature of life. In addition, a mania for tulips, shells, and other exotic items seized the Dutch in the early part of the century. As a result of the financial catastrophe caused by speculation in these items, they became commonplace symbols of foolishness and luxury. Tulips and shells appear among Visscher's emblems bearing the complementary mottoes "A fool and his money are soon parted" and "It's astonishing what use a fool can make of his money." Emphasizing the transitory nature of fortune, these objects affirm the vanity of material wealth.[13] In this context, the vanity of worldly learning and the arts is suggested by the artist's palette and brushes, the weighty books, and also musical instruments, which themselves became a frequent *vanitas* emblem.[14] Music performed is inherently fleeting, and therefore the theme of transience is underscored by the instruments. Also, the common analogy between making music and making love is recalled by the recorder, guitar, and especially the lute, which allude to the voluptuous life because of their legendary capacity to incite lust. However, because it is an art of proportion and harmony, the reference to music also cautions the viewer regarding the need to temper desire.

The carved putto serves a dual function. Among the emblems for the arts, it symbolizes sculpture. In addition, the juxtaposition of the carved putto and the skull represents a clever adaptation of a *memento mori* motif invented in the fifteenth century. The contrast between an exuberant child and a death's head bluntly reiterates the central theme of humanity's inevitable fate.[15] The putto's energetic gesture also draws attention to the glistening bubbles. Common metaphors for life's brevity, they have added resonance in this composition, because they also echo the shape of the portrait miniature. Having its origin in classical antiquity, the proverb "Man is a bubble" was revived in the sixteenth century and introduced into the pictorial repertoire by artists such as Hendrick Goltzius (1558-1617), teacher of Bailly's colleague de Gheyn II, who used the theme most dramatically in *Humana vana*.[16] The implications of the motif are poignantly expressed in the verse by Franco Estius appended to *Quis evadet* (*Who Will Be Spared?*), a 1594 engraving of this subject from the school of Goltzius: "The fresh silvery flower, fragrant with the breath of spring, / Withers once its beauty wanes; / Likewise the life of man, already ebbing in the newborn babe, / Vanishes like a bubble or like fleeting smoke."[17]

Bailly's *Vanitas with Negro Boy* is a picture designed to serve a serious moral purpose. To borrow a phrase from Simon Schama, it is "congested with meaning." It includes an encyclopedic compendium of *vanitas* motifs which Bailly has manipulated with intelligence and ingenuity. His technical skill and compositional mastery have imbued these conventional symbols with a new and powerful eloquence.

Dutch, 1619/20-1678

arseus, inventor of the woodland still life (*bosstilleven*) or "herb piece,"[1] was a fascinating individual to whom relatively little scholarly attention has been devoted. Most of our information derives from Arnold Houbraken, a painter and biographer who interviewed the artist's widow, but the chronological details in his account are imprecise. Marseus evidently worked not only in his native Holland but also in England and France and, most importantly, in Italy. He traveled there in 1648, accompanied by his pupil Mathias Withoos (1627-1703). Between 1652 and 1663 the pair worked in Florence for Grand Duke Ferdinand II de' Medici (1621-1670) and his brother, Cardinal Leopoldo de' Medici, who were especially interested in Dutch painting. They were also patrons of the Accademia del Cimento, the first scientific society devoted to empirical experimentation, and their fascination with Marseus's paintings was presumably related to their enthusiasm for science. Marseus also visited Naples and Rome, where he was associated with the Dutch painters known as the Bentvogels. They gave him the nickname de Snuffelaar (The Sniffer) because he "sniffed around everywhere for strange colored or speckled snakes, lizards, caterpillars, spiders, butterflies, and strange plants and herbs." Noting the artist's interest in "the most despised and horrible objects," Houbraken remarked that he "painted almost nothing other than poisonous snakes, toads, and lizards." Visiting Marseus in Rome, Samuel van Hoogstraten recorded his astonishment at the "many strange monsters he kept and fed, whose nature he also so wonderfully understood, as if he could imagine their thoughts."[2]

In 1657, Marseus returned to Holland, accompanied by his pupil in Florence, Willem van Aelst (1627-ca. 1683), who later became the teacher of Rachel Ruysch (cat. no. 7). At his house at Diemen, known as Wateryk, Marseus bred snakes and had a vivarium for the animals he used in his paintings. He also had a cottage on the outskirts of Amsterdam that he used when collecting zoological specimens.

Marseus's earliest surviving works are flower paintings that conform to the conventions established by such artists as Ambrosius Bosschaert the Elder (1573-1621) and van der Ast. These paintings depict bouquets displayed in vases located on ledges in unspecified interior settings. Typically, these pictures are animated by the presence of various insects and reptiles, which might have allegorical meanings that complement the symbolic significance of the flowers.[3] Marseus's best-known works, however, are his woodland scenes, in which the botanical specimens are depicted in naturalistic outdoor settings inhabited by butterflies, beetles, snails, lizards, and snakes. His signed but undated *Plants, Butterflies, Snake, Insects, and Lizard* and *Plants, Butterflies, and Lizard* (formerly in the collection of Cardinal Leopoldo; Florence, Palazzo Pitti) indicate that Marseus invented this genre while in Italy, although known dated examples were created between 1660 and 1677, after his return to Holland.

Because of its monumental scale, *Still Life with Thistle* is an especially impressive example of Marseus's unique contribution to the still life tradition, exemplifying as well a format favored by his student Withoos.[4] The composition is dominated by a magnificent thistle growing at the base of a rock. The threatening sky seen at the left accounts for the crepuscular atmosphere within the grottolike space and hints that lightning may be the cause of the intense chiaroscuro that highlights the plant's angular contortions. The phosphorescent glare also illuminates the wings of butterflies flitting among the spiky leaves, adding notes of color to the somber green and brown tonalities of the picture. The lower leaves have suffered from the depredations of snails that crawl along the stems, and from beneath these decaying leaves, a lizard emerges to threaten a grasshopper.

The bosky scene is replete with meaning. The contrast between the decomposing foliage and the healthy leaves suggests the idea of transience, as does the depiction of blossoms in various stages of their life cycle. Other elements of the composition also possess figurative meanings. The thistle is a symbol of earthly sorrow because of the curse pronounced against Adam in Genesis 3:17-18 ("Cursed is the ground for thy sake…thorns also and thistles shall it bring forth to thee"). Because of its thorns, it is also a symbol of the Passion of Christ, recalling the crown of thorns. As the instrument of humanity's fall, the snake seen emerging from amidst the thorns is a commonplace symbol of evil. However, because they shed their old skin and become "new," snakes were also thought of as analogous to those who "throw off for Christ the old man…through much abstinence and tribulation."[5] Because of its mythic ability to restore its sight by gazing at the sun, the lizard was a "seeker after salvation."[6] Although conventionally a symbol of sloth, the snail emerging from its shell was also a symbol of resurrection.[7] A common symbol of the human soul, the butterfly also represented resurrection, because it emerged from a tomblike chrysalis and resembled

Still Life with Thistle,
ca. 1670
Oil on canvas, 49 1/2 x 40 in.
(125.7 x 101.6 cm)
Herbert F. Johnson Museum of Art,
Cornell University, Gift of Mr. and
Mrs. H. A. Metzer, 60.195

Plate 3

the redeemed soul ascending to eternity. Grasshoppers— or locusts—were among the plagues that persuaded Pharaoh to free the Hebrews, and this insect became a symbol for the conversion of nations to Christianity.[8] If it is read as a conglomeration of visual metaphors, the meaning of *Still Life with Thistle* is the hope of redemption afforded by Christ's sacrifice.

Symbolic expression is pervasive in the still life tradition, but the meanings are rarely explicit and must be teased out from their context. In the case of Marseus, it would be anachronistic to characterize the artist as an early scientist, objectively recording observed phenomena. Though the thistle is a masterpiece of illusionistic painting, and the fauna are undoubtedly based on studies from nature, the composition as a whole is entirely artificial, the product of imaginative

amalgamation and transformation in the studio. Curt Habicht suggested that Marseus discovered in the secluded world of the forest undergrowth a microcosm of the human world.[9] This interpretation was expanded by Ingvar Bergström, who suggested that this consummate naturalist discovered a reflection of the human condition in the small dramas occurring in the forest undergrowth and in bogs, and that he painted his strange pictures to represent in a general sense the human soul struggling for salvation.[10] The congruence of related themes encompassed in the imagery of *Still Life with Thistle* suggests that the artist was aware of the Christological connotations incorporated in its details, and that he composed the painting with the intention of conveying a message of pious hope.

Dutch(?), seventeenth century

aving their origins in manuscript illuminations, religious paintings, tapestry designs, and model books, floral still lifes emerged as an independent genre in the northern Netherlands around 1600. Among the earliest surviving examples is Roelant Savery's *Flower Still Life* of 1603 (Utrecht, Centraal Museum), which shows a bouquet in a glass vase set within a stone niche and accompanied by various reptiles and insects.

Naturalistic accuracy was fundamental to the genre, but within an intellectual environment devoted to allegory, such paintings were more than charming decorations. Depending on their context, they might represent the sense of sight or smell, a particular season or continent, or some combination of these and correlative ideas. Because of the brevity of their lives, flowers were easily associated with the concept of transience, and floral still lives were thus generally aligned with the *vanitas* theme. Moreover, individual plants and flowers possessed traditional symbolic connotations, and an artist might allude to particular theological or moral notions by means of the plants and flowers selected for a pictorial bouquet. Finally, the development of the genre coincided with the emergence of botanical science, and the paintings might document rare or exotic specimens treasured among collections of curiosities.[1]

The earliest still lifes—created by artists such as Bosschaert the Elder, de Gheyn II, and van der Ast between about 1600 and 1620—tend to be organized symmetrically. Usually occupying a costly vessel on an unadorned table top, an individual blossom or modest bouquet is set against a monochrome background that contrasts with the evenly illuminated subject. Legibility is crucial to these early still lifes, and the flowers are commonly arranged to minimize overlapping. Light is used primarily for descriptive rather than dramatic purposes, and the blossoms themselves are depicted in a manner that offers the clearest possible reading of their distinct forms. Although compositions tended to become more opulent and complex as the genre matured, atavism, as Sam Segal has noted, was a feature in later periods.[2] While the pristine simplicity of the early examples may have had an enduring appeal among painters, other reasons for this retrograde tendency may have included training by older masters or a desire to appeal to connoisseurs anxious to enhance the historical appearance of their painting collections.

The composition of the Utica painting recalls formulas prevalent during the first decades of the seventeenth century. Although the absence of a tulip in a mixed bouquet is somewhat unusual, the lilies, rose, narcissus, iris, and other flowers are common in early flower pieces. Pointing to the opaque application of paint and the rather stiff composition, Susan Kuretsky suggested that the author may have been Ernst Stuven (1657-1712), a German student of van Aelst and Abraham Mignon (1640-1679), who is recorded in Amsterdam in 1675 and is known to have collaborated with Rachel Ruysch (cat. no. 7).[3] The amusing vase resembles vessels found, for example, in paintings by Giacomo Recco (1603-1653), one of the first Neapolitan still life painters to specialize in floral subjects, and in works by his followers. The importance of the Netherlands as a center for international trade would account for its presence—as well as its value as an exotic item—in the North. A similarly rich, ornamental urn occurs, for example, in *Flower Still Life* (Copenhagen, Statens Museum for Kunst) by Jacob Marrell (1613/14-81).[4]

▶

Still Life with Lilies and Iris,
ca. 1675-1700
Oil on panel, 15 1/4 x 10 in.
(38.7 x 25.4 cm)
Munson-Williams-Proctor Institute
Museum of Art, PC 949

PROVENANCE:
William C. Doscher Co., New York;
Proctor collection.[5]

raceful, imaginative compositions and fidelity to nature in the depiction of glorious botanical specimens are the qualities that underlie Ruysch's renown as one of Holland's greatest flower painters. Her expertise derived from two sources. Her knowledge of nature and enthusiasm for botanical subjects were nurtured by her father, Dr. Frederick Ruysch. A scientist of wide interests, he was a renowned anatomist as well as director of Amsterdam's botanical garden. He also maintained a famous *Wunderkammer*—a sort of early natural history museum—in which he exhibited his immense collection of anatomical and natural curiosities which his daughter helped him to prepare and display.[1] Her proficiency as a painter was acquired from Willem van Aelst, a versatile still life artist specializing in fruit and flower pieces, whose apprentice she became at age fifteen. In 1701, Ruysch entered The Hague's painters' guild, and in 1708, she was named court painter by the Elector Palatine Johann Wilhelm von Pfalz, visiting his court in Düsseldorf. After the elector's death in 1715, Ruysch and her husband since 1693, the portrait painter Juriaen Pool II (1666-1745), settled in Amsterdam with their large family. Ruysch continued to paint until at least 1747, when she was eighty-three, carrying the tradition of fruit and flower painting well into the eighteenth century.[2]

Floral Still Life is one of about a dozen woodland still lifes (*bosstillevens*) Ruysch painted early in her career. Her later works are sophisticated but more conventional flower pieces, each featuring an elaborate bouquet in a vase set in a niche or on a marble ledge. In the woodland still lifes, floral elements are located in a naturalistic outdoor setting inhabited by insects, reptiles, and amphibians. She was probably introduced to this theme by students of Otto Marseus van Schriek, the painter who had invented the genre at midcentury (cat. no. 5). The Rochester composition is related to the left half of *Flowers and Amphibians near a Pool of Water* (Vaduz, collection of the Prince of Liechtenstein), a painting by de Heem (cat. no. 3) on which Abraham Mignon may have collaborated with his teacher; it is likewise related to *Flower Composition in a Landscape* (Bamberg, Staatsgalerie), Mignon's own copy of de Heem's composition. Ruysch's familiarity with this composition is affirmed by the general design of *Floral Still Life* and by details such as the snake and frog motif in the lower left, which is quoted directly from the earlier compositions. The means by which Ruysch became familiar with this composition remain uncertain. Berardi's hypothesis that she may have known it through her future husband, who was Mignon's adopted son, seems less likely than the suggestion of Fred Meijer and Sam Segal that the intermediary was Ernst Stuven (see cat. no. 6), a pupil of Mignon with whom Ruysch collab-

orated. Ruysch's fascination with the motif is suggested by the Rochester painting and two related compositions (Kassel, Gemäldegalerie; Rotterdam, Museum Boymans-van Beuningen).[3]

Floral Still Life is an entirely artificial construct in which an illusion of naturalism has been achieved through the realistic depiction of details. The spotlighted roses, lilies, iris, morning glories, morning bindweed, opium poppies, and inkcap mushrooms, for example, are painted with the same meticulous precision lavished on the trunk of the elder tree from which they unnaturally spring. Although some of the plants do grow in or near water, the cultivated blooms are not indigenous to this woodland environment, nor do they grow in this fashion. Although the physical description of the various zoological specimens is precise, the denizens of such swampy landscapes do not act in the manner portrayed—the rearing snail and fire-spitting frog are fanciful inventions added for dramatic effect.

The drama of the composition is heightened as well by the lighting, which accents the forceful modeling of the foreground elements. In contrast to the rocky background and sky, which are rendered in a flat and cursory manner, the detailed delineation of flora and fauna suggests that these elements are based on the observation of specimens to which the artist's father may have provided access. *Floral Still Life*, with its disjunction between foreground and background elements, may give some indication of the dioramas Ruysch helped design for her father's Wunderkammer.

The discrepancy between foreground and background emphasizes as well the artificial structure of the composition, revealing the artist's intention while betraying the painting's origin in the studio. Unlike Marseus or Mignon, who depicted complex and integrated environments replete with metaphoric overtones, Ruysch's primary interest was in the display of the precious blossoms, for which the swampy grotto served as an atmospheric backdrop. Her composition has its conceptual source in the artistic inventions of her predecessors rather than in nature. Her painting also lacks the iconographic elements that inform de Heem's or Mignon's paintings. Although she included the grasshopper, a common symbol of gluttony[4] as well as a symbol of resurrection (because it sheds its skin), Ruysch deleted the fir tree and goldfinch, which have traditional Christological connotations.[5] She may have been aware as well of the moral implications of the bestial confrontations and floral imagery, but allegory was not her primary concern. Rather, Ruysch seems to have discovered in de Heem's innovative composition a theme she ably adapted for her own purpose—the contrast between the grotesque and the beautiful in nature.

► *Floral Still Life,*
1686
Oil on canvas, 45 x 34 in. (117 x 87 cm)
Inscribed, l.r.: *R Ruysch / 1686*
Memorial Art Gallery of the University of
Rochester, Acquired with contributions
made in memory of Brenda Rowntree by
her friends, the Acquisition Fund of the
Women's Council, and the Marion
Stratton Gould Fund, 82.9

Cover

SELECTED BIBLIOGRAPHY:
M. Berardi, "The Nature Pieces of Rachel
Ruysch," *Porticus* 10/11 (1987-88), pp. 3-15;
M. H. Grant, *Rachel Ruysch, 1664-1750*
(Leigh-on-Sea, 1956), p. 25, no. 9
(misdated 1680); S. D. Peters, ed., *Memorial
Art Gallery: An Introduction to the Collection*
(Rochester, 1988), pp. 94-95; S. Segal,
A Flowery Past, exh. cat. (Gallery P. de
Boer, Amsterdam, 1982), p. 52, no. 60.

Dutch(?), eighteenth century

*I*t is difficult to ascribe this unusual composition to a specific national school or period. There is some slight affinity to compositions by Elias van den Broeck (ca. 1650-1708) and later works by Rachel Ruysch (cat. no. 7), however, and the relatively light palette and balanced serpentine design suggest its origin in eighteenth-century Holland.

Located on an unadorned stone plinth, a bouquet is set before a monochrome background, occupying the center of the panel. Light enters from the left, creating tonal differences that enhance the visual impact achieved by variations of scale, texture, and color. The axis of the composition is formed by a curving arrangement of stock, scabiosa (pincushion flowers), primroses, lilies-of-the-valley, and other blossoms that form a richly variegated structure dominated by the brilliant saffron of the marigolds.[1] The bright colors and multitude of small, varied forms contrast dramatically with the smooth, broad, gently curving forms of the tulip. Past its prime, its red-tinted, milky-white petals open out to dominate the center of the composition.

The author of this painting was concerned with the decorative value of the composition, not with establishing a narrative based on floral symbolism. As had been typical of the genre since its inception, the unique features of each flower are meticulously imitated. Though there is considerable detail, a crisp but rather broad manner was used in deploying the unmixed, opaque colors favored by this artist.

▶

Flower Still Life,
eighteenth century
Oil on panel, 17 x 12 1/4 in.
(43.2 x 31.1 cm)
Munson-Williams-Proctor Institute
Museum of Art, PC 120

PROVENANCE:
Proctor collection.[2]

61

eyond the outline of his successful career, biographical details concerning Spaendonck are sparse. Born in Tilburg, he was the younger brother of Gerardus van Spaendonck (1749-1822), an influential still life painter specializing in floral subjects. Gerardus moved to Paris, where his success paved the way for his brother. In 1774, Gerardus was appointed miniaturist to Louis XVI (1754-1793), and after the Revolution he served as administrator for the former royal park, the Jardin des Plantes, with responsibilities for teaching the iconography of flowers. Under Napoleon (1769-1821), Gerardus became a member of the Legion of Honor in 1804, and in 1808, he was invested with the title of count.

Cornelis followed his brother to France in 1773 and, except for the years 1818-25, when he returned to Holland, also enjoyed an enviable career in his adopted country. He made his Salon debut in 1789 and became a member of the Académie that same year. Between 1795 and 1800, he served as director of the Sèvres porcelain works, and he continued to produce designs until 1808. The brothers were close and sometimes collaborated, but unlike Gerardus, who favored watercolors, Cornelius continued to work in oils as well as gouache and exhibited frequently. Though it is dated 1793 and has somewhat smaller dimensions than those listed in the Salon catalogue, the Ithaca canvas is believed to be the painting Cornelis displayed there in 1795 (as no. 697).[1]

Floral still lifes first appeared in Holland during the early years of the seventeenth century. The relatively uncomplicated compositions of the earliest examples, which were designed for the clearest possible display of individual specimens, became much more complex as the genre matured. In the early compositions, too, flowers as well as insects and other elements were selected not only for their aesthetic appeal but also for their symbolic meanings. By the accretion of these metaphorical connotations, flower pieces were often imbued with specific religious and moral ideas in addition to the general notion of transience. New layers of significance were added to flower paintings as the century progressed. Reflecting the pride of amateur botanists and the emergence of empirical science, they served to document rare or exotic specimens. By including blossoms from different parts of the globe or from different seasons, for example, flower paintings also served as emblems of Dutch mercantile success or as a sort of floral microcosm or calendar. As with other still life genres over the course of the century, flower pictures became more decorative than didactic. Even as the range of potential meanings expanded, the spiritual and figurative values implanted in such still lifes were sublimated as they became more opulent in accordance with their role as luxury items. Commensurate with this change of function, they became vehicles for the display of artistic virtuosity. Luxuriousness was articulated in the ostentatious craftsmanship essential to the creation of these lavish floral confections.[2]

Rachel Ruysch (cat. no. 7) in her later work and, especially, Jan van Huysum (1682-1749) were consummate masters of this lush tradition, carrying it into the eighteenth century to be perpetuated by Jan van Os (1744-1808) and the Spaendonck brothers. Featuring a profusion of magnificent blossoms, Cornelis's *Still Life of Flowers* is the product of this rich legacy.[3] The composition is stabilized by its triangular arrangement, the apex of which is defined by the flowers in the alabaster vase. The polished surface of the variegated marble ledge serves as its base, while the ceramic vase and precariously balanced crystal dish demarcate its sides. This configuration is animated by the curvilinear floral arrangement. The flowers sweep up to the left along the sinuous stem of the poppy and spiral around to culminate in the asymmetrical bouquet in the alabaster vase. Lilacs and tulips rise from the vase, while the curving design is continued by the highlighted roses and peonies that cascade down from this elegant container. Light is used to dramatize the composition. Compositional unity is achieved by a harmony of warm tones invigorated by judiciously balanced areas of rich, saturated color.

The alabaster vase is set on a stone socle embellished with a trompe l'oeil bas-relief of a sleeping bacchante and baby satyr. In their discussion of this painting, Boven and Segal suggest that the juxtaposition of these sleeping figures with the poppy, another symbol of sleep, connotes ignorance.[4] The meaning of the painting arises from the contrast between this element and the symbolic meanings contained in other elements of the composition, most notably those in the crystal bowl above the relief. Grapes traditionally represent the Eucharist, and pomegranates conventionally symbolize the Church and the Resurrection. Other flowers have related connotations. The peony, for example, represents transitory voluptuousness, the white rose adjacent to it symbolizes purity, the hyacinth represents prudence, and the anemone the Passion of Christ. Cornelis's composition and choice of flowers indicate that he was conversant with the traditional language of allegory of

Still Life of Flowers,
1793
Oil on canvas, 31 1/4 x 25 in.
(79.4 x 63.5 cm)
Inscribed, l.r.: *Corneille / Van
Spaendonck.1793*
Herbert F. Johnson Museum of Art,
Cornell University, Gift of the Estate
of David B. Goodstein, 86.30.8

Plate 4

PROVENANCE:
Comte Oscar de l'Espine(?); Princess
Louis de Croy (by 1892[?]); her sale,
Charpentier, Paris, March 22, 1933,
lot 57; sold Sotheby's, London, March
26, 1969, lot 45; Leggatt Brothers,
London; private collection, England
(by 1980); David B. Goodstein, New
York.

SELECTED BIBLIOGRAPHY:
M. van Boven and S. Segal, *Gerard &
Cornelis van Spaendonck: Twee
Brabantse Bloemenschilders in Paris*
(Maarssen, 1980), no. 202.

which his brother was a master. To assume that his audience was equally familiar with the language of floral symbolism is probably incorrect.

In his standard history of Dutch still life painting, Ingvar Bergström identifies the attempt "to separate the customary symbols from the religious scene and to give them an independent existence as a symbolical still life" as fundamental to the emergence of still life as an independent genre.[5] Recognizing visual metaphors as prevalent in seventeenth-century still lifes is justified by our knowledge of contemporary habits of thought as well as by the writings of theoreticians such as Gérard de Lairesse, who as late as 1707 advised still life painters to infuse their works with hidden meanings.[6] Bearing in mind Edouard de Jongh's warning that "congruencies in form between an emblem and a painting do not automatically imply congruent contents,"[7] we are justified for the most part in trying to

decipher the meaning of individual objects in these paintings and in trying to discern the programmatic connotations of such artfully contrived conglomerations of objects.

By the end of the seventeenth century, however, the tradition of "disguised symbolism" had become diluted as the religious and social impulses informing the development of the genre lost potency. The iconographic relevance of objects became subsidiary to their importance as part of the conventional repertoire of still life painters. At the same time, the tradition of moral and philosophical allegory was superseded by other paradigms. Although some of its components may have retained a residual significance, it seems more likely in the context of the late eighteenth century that *Still Life of Flowers* was appreciated primarily as an exquisite ornament.

American, 1810-1899

Theorem painting was especially popular during the first half of the nineteenth century, when the technique was used extensively for domestic ornamentation. According to Louise Karr, the vogue coincided with the temporary eclipse of embroidery and the concurrent rise of painting and drawing as skills essential to the education of genteel young women.[1] Pitkin, a native of Saratoga County, New York, was fifteen when she made this "theorem" for a sofa pillow.[2]

Theorem paintings were created by an essentially mechanical process that involved first tracing a design on transparent paper, then cutting out the pattern to produce a stencil. The stencil itself was known as a "theorem"; paintings created by the "theorem method" became known as "theorem paintings." Instructions for making the transparent paper and recipes for the colors were widely available in publications such as J. W. Alston's *Hints to Young Practitioners in the Study of Landscape Painting, to Which Are Added Instructions in the Art of Painting on Velvet* (Edinburgh, 1804) and Maria Turner's *Young Lady's Assistant in Drawing and Painting* (Cincinnati, 1833). Prints were the recommended source for the designs, although ready-cut stencils could be purchased.

The whole design was reduced to a set of theorems, or stencils, each including noncontiguous parts. This was done to prevent wet colors from bleeding into one another. The theorems were placed successively on velvet and the material within each aperture was painted according to the following instructions: "Take plenty of paint...on your brush, and paint in the cut leaf of the theorem; hold the brush upright, and manipulate quickly with a circular motion." Shading was added in a second stage that was followed by the addition of stalks and other linear elements.

The artist could combine templates derived from a variety of sources to create an original composition. The precise source of Pitkin's design is unknown. The bouquet enriched with a peony and tulip, lush pile of fruit, and bird's nest set on a marble ledge are all familiar elements within the tradition of still life painting. As a household ornament, Pitkin's pillow cover offers charming testimony of the continuing appeal outside the Netherlands of compositions originating in the bourgeois world of seventeenth-century Holland.

▲

Still Life on Velvet,
1825
Oil on velvet, 12 3/4 x 20 in. (32.4 x 50.8 cm)(oval)
Inscribed (on a detached fragment): *Painted in 1825*
by Elizabeth Pitkin
Albany Institute of History and Art,
Gift of Emily S. Penfield, 1961.15

PROVENANCE:
Emily S. Penfield (artist's granddaughter).

American, 1805-1876

ohn Vanderlyn, Jr. (or II) was the nephew and godson of the cantankerous and frustrated history painter John Vanderlyn (1755-1852). Details of the younger Vanderlyn's life are sparse. He worked in Savannah, Georgia (1833), and possibly Charleston, South Carolina (1836), and also in the Albany region.[1] According to Hasbrouck family tradition, Vanderlyn was "overly fond of the bottle and when he was down and out, 'Abraham of the Strand' [Abraham Hasbrouck], as he was called, would take him in until he recovered." Vanderlyn, who is known primarily as a portrait painter, exchanged paintings for this beneficence.[2]

The present example may have been one of two fruit still lifes exhibited by "John Vanderlyn" in Albany in 1858. That this refers to John Vanderlyn, Jr., is suggested by the stamp of Goupil and Co. on the reverse, giving their address as 366 Broadway. The dealer and art supply company moved to this address in 1854, two years after the death of the older Vanderlyn, and remained there as Goupil only until 1858.[3] Internal evidence supports a midcentury date as well. Richly veined marble was especially desirable at this time, and the design of the marble-topped sideboard, with its serpentine pattern and ogee beveled edge, is typical of American furniture made in the 1850s and 1860s. The glass and latticework ceramic bowls as well as the silver platter are contemporary with the sideboard. The "Grecian"-style molding that frames the window was a common architectural embellishment that may have derived from a pattern book published between the 1840s and 1860s.[4]

Although it was a favorite genre among the Peale family, still life production in America experienced something of a hiatus during the third and fourth decades of the nineteenth century, only to reemerge in the 1850s. Vanderlyn's *Still Life* is typical of the intermediate period between the modest and restrained compositions of the Peales (cat. no. 12) and the more elaborate compositions of the later period, which culminated in Severen Roesen's lavish paintings (cat. nos. 13, 14).[5] Vanderlyn's composition is somewhat unusual, however.

Whereas interior settings are common in the majority of contemporary still lifes, he located his subject before an open window, recalling a seventeenth-century format most closely associated with Jan de Heem (cat. no. 3).[6]

Enriched by its architectural setting and embellished by an opulent swag of red drapery, this painting focuses on generous piles of fruit set on a sideboard before a window that opens onto a luminous, cloud-streaked sky. All the fruit is large, unblemished, and perfectly ripe. Each is uniformly illuminated by the clear, bright light that pervades the entire composition, crisply defining all of the surfaces and highlighting the radiant colors. The light reflects off the glossy skins of the apples, grapes, and pears and reveals the subtle texture of the peaches and the waxy surfaces of the melons. Although each object is carefully painted in brilliant, subtly varied local colors, the direct illumination minimizes the shadows that would suggest volume and density. The absence of effective chiaroscuro results in a peculiarly "weightless" effect. The fruits appear to float precariously, as though each had been painted from a separate model and only subsequently arranged in this configuration.

▲

Still Life: Fruit in a Classical Setting,
1854-58
Oil on canvas, 30 x 42 in. (76.2 x 106.7 cm)
Albany Institute of History and Art, 1983.11

PLATE 5

PROVENANCE:
Abraham Hasbrouck, Kingston, New York;
by descent to Jansen Hasbrouck; to his daughter,
Mary Hasbrouck Preston; to her daughter,
Susan Preston Hasbrouck; to her son Preston
Hasbrouck; Vose Galleries, Boston.

American, 1784-1865

ubens Peale was the fourth son of Charles Willson Peale (1741-1827), a painter, scientist, and cultural entrepreneur noted for his diverse interests and impressive energy, from whom Rubens learned the rudiments of painting. Unlike his siblings, whom painting became a primary enterprise, Rubens devoted himself to other aspects of his family's enthusiasms because of his notoriously poor eyesight and fascination with botany. He became a dedicated naturalist, and it is in this capacity that he is celebrated in *Rubens Peale with a Geranium* (1801; Washington, D.C., National Gallery of Art), a portrait by his brother Rembrandt (1778-1860) in which the young scientist displays a prize plant and peers at us over his spectacles.[1] Rubens also managed his father's museums in Philadelphia and Baltimore, and then his own museum in New York that failed during the financial panic of 1837. Following this catastrophe, Rubens retired with his wife and children to a Pennsylvania farm, where he continued his horticultural experiments. With the encouragement of his daughter Mary Jane, he also resumed painting.

Rubens fastidiously noted the progress of each picture in a journal. Work on *Number 26* began on February, 3, 1857, when his son George "dead colored" the tin support, that is, laid in the grey or brown underpainting. Rubens completed the work on January 30 of the following year.[2] The finished painting has a soft radiance that may result in part from the reflective nature of the tin. Rubens's technique was painstaking. The pearly luster of the silver basket and the glowing ripeness of the fruit were achieved by patient layering of pigments and oil glazes.

Rubens was proficient but not inventive. The composition, in which fruit is displayed on a simulated shelf, can be traced back to ancient Greek still lifes described by Pliny the Elder and imitated by the Romans in wall paintings executed between the first century B.C. and fourth century A.D.[3] Of more immediate relevance is the fact that the majority of

Rubens's still lifes are typical of the Peale dynastic style, reflecting in particular the influence of his uncle, James (1749-1831), and his brother Raphaelle (1774-1825), who specialized in the genre, and whose compositions are themselves indebted to early seventeenth-century Netherlandish prototypes.[4] The silver basket in *Number 26*, for example, appears first in James's *Fruit and Grapes* (location unknown), a painting Rubens may have owned.[5] Likewise, *Number 26* is reminiscent of such characteristically austere compositions as Raphaelle's *Still Life with Raisins, Yellow and Red Apples, and Porcelain Basket* (Baltimore Museum of Art) and *Still Life with Oranges* (Toledo Museum of Art),[6] in which a few centrally located specimens are isolated on a bare ledge.

Occupying the center of the composition, the basket here is placed before a monochromatic background. The fruits are illuminated by clear, direct light, their forms modeled primarily by modulations in color rather than by contrasts of light and shadow. Rubens's rendering of fruit was less sophisticated and somewhat harsher than Raphaelle's, and he failed to achieve the sense of atmosphere and illusion of palpable reality obtained by his brother. However, the luminous hues and symmetry of *Number 26* exemplify the tonal harmony and serene balance that constitute the virtues unique to his paintings. Created in the quiet of rural retirement, *Number 26* was already unfashionable when it was finished in 1858. It embodies the modesty and restraint of an earlier era that had been overwhelmed by the exuberant and lavish still lifes favored by Severin Roesen (cat. nos. 13, 14) and his contemporaries.

▲
Still Life Number 26: Silver Basket of Fruit,
1857-58
Oil on tin, 13 x 19 in. (33 x 48.3 cm)
Inscribed, l.r.: *26*
Memorial Art Gallery of the University of Rochester,
Gift of Helen Ellwanger, 64.40

Plate 6

PROVENANCE:
Rubens Peale; his son, Charles Willson Peale II; his daughter,
Clara Elizabeth Peale (Mrs. Charles Karsner Mills); her son,
Albert Burd Mills; by whom given to Helen Ellwanger.

SELECTED BIBLIOGRAPHY:
P. Anderson, "Rubens Peale's *Still Life Number 26: The Chronicle
of a Painting*," *Porticus* 6 (1983), pp. 32-36; C. C. Sellers, "Rubens Peale:
A Painter's Decade," *Art Quarterly* 23 (1960), pp. 139-50; *The Peale Family:
Three Generations of American Artists*, exh. cat. (Detroit Institute of Arts,
1967), pp. 116-18.

American (born Germany), ca. 1815-after 1872

hough his paintings are numerous, biographical information on Roesen is sparse. Born in Germany, he was probably trained as a painter on enamel or porcelain, and his work constitutes an extension of the still life tradition represented, for example, by the congested and opulent floral compositions of Joseph Nigg (1782-1863). Roesen may have exhibited a flower piece in Cologne in 1847, a year before he emigrated to the United States to escape political unrest in his homeland. He first settled in New York, where his works were exhibited and acquired by the American Art Union. In 1857, he abandoned his family and traveled first to Philadelphia and then to Harrisburg and Huntington before settling in Williamsport, Pennsylvania, in 1862. Following his departure a decade later, all traces of the painter are lost. Scholars continue to sort out his works from those produced by numerous imitators and forgers; it is currently estimated that Roesen produced between three and four hundred paintings during his American career, some of which he sent to exhibitions in Brooklyn, Philadelphia, and Baltimore.[1]

Roesen is thought to have painted portraits, but all of his surviving works are still lifes featuring flowers or fruits, which are sometimes the subjects of paired canvases or intermingled in single compositions. Like the Dutch masters to whom his work is indebted, Roesen's method of composing was synthetic; individual pictures are not based on the immediate observation of nature. For example, though they are separated by a decade, the Syracuse and Utica paintings contain many common motifs, including the champagne glass and the ceramic epergne with wild strawberries, suggesting that he may have worked from templates or, more likely, that he reused a collection of props filled variously with fruit or flowers.[2] Since the scale of many of his pictures and the multiplicity of fruits and flowers preclude the possibility of individual studio setups, he also may have used highly finished drawings as models for the various parts of their compositions, a Netherlandish tradition that persisted in the ateliers of porcelain painters.

Both pictures incorporate a characteristic device: the bounty of nature cascading into the foreground from two marble tiers. In the Utica canvas, the fruit is arranged in a generous pyramid, its apex formed by the open magnum of champagne and its base stabilized by a luscious section of watermelon and the inviting pilsner of champagne. The vertical structure of the Syracuse canvas is emphasized by two

grape clusters that extend downward from the stem of the white epergne and demarcate the central axis of the composition. In both paintings, the underlying geometry gives order to a seemingly haphazard arrangement, while the formality of the structure is relaxed by the decorative arabesques described by the tendrils of the grapevines.

The scales of the pictures differ, but in each the individual elements are more or less life-size. The idealized fruits are depicted with almost scientific objectivity. The effervescing champagne within its fragile crystal, the pulpy texture of the lemon rind, and the glistening dewdrops, for example, are rendered with the precision of a miniaturist. As though contained in decorative bell jars, which became popular at this time, these naturalistic elements are arranged in a flamboyantly artificial manner, affording the artist ample opportunity to demonstrate his virtuosity in depicting the play of light over diverse surfaces and textures. With their abundant masses of fruits and flowers, Roesen's pictures are heirs to the opulent still lifes that first appeared in mid-seventeenth-century Antwerp and persisted in ornate compositions by such artists as Cornelis van Spaendonck (cat. no. 9). If they lack the specific moral connotations that often reside in their Netherlandish predecessors, Roesen's paintings achieve a similar level of decorative grandeur, delighting the viewer by the almost palpable reality of the sumptuous displays and portraying the material abundance fundamental to bourgeois well-being. The Utica and Syracuse examples affirm the interpretation of Roesen's still lifes as expressions of plenitude, "the ultimate embodiment of mid-century optimism, representing the richness and abundance of the land, the profusion of God's bounty in the New World, [and] his blessing upon the American Eden."[3] Dramatized by the play of light, the pictures have a commanding presence. Although little is known concerning Roesen's patrons, the pictures were clearly intended as dominating elements in the decoration of Victorian homes.

▶

Still Life with Fruit and Champagne,
1853
Oil on canvas, 30 x 44 in. (76.2 x 111.8 cm)
Inscribed, l.r.: *S. Roesen / 1853*
Munson-Williams-Proctor Institute
Museum of Art, 82.53

Plate 7

PROVENANCE:
Alexander Gallery, New York; Mr. and
Mrs. Erving Wolff, New York; sold
Sotheby's, New York, April 23, 1982, lot 7.

SELECTED BIBLIOGRAPHY:
P. Schweizer, ed., *Masterworks of American
Art from the Munson-Williams-Proctor
Institute Museum of Art* (New York, 1989),
no. 20.

▶

Still Life with Fruit, ca.
1860-65
Oil on canvas, 30 x 25 in. (76.2 x 63.5 cm)
Everson Museum of Art, Purchased with
funds from the J. Stanley Coyne
Foundation, Inc., 85.55

PROVENANCE:
Ira Spanierman Gallery, New York;
The Fanlight Inc., Manlius, New York.

American, 1848(?)-1892

arnett is unquestionably among the most important American still life painters active during the last quarter of the nineteenth century.[1] Carrying the scrupulous observation of objects farther than earlier artists, his works achieve a deceptive level of illusionism. The success of his trompe l'oeil compositions influenced many of his contemporaries, including John Haberle and John Peto (cat. nos. 19, 20). Some emulated his subject matter as well as the rich, dark tonality that he favored (cat. no. 16); others were inspired to create unique and personal works within the still life tradition Harnett had transformed.

Harnett was instrumental in introducing a sharply delineated realism to still life painting and shifting its focus from the fruits and flowers favored by the Peales and Roesen (cat. nos. 12-14) to man-made objects. Nevertheless, his reputation declined rapidly after his death. He was only rediscovered in the 1930s by the dealer Elizabeth Halpert and, later, by critics such as Alfred Frankenstein, who in the mid-1940s were impressed primarily by the artist's mimetic skill and elegant compositions. In the 1970s, scholars first acknowledged the psychological impact produced by these paintings, suggesting that "Harnett's books and music are not only examples of amazing trompe l'oeil illusionism, but…also symbols of man's achievements."[2] Subsequently, art historians began to explore not only the social context with which these virtuoso paintings are associated but also their iconographic connotations.[3]

Harnett emigrated from Ireland, probably as a result of the potato famine, to settle in Philadelphia with his family in 1849. Apprenticed to an engraver, he became proficient at this trade. In January 1866, he enrolled in the "antique class" at the Pennsylvania Academy of the Fine Arts before moving in 1869 to New York. Supporting himself by engraving silver for such notable jewelry firms as Tiffany's and Wood and Hughes, Harnett attended the Cooper Union Free School and the National Academy, where he first exhibited publicly in 1875. In an undated interview, the artist recalls that he had been unable to afford a model and had therefore painted a still life. The sale of *Fruit* (location unknown) and other still lifes encouraged him to make a career of painting and to devote himself exclusively to this genre.[4] Returning to Philadelphia in 1876, he exhibited in the Philadelphia Centennial Exposition and established himself as a still life painter. By 1880, Harnett was able to sail to Europe, where he visited London and Frankfurt but stayed longest in Munich and Paris, returning to New York in 1886. Afterwards, he enjoyed considerable success, but ill health evidently impinged on his productivity (though not on the quality of his work) during the six years preceding his death.

Harnett's earliest paintings are fruit pieces, but he soon became preoccupied by other subjects—beer steins, smoking paraphernalia, books, money, and the accessories of letter-writing. During his brief career, his game and trophy pictures, trompe l'oeil musical instruments, and table-top subjects pioneered in America a resurgence of still life themes familiar from the tradition that had evolved in seventeenth-century Europe. Painted in 1878, *Music and Literature* demonstrates the

▲

Music and Literature,
1878
Oil on canvas, 24 x 32 1/8 in. (61 x 81.2 cm)
Inscribed, l.r.: W Harnett / 1878
Albright-Knox Art Gallery, Gift of Seymour H.
Knox, 41.10

Plate 8

PROVENANCE:
Discovered in a music shop, Rittenhouse Square,
Philadelphia, 1930s; Edith Halpert, The Downtown
Gallery, New York.

SELECTED BIBLIOGRAPHY:
S. A. Nash, *Albright-Knox Art Gallery: Painting and Sculpture
from Antiquity to 1942* (New York, 1979), pp. 288-89; A.
Frankenstein, *After the Hunt: William Harnett and Other
American Still Life Painters 1870-1900,* rev. ed. (Berkeley, 1969),
pp. 15, 48, no. 35; W. H. Gerdts, *Painters of the Humble Truth:
Masterpieces of American Still Life 1801-1939,* exh. cat. (Philbrook
Art Center [Tulsa], Columbia, Mo., 1981), pp. 153-60, 178-79;
H. W. Williams, Jr., "Notes on William M. Harnett," *Antiques* 43
(June 1943), pp. 260-62.

artist's technical virtuosity as well as his familiarity with the traditions of the genre. His adaptation of this subject matter parallels the growing taste for old master paintings among American collectors.[5] He may have studied seventeenth-century examples in private collections at the same time that he could have seen them displayed in the galleries opened at the Pennsylvania Academy of the Fine Arts in 1876, at the New-York Historical Society, and at the recently established Metropolitan Museum of Art, New York.

In its essential elements, *Music and Literature* is a traditional book still life.[6] Although the objects appear to be chaotically disposed, the composition is stabilized by its pyramidal arma-ture: the base is established by the table on which the objects rest and the worn sheet of music that extends forward; the apex is defined by the central pile of books. This structure is animated by the zigzagged spines of the central volumes and the diagonals formed by the precariously perched flute, the gold-embossed spine of *Don Quixote*, and the rolled score of Giuseppe Verdi's *La Traviata*. The surface is further enlivened by the contrasts of light and shadow which emerge from the diffuse lighting. Harnett's harmonious chiaroscuro serves to unify the composition and to affirm the solidity of the forms.

The ink dripping from its pot and the fanned pages of the volume in the foreground suggest that we are witnessing a transient moment frozen in time. The drama of this unique effect is enhanced by the rich harmony of colors and the lacquered precision with which Harnett rendered the most minute surface details. The distinctive matte textures of paper and leather are imitated precisely; the differing reflective capac-ities of the silver candlestick, ivory and ebony flute, and worn gold of the embossed bindings are depicted with equal care.

Attention to detail and precision in the replication of appearances were essential to the "almost magical illusionism" Harnett achieved "in the deceptive rendering of three-dimen-sional objects on his flat painted surface."[7] Trompe l'oeil was not, however, an end in itself, for Harnett, a devote Catholic, may have been familiar with the traditional language of *vanitas* iconography. Aware of the spiritual and symbolic connota-tions of objects, he was also extremely sensitive to the contem-plative potential inherent in such assemblages.

The polished veracity with which the elements of the composition are depicted contribute to the emotional impact of *Music and Literature* by establishing a degree of conviction that was crucial to Harnett's purpose. The artist's microscopic precision convinces the viewer that every detail has been replicated with absolute fidelity, but the realism of the image is deceptive. Harnett believed that "the whole effect of still life painting comes from its tone, and the nearer one attains perfection, the more realistic the effect will be."[8] In making "an artistic composition," the perfection Harnett sought was not measured in terms of verisimilitude but by its psychological impact. Achieving the desired effect depended ultimately on the choice of objects rather than their arrangement, but he recognized that their evocative potential derived as much from their appearance as from their intellectual or emotional associations. "I want my models to have the mellowing effect of age," he said, because "models selected without judgement...would be utterly devoid of picturesqueness, and would mar the effect of the painting." He therefore transformed nature "to make the composition tell a story."

Harnett achieved his narrative purpose by selecting objects exhibiting "the rich effect that age and usage give" and by purposeful manipulation: "In painting from still life I do not closely imitate nature. Many points I leave out and many I add." Harnett's declaration makes it impossible to be certain whether his models in fact possessed the characteristics the artist required to harmonize "well with the tone of the painting." Harnett may have been referring to *Music and Literature* when he explained that "the flute that served as a model is not exactly like the one in the picture. The ivory was not on the flute at all, and the silver effects for the keys and bands I got from a bright silver dollar." This synthetic method of creation resembles the procedures of his seventeenth-century predecessors, who composed their vivid flower pieces more frequently from different pages of sketchbooks than from actual models. Harnett's consummate artistry lay in his ability to organize observed phenomena into a coherent, convincing unit capable of inspiring thoughts on mortality and the value of human achievement.

J. M. Schmidt(?)
16

American, active ca. 1879

his picture is indistinctly signed in dark red paint over the dark green of the tablecloth. Although the date 79 can be distinguished with some certainty, the signature itself has been deciphered variously as "J. M. Schorr" and "J. M. Scherrah." "J. M. Schmidt" is being used currently by the Herbert F. Johnson Museum of Art.[1] None of these readings correspond with the names of professional American artists active during the final quarter of the nineteenth century.

Whoever he or she may have been, "Schmidt" was clearly familiar with paintings William Harnett created after returning to Philadelphia from New York in 1876. The composition and components of this 1879 still life are dependent on Harnett's table-top still lifes such as *Banker's Table* (1877; New York, Metropolitan Museum of Art) and *Writing Table* (1877; Philadelphia Museum of Art),[2] compositions that reflect the intimacy of the Peale tradition (cat. no. 12) while presaging the more elaborate assemblages Harnett would begin to develop in compositions such as *Music and Literature* (cat. no. 15).

Harnett boldly arranged his objects asymmetrically and parallel to the picture plane to emphasize the horizontal format. The design of Schmidt's *Still Life* is more conventional. The centralized pyramidal composition is anchored by two stout volumes surmounted by a smaller book and folded piece of paper. From left to right in the foreground are a folded one-dollar silver certificate, a conical bottle of Arnold's ink, a quill pen that leans against the books, three silver coins, a folded

letter adjacent to its torn envelope, and some small cigars and matches. Familiar from Harnett's earlier paintings, these attributes are set on a deep green cloth decorated with a looping gold band. The red ink label, blue folded paper, and yellow envelope punctuate and enliven the surface with a classical triad of saturated colors. As though the frame were indeed a window, the various shapes and volumes are defined by light that enters from the viewer's space to illuminate the foremost surfaces. This light dissipates quickly, and the objects recede into shadows that merge with the dark monochrome background.

Like many of Harnett's emulators, the author of *Still Life* was intrigued primarily by the decorative potential of Harnett's compositions and was less scrupulous in rendering minute details. The torn binding of the book bearing the title *Aldemus* and the various textures have been imitated with less conspicuous precision than in Harnett's paintings, and throughout, only the largest letters are legible. In contrast, Harnett focused on such details because of their evocative potential, using them as opportunities to underscore the narrative implied by each conglomeration of objects. If Schmidt failed to appreciate a deeper purpose in Harnett's skillful trompe l'oeil paintings, his *Still Life* nevertheless attests to their immediate influence.

▲

Still Life,
1879
Oil on canvas, 11 1/2 x 16 1/2 in. (29.2 x 41.9 cm)
Inscribed, l.l.: *J. M. Schmidt[?]* / *Philada 79*
Herbert F. Johnson Museum of Art, Cornell University,
Herbert F. Johnson Bequest Fund, 80.22

PROVENANCE:
J. B. Neumann, New York; Schweitzer Gallery,
New York.

SELECTED BIBLIOGRAPHY:
A. Frankenstein, *After the Hunt: William Harnett and
Other American Still Life Painters 1870-1900*, rev. ed.
(Berkeley, 1969), p. 186, no. 25.

*V*ollon was a native of Lyons, an important center for still life painting during the nineteenth century.[1] In 1850, he enrolled in the local Ecole des Beaux-Arts and nine years later moved to Paris. There he made the acquaintance of the Realist painters François Bonvin (1817-1887) and Théodule Ribot (1823-1891), who influenced his work perhaps as much as Jusepe de Ribera (1588-1652), Diego Velázquez (1599-1660), and Frans Hals (1580-1666), the seventeenth-century Spanish and Dutch painters he most admired. Vollon exhibited consistently at the Salon after his debut in 1864. His numerous official honors included the grand prize at the Paris Exhibition Universelle in the year of his death.

Though he painted landscapes and portraits as well, Vollon remains most famous for his vivid still lifes. In his encyclopedic *History of Modern Painting*, first published in 1893, Richard Muther declares Vollon to be "the greatest still life painter in the century." Arthur Bye, author of the earliest survey of the genre, thought him to be "the greatest painter of still life since Chardin, and one of the most accomplished painters of the nineteenth century."[2] The American critic and artist Kenyon Cox was even more effusive, explaining that Vollon "may not be a draughtsman—he may not be a colorist; but he is a painter. Vollon is, perhaps, the greatest painter living."[3]

Still life, traditionally the lowest rung in the academic hierarchy of pictorial genres, began to enjoy a more elevated status in mid-nineteenth-century France. Coinciding with the advent of Realist painting, this shift in critical values was reflected in a reevaluation of the forerunners of the new pictorial tendencies. Along with the Spanish artists whom Vollon especially admired, Chardin was among the painters who benefited most from this process. Writing in 1856, the influential critic Théophile Gautier emphasized that "the greatness of Chardin's talent lies in his broad and simple understanding of nature, his emphasis on local color, his robust use of paint."[4] Critics recognized similar qualities in Vollon's atmospheric compositions. Citing his proclivity for still lifes featuring domestic articles and his vigorous, painterly technique, they praised Vollon as the "Chardin of the nineteenth century."[5] Cox was more astute, however, when he observed that "Vollon's manner approaches much nearer to that of Velázquez."[6] What these artists were seen as sharing was mastery of a virtuoso technique that enabled them to transcribe their impressions of nature directly and precisely. The Buffalo *Still Life* is typical of paintings which the critic Jules Clarétie admired as "faithful to an exact interpretation of nature."[7]

Reminiscent of such paintings as Chardin's *Kitchen Table* (fig. 10; Boston, Museum of Fine Arts),[8] *Still Life* is linked to Chardin's pictures on several levels. Both feature commonplace domestic utensils that graphically demonstrate the material continuity underlying the entire still life tradition.[9] Also, the objects depicted by both painters were selected and arranged not for a narrative purpose, as might have been the case in a seventeenth-century Dutch painting, but for their intrinsic visual appeal and for the formal contribution they would make to the composition.

Less geometrically rigorous than Chardin's paintings, Vollon's *Still Life* features five simple objects remaining on a plain table after a meal. The linen tablecloth had been folded back to avoid soiling, and a few empty mussel shells remain among the vessels. The glazed pot, copper cauldron, earthenware wine pitcher, glass, and plain white platter are illuminated from left of center. The light penetrates no farther than these objects, which appear randomly placed but which actually constitute a carefully balanced design within the frame. The containers are isolated within a glowing atmosphere and silhouetted against a dark background. The contrast enhances the three-dimensional presence of the rotund forms, enriching the harmony of their browns, golds, and creamy whites.

Vollon employed a variety of brush strokes to imitate the distinct play of light on the glossy surface of the copper or the matte wine pitcher. He virtually molded each object with his brush, often building up a thick impasto, and by this means he represented each surface in a way that suggests its tactile qualities. Emile Zola accepted this mimetic naturalism literally and failed to understand Vollon's accomplishment. In his review of the 1866 Salon, he complains that Vollon's "realism consists in choosing vulgar subjects."[10] However, Clarence Cook, another contemporary critic, recognized that Vollon's "aim in painting is not imitation, least of all deception.... It is the beauty or curiousness of the reflections and color combined that charm him."[11] For Cox, Vollon's still lifes encompassed more than the record of the artist's perception. He suggested that they shared the poetic expressiveness of Chardin and Velázquez, transcending literal transcription.

The humble objects in this or related pictures, such as *Poteries* (1886; Canada, private collection),[12] are not properly the subject of Vollon's paintings, nor is their naturalistic appearance an end in itself. The Buffalo *Still Life* is not about pots and pans but about the poetry Vollon discovered within a deceptively commonplace matrix. Its subjects are form and color and light. Acknowledging the nobility Vollon bestowed on commonplace objects, the connoisseur Michel Faré concluded that the artist knew "how to bring out the hidden beauty of inanimate things. His technical virtuosity had a share in this enchantment."[13]

▲
Still Life,
1880-85
Oil on canvas, 25 3/4 x 32 in. (65.4 x 81.3 cm)
Inscribed, l.l.: *A. Vollon*
Albright-Knox Art Gallery, George B. and
Jenny R. Mathews Fund, 52.13

PROVENANCE:
Private collection, Paris; Robert Frank,
London (dealer).

SELECTED BIBLIOGRAPHY:
S. A. Nash, *Albright-Knox Art Gallery:*
Painting and Sculpture from Antiquity to 1942
(New York, 1979), p. 279.

American, 1840-1910

orn in Albany, Goodwin began painting around 1862 after injuries obliged him to leave the Union army. For the first twenty-five years of his artistic career, he followed the example of his father, the prolific portrait painter Edwin Wyburn Goodwin (1800-1845). Peripatetic by nature, the younger Goodwin traveled from Maine to Florida and from coast to coast, residing at least briefly in various western New York cities, including Ithaca, Syracuse, and Rochester, as well as in New York City, Washington, D.C., Colorado Springs, Chicago, Los Angeles, San Francisco, and Portland, Oregon. Goodwin painted numerous portraits as well as landscapes but is best known today for his trompe l'oeil still lifes. Explaining that "his wonderful coloring gave brilliancy to his subjects," the anonymous author of an obituary praised Goodwin's paintings as "so realistic…that the beholder was captivated by their close resemblance to nature."[1]

Goodwin specialized in game pieces, which depended on a tradition extending back to seventeenth-century Holland (cat. no. 2). Evidence suggests that he began to paint them around 1881, when he established a studio in Syracuse. His game pieces vary considerably in complexity, although all feature realistic depictions of dead game—most often birds, on occasion fish or rabbits. His most elaborate compositions, his cabin doors, reflect the influence of Harnett's *After the Hunt* and feature all manner of hunting paraphernalia realistically painted against wooden doors or panels. Among these, Goodwin's most famous composition is *Theodore Roosevelt's Cabin Door* (1905), a version of which is now in the Museum of Art, Springfield, Massachusetts.[2] Less complicated pictures resemble seventeenth-century compositions by Jan Baptist

Weenix or Hondecoeter. These feature individual or small groups of animals suspended from nails affixed to illusionistic wooden doors or plaster walls, as in the present example.[3]

Among the most pristine and elegant of Goodwin's compositions, *A Brace of Ducks* resembles the painting that appears in the upper right corner of Goodwin's Syracuse studio in an anonymous photograph dated 1887-89.[4] The ducks are silhouetted against a wall. The terra-cotta color of this smooth surface complements the grey, brown, and golden hues of the birds' plumage, and the harmonious blending of all these warm tones gives atmospheric unity to the composition. The play of light over the downy feathers highlights the graceful volumes of the plump birds, which cast deep shadows that enhance the trompe l'oeil effect.

Goodwin emphasized the weight of the birds by the positions of their sagging wings and feet and by his crisp rendering of the string that holds them suspended. He differentiated the leathery texture of the feet from the sleek feathers and offered mirrored front and back views. This provided an opportunity to describe the birds' distinctive markings completely, although Goodwin's purpose was not to achieve ornithological exactitude.[5] Viewed from a certain distance, the illusion of comprehensive detail is convincing; examined closely, however, the feathers disintegrate into thick-textured, staccato brush strokes. As is typical of his works in this genre, Goodwin eliminated all reference to the kill itself, presenting the pair as a beautiful trophy.

▶

A Brace of Ducks, 1885
Oil on canvas, 30 1/4 x 25 1/4 in.
(76.8 x 64.1 cm)
Inscribed, l.r.: *R. Lebarre Goodwin /
1885*
Memorial Art Gallery of the
University of Rochester,
Marion Stratton Gould Fund, 64.36

PROVENANCE:
Dr. Charles Strowger; Rochester
Stationary Company, Rochester;
Prof. Howard Merritt, Rochester.

SELECTED BIBLIOGRAPHY:
A. Frankenstein, *After the Hunt:
William Harnett and Other American
Still Life Painters 1870-1900*, rev. ed.
(Berkeley, 1969), pp. 131-35.

 hen he was fourteen years old, Haberle was apprenticed to a lithographer in his native New Haven. He practiced this craft in Montreal, Quebec; Providence, Rhode Island; and New York before returning in 1880 to work as a preparator and illustrator at Yale University's Peabody Museum. In 1884, he was again in Manhattan for a year of study at the National Academy of Design; he then settled permanently in New Haven, where he devoted himself to painting. The precision demanded by his work as a lithographer and illustrator manifests itself in Haberle's painted oeuvre.

The majority of his illusionistic pictures were produced between 1887 and 1895, after which Haberle tended to paint more conventional still lifes.[1] He displayed his trompe l'oeil pictures in various local and national exhibitions as well as in hotels, book and stationary shops, theaters, and saloons, attracting a clientele of affluent businessmen to whom realistic paintings of smoking paraphernalia, "girlie" pictures, playing cards, and hunting trophies appealed.

Haberle generally shares honors with Harnett and Peto (cat. nos. 15, 20) as the most distinctive and proficient of the late nineteenth-century American painters specializing in trompe l'oeil. Though the objects they portray are often similar, Haberle's crisp style appears straightforward and objective, differing from both the bell jar atmosphere and enameled perfection of Harnett and the tactile volumes and poignant ambience achieved by Peto. Also, unlike the other members of this triumvirate, Haberle consistently favored relatively flat subjects, establishing his reputation with deceptive paintings of paper currency. Among his most convincing illusions are pictures of clock faces and smudged blackboards, but his favorite subjects include worn money, playing cards, photographs, canceled stamps, torn stickers, and miscellaneous printed ephemera affixed to bruised surfaces. The frequently witty juxtaposition of texts and images complements the visual trickery of his rack paintings and typifies the artist's pervasive humor.

Torn in Transit is possibly the earliest of three innovative "package paintings," the other two dating from the first half of the 1890s.[2] The Rochester example represents a slim package tied up with soiled, slightly frayed string. The flatness of the objects offered Haberle perfect control over the illusion, and in this case the appearance of three-dimensionality suggested by the layered surfaces has been augmented by the clever device of having the painted wrapping and string continue onto all four edges of the stretcher. *Torn in Transit* depicts the "top" of the package. The wrapping paper is apparently torn, forming, so to speak, a ragged frame surrounding the exposed contents.

The package appears to contain an atmospheric landscape, perhaps a fashionable Hague School river scene or, according to Sill (1985), a view of an Alpine lake which Haberle may have copied from a postcard. This "painting" appears to have been carelessly removed from its stretcher—the left and bottom edges have been carefully cut, but the top edge is frayed, and the tacking edge survives only on the right. The tattered canvas has been carelessly attached to a rough pine support with tacks and a thumbtack that are depicted with microscopic precision. The upper right corner of the canvas curls back to reveal a cigarette-package beauty secured under it. Though this small monochrome card has been painted with great care, the artist's attention to detail is most dramatically demonstrated by his subtle imitation of the slight impression the card would have made pressing against the outer wrapping. Narrow but dense shadows have been employed to distinguish the overlapping layers of paper, canvas, and wood, and the distinct textures of these materials are carefully differentiated.

The tradition of trompe l'oeil pictures of pictures extends back to seventeenth-century Europe. They enjoyed a particular vogue in eighteenth-century Holland and France and then became part of the repertoire of American trompe-l'oeil painters.[3] In his treatment of the motif, Haberle demonstrated considerable skill and wit. Because it covers such a large proportion of the picture surface, it has been suggested that the painterly landscape was incorporated by the artist to compensate for his failing eyesight. However, the meticulous detail in other areas of *Torn in Transit* suggests instead that the motif was chosen as an amusing vehicle for displaying his extraordinary talent for descriptive imitation. By using his own precise technique to depict a loosely painted picture, Haberle created a visual paradox that is equally a clever trompe l'oeil invention and a thought-provoking demonstration of his virtuosity. In addition to the wit implicit in this pictorial conceit, *Torn in Transit* offers a wry commentary on the stylistic innovations of the Barbizon and Impressionist painters. The paradoxical nature of the work is enhanced by the complexity of the deception Haberle has perpetrated: a two-dimensional surface painted to imitate three dimensions is attached to a stretcher, so that it actually becomes a three-dimensional simulacrum of a package.

▶

Torn in Transit,
ca. 1888-89
Oil on canvas, 14 x 12 in.
(35.6 x 30.4 cm)
Inscribed, l.r.: *from Haberle-*
Memorial Art Gallery of the
University of Rochester,
Marion Stratton Gould Fund, 65.6

Plate 9

PROVENANCE:
Mrs. A. J. Fresneda, New Haven, Conn.
(artist's daughter); Mrs. Vera Haberle
Demmer, New Haven, Conn. (artist's
daughter).

SELECTED BIBLIOGRAPHY:
A. Frankenstein, *After the Hunt: William
Harnett and Other American Still Life
Painters 1870-1900,* rev. ed. (Berkeley,
1969), pp. 115-22; W. H. Gerdts and R.
Burke, *American Still Life Painting* (New
York, 1971), p. 158; W. Gerdts, *Painters
of the Humble Truth: Masterpieces of
American Still Life Painting 1801-1939,*
exh. cat. (Philbrook Art Center [Tulsa],
Columbia, Mo. 1981), pp. 196-98; R. F.
Chirico, "John Haberle and Trompe-
l'Oeil," *Marsyas* 19 (1977-78), p. 40; J.
Wilmerding, *Important Information
Inside: The Art of John F. Peto and the
Idea of Still-Life Painting in Nineteenth-
Century America,* exh. cat. (National
Gallery of Art, Washington, D.C.,
1983), p. 214; G. G. Sill, *John Haberle:
Master of Illusion,* exh. cat. (Museum of
Fine Arts, Springfield, Mass., 1985),
no. 28.

ike his friend William Harnett (cat. no. 15), Peto studied painting at the Pennsylvania Academy of the Fine Arts and specialized in painting still lifes. Peto remained in his native Philadelphia until 1889, when he moved to Island Heights, New Jersey. His self-imposed isolation from the centers of artistic activity seems to have been characteristic of this retiring artist, about whose life we know little. He was evidently well liked in his community, a conscientious family man, an affectionate father, and a talented musician, but otherwise there remain few biographical details beyond the tantalizing hints offered in his introspective and frequently enigmatic paintings.

Peto admired Harnett and was influenced by his accomplishments. However, Peto's table-top subjects and illusionistic office doors inevitably bear the unique, somewhat quirky stylistic and psychological imprint of their maker. Moreover, Peto is generally credited with reintroducing the rack picture— a motif that flourished in seventeenth- and eighteenth-century Europe—into the repertoire of American trompe l'oeil painters.[1] Nevertheless, when works by the latter were being rediscovered in the 1940s, Peto was inaccurately characterized as a follower of Harnett, and similarities in subject matter resulted in purposeful as well as unintentional confusion of Peto's works with those of his more famous colleague. The need to disentangle their oeuvres resulted in a clearer understanding of Peto's artistic personality and of the stylistic attributes unique to each painter.[2]

In an article notable for its brevity, Lloyd Goodrich summarizes distinguishing stylistic attributes that can be discerned, for example, when *Fish House Door* is compared with Harnett's *Music and Literature* (cat no. 15). The Harnett offers what appear to be "portraits" of specific, frequently luxurious objects. The conviction he achieved through his emphasis on local color, surface texture, and surface details suggests a vision resembling that of a high-resolution camera in its objectivity, clarity, and precision. Peto's manner of depicting objects makes them appear no less real but altogether more self-contained, mysterious, and seemingly introspective. He was generally more attentive to the decorative potential of shade and light, which emanates mysteriously and falls with almost tangible weight on selected surfaces. Rather than augmenting the appearance of three-dimensionality as it does in Harnett's work, the dramatic and sometimes inconsistent illumination in Peto's paintings simplifies forms and flattens volumes; these contradictions enhance the works' enigmatic quality. Surfaces are sharply divided into broad areas of light and shade which appear determined less by the demands of representational accuracy than by their contribution to the geometric structure of each composition. Unlike Harnett, who delighted in specificity and in depicting the polished surfaces of elegant, shiny objects, Peto's objects are more commonplace, rarely individualized, and cast in a luminous atmosphere that renders uniform the dusty opacity of their surfaces.[3]

The notoriety of the fourth version of Harnett's *After the Hunt* (fig. 13), exhibited at the 1885 Salon and sold to Theodore Stewart after Harnett's return to the United States, inspired a vogue for similar large-scale trompe l'oeil paintings. It has been suggested that still life photographs by Adolphe Braun (1812-1877) were the immediate source for Harnett's composition, but it is equally likely that during his European travels, he may have seen seventeenth-century paintings such as *Still Life with Hunting Attributes* (Groningen Museum) by Johannes Leemans (ca. 1633-1687/88) or similar subjects by Cornelius Norbertus Gijsbrechts (1610-after 1675) that established this pictorial tradition.[4] In any case, Peto was among those influenced by *After the Hunt*, but characteristically, he personalized the subject, perhaps to reflect his own interest in fishing.

According to Frankenstein, Peto painted several versions of *Fish House Door*, and the Utica painting is "the largest of the series and, in my opinion, the best."[5] Instead of a celebratory trophy picture, Peto offered an imposing, life-size image whose melancholy tone is enhanced by what is probably the original distressed frame. The dense shadow that divides the composition and the mysterious interior revealed by the partially open door are typical of Peto's melodramatic lighting effects. The dominant element is the blue-green door, of which we are shown the lower portion. Its paint is severely chipped and weathered, and its scarred wood has deteriorated; the rusted lower hinge has been moved to a more secure position. Hanging from a rusted nail is a brilliantly highlighted wicker eel basket—though, oddly, the twine supporting the basket casts no shadow. Suspended from the same nail is a dark lantern, its glass clouded with dust. Behind it hangs a yellow slicker and a precariously balanced fishing pike. Papers have been torn away, leaving only fragments and a tattered print of a stormy sea affixed to the door. *Fish House Door* is the product of a unique and private imagination. Its colors are deftly balanced and the shapes rhythmically arranged; their juxtaposition is evocative. Rather than merely describing the physical world, Peto transformed commonplace objects and, as John Wilmerding observed, imbued deterioration with a symbolic power that invites contemplation.[6]

Fish House Door with Eel Basket,
1890s
Oil on canvas, 60 1/4 x 43 in.
(153 x 109 cm)
Munson-Williams-Proctor Institute
Museum of Art, Purchase by exchange,
65.15

PROVENANCE:
Mrs. George Smiley, Island Heights, N.J.
(artist's daughter); M. Knoedler and Co.,
New York.

SELECTED BIBLIOGRAPHY:
A. Frankenstein, *After the Hunt: William
Harnett and Other American Still Life
Painters 1870-1900,* rev. ed. (Berkeley,
1969), pp. 99-111; P. D. Schweizer, ed.,
*Masterworks of American Art from the
Munson-Williams-Proctor Institute* (New
York, 1989), no. 41; J. Wilmerding,
*Important Information Inside: The Art of
John Peto and the Idea of Still Life Painting
in Nineteenth-Century America,* exh. cat.
(National Gallery of Art, Washington,
D.C., 1983), esp. pp. 150-58.

French, 1877-1953

ufy was immensely prolific, producing some five thousand paintings, drawings, and watercolors, and an additional fifty-three hundred illustrated books, ceramics, tapestry cartoons, stage sets, and fabric designs.[1] He is best known for his highly decorative pictures celebrating the pleasures of the wealthy. Aficionados of horse races, gambling casinos, yacht races, and musical concerts are represented by calligraphic lines that convey form and movement with abbreviated precision. Bright colors splashed on in broad, luminous masses suggest an expansive panorama quickly surveyed, enhancing the festive ambience and adding a sense of immediacy to our enjoyment of these light-hearted subjects. His art is representational but not realistic. Its essence is best captured by Gertrude Stein: "think of Dufy, nobody calls him abstract but he is he does not paint what he sees, he paints what he is, and certainly it is not what anybody else sees.... One must meditate about pleasure. Raoul Dufy is pleasure."[2]

As Stein's ruminations on the artist and abstract painting suggest, the charm of his works depends in part on the frothy air of spontaneity which somehow suggests that each painting was blithely dashed off. However, the effortless joy and benign modernity encapsulated in his work belie the serious study and experimentation that culminated in his distinctive style.

Dufy was born into a large family, which he helped support while studying painting in the evening in the art academy of his native Le Havre. In 1900, he received a scholarship that enabled him to attend the Ecole des Beaux-Arts, Paris, where his academic training was augmented by encounters with Impressionist paintings in the galleries. Seeing Matisse's *Luxe, calme et volupté* (1905; Paris, Musée d'Orsay) at the 1905 Salon des Indépendants was a revelation: "Impressionist realism lost all its charm for me, when I contemplated the miracle of the imagination that had penetrated both line and color. Immediately I understood the mechanics of the new painting."[3]

Impressed especially by Matisse's arbitrary use of color, Dufy came to believe that painting required the artist not to imitate observed reality but to reinvent it: "Painting means creating an image which is not the image of the appearance of things, but which has the power of their reality."[4] During the next several years, he searched for an appropriate pictorial language, experimenting with Fauvist and Cubist idioms. Eventually, he discovered a formula for translating nature into art "by means of colors applied in planes and given a plastic role, while forms are simplified and reduced to their pictorial expression."[5]

Applicable in a variety of media, this basic insight informs all of Dufy's subsequent work. Although based on perceived reality, objects are stripped of naturalistic details and simplified. Rather than imitating natural appearances by means of aerial perspective or chiaroscuro, broad areas of flat color are used to indicate space and volume. The impact of these abstractions is augmented by the subjective and expressive use of color, which serves as well to enhance the decorative coherence of compositions. Light and airy in appearance, the style Dufy perfected served to communicate the lyrical beauty he joyfully perceived: "Mere anecdote...is not the real aim of my pictures. The subject itself is of no account; what matters is the way it is presented."[6]

Like Cézanne and the modernist painters influenced by him, Dufy found still life to be an apposite genre for investigating complicated issues of pictorial representation. The Ithaca *Still Life* is related in form and motif to a group of still lifes with bananas dating from the years 1908-09.[7] It exemplifies the formal issues that preoccupied Dufy during a period of especially assiduous experimentation that lasted from 1906 until 1915. He assimilated the subjective colors of the Fauves and the geometric abstractions of the Cubists as he worked to develop a personal artistic vocabulary, but by 1908, his attention was focused on the implications of Cézanne's response to the problem of representing three-dimensional reality on a two-dimensional surface.[8]

As in the related *Still Life with Lemon, Pears, and Bananas* (1909; Copenhagen, Statens Museum for Kunst),[9] for example, Dufy was concerned in the Ithaca canvas with organizing into a coherent and cohesive composition geometric shapes and the spaces surrounding them. Traditional laws of perspective were rejected and no effort was made to establish an illusion of spatial depth. Rather—as seen here—the objects were arranged parallel to the picture plane. Though they have been reduced to geometrical schemata, they remain clearly identifiable: melons, bananas, and other fruits set on a table alongside a bulbous terra-cotta pitcher. Volumes are suggested by thick, parallel, form-defining brush strokes that also serve as a decorative leitmotif to unify the composition. The colors, too, are not entirely arbitrary. The hot orange of the pitcher, bright green of the bananas, and brilliant saffron of the melon are exaggerations of natural hues, made more intense by contrast with the vibrant blue surface on which they rest.

Coupled with Dufy's innate sense of design, the result of these manipulations is a painting of considerable decorative power. Visual reality has been translated by means of abstracted forms and brilliant colors into a pictorial reality that is both pleasurable and expressive.

▲

Still Life,
1908-09
Oil on canvas, 25 3/4 x 31 3/4 in. (65 x 81 cm)
Inscribed, l.r.: *Raoul Dufy*
Herbert F. Johnson Museum of Art,
Cornell University,
Gift of Mrs. Bernard F. Gimbel, 56.82

PROVENANCE:
Charles-August Girard, France; Mrs. Bernard F. Gimbel,
Greenwich, Conn. (by 1951).

SELECTED BIBLIOGRAPHY:
M. Laffaille, *Raoul Dufy: Catalogue raisonné de l'oeuvre peint,*
4 vols. (Geneva, 1972), vol. 3, p. 323, no. 1318.

French, 1844-1910

riting in 1948, the poet Tristan Tzara described Rousseau as "among the most picturesque characters of his period" and offered the most concise explanation for the fascination exerted by this artist's paintings: "Fantasy and common sense join…in building that spontaneous unreality which is the astonishingly natural and powerful lyrical world of the Douanier."[1] Implicit in this appraisal is the recognition of the importance of Rousseau's reputation as a "primitive." The belief that he worked without theory but was "deeply imbued with the conception of the total artist" enabled a varied audience to appreciate his paintings as expressions of a pure inner vision.[2]

The son of a tinsmith, Rousseau began his career by studying law. A legal peccadillo, however, forced him to abandon this profession and enter the army. The critic and poet Guillaume Apollinaire perpetuated the legend that Rousseau was among the troops sent to support Maximilian in Mexico, but in fact, the artist never saw foreign service. The exotic vegetation in his jungle scenes was actually based on plants studied in the botanical garden of Paris. After leaving the army in 1871, he was employed by the municipal toll service (the source of his nickname, Le Douanier [Customs Inspector], which is a misnomer) and began his artistic life as a Sunday painter. In 1885, he left the municipal service to devote himself entirely to painting. It was at this time, too, that Rousseau began to host gatherings at which the artistic and intellectual elite mingled with the neighborhood bourgeoisie in his humble apartment.

Rousseau conscientiously exhibited at the Salon des Indépendants from 1886 until 1910, and for years his contributions were ridiculed. Wilhelm Udhe, an early admirer and patron, reported that "Paris crowded in to look and laugh …. Curiosity-seekers craned their necks at his pictures as at some comic incident."[3] In the early years of the twentieth century, a shift in attitude occurred that may conveniently be tracked in the critical writings of Apollinaire. In 1908, he was condescending: "M. Rousseau's exhibit is at once touching and amusing…. One cannot quite abandon oneself to his ingenuousness. One is too aware of its hazardous and even of its ridiculous aspects."[4] Two years later, however, Apollinaire affirmed that the beauty of *The Dream* (New York, Museum of Modern Art) is "incontestable" and added, "I think that this year no one will laugh…. Ask the painters. Their admiration is unanimous."[5] Finally, in 1914, Apollinaire stated his belief that Rousseau's "artistry and freshness are inimitable."[6]

There are elements of irony in this change in Rousseau's critical fortune, for it is linked to the appearance of artistic tendencies that differ radically from the aesthetic predilections of Le Douanier, who admired the formal perfection achieved by Jean-Léon Gérôme (1824-1904) and other nineteenth-century academicians. Rousseau was self-taught. Though his style is autochthonous, he emulated academic practice, training himself by copying paintings in the Louvre. In 1895, he described himself as "on the way to becoming one of our best realist painters."[7] His own work is always representational, but its stylized quality intrigued sophisticated young painters, who were fully aware of their position in history and who consciously sought to transform the naturalist tradition inherited from the Renaissance. Artists as different in their formal aspirations as Picasso (cat. no. 36), Robert Delaunay (1885-1941), and Wassily Kandinsky (1866-1944) were among Rousseau's most enthusiastic admirers. Fernand Léger (cat. no. 31) described Rousseau as "a formidable man" who painted "straightforwardly like Jacques-Louis David."[8] As Léger's statement suggests, what these members of the modernist vanguard seem to have admired about Rousseau was the fact that his pictures were simultaneously convincing in their representations and obviously flat, patterned surfaces. Equally significant, they admired the integrity with which he painted, the purity of his vision, and the self-consistent reality he achieved in his compositions. According to Apollinaire, "Rousseau's lack of technical knowledge was amply compensated for by an abundance of artistic qualities and by a forcefulness that derived, if not from academic knowledge, at least from his consciousness," which made his paintings mysterious, haunting, and lyrically sentimental.[9] He is said to have considered himself "the most powerful painter of his time," and indeed, especially during the first half of the century, he exerted a persistent, if sometimes surreptitious, influence on artists of diverse aesthetic persuasions.[10]

Rousseau is most famous for mysterious jungle scenes with lurking beasts, such as *The Dream* or *The Snake Charmer* (1907; Paris, Musée d'Orsay). He also painted portraits and urban landscapes as well as still lifes. More numerous late in his

Flowers in a Vase,
1909
Oil on canvas, 18 3/8 x 13 1/4 in.
(45.4 x 32.7 cm)
Inscribed, l.l.: *Henri Rousseau / 1909*
Albright-Knox Art Gallery, Room of
Contemporary Art Fund, 39.17

PROVENANCE:
Count Sandor, Hungary (1911-39); by
descent to his niece, Countess Sandor;
Arthur Tooth and Sons, London; Knoedler
and Co., London (1939); purchased from
Knoedler and Co., New York.

SELECTED BIBLIOGRAPHY:
G. Artieri and D. Vallier, *L'opera completa
di Rousseau il Doganiere* (Milan, 1969), p.
110, cat. no. 232; H. Certiguy, *Le Douanier
Rousseau en son temps: Biographie et
catalogue raisonné,* 2 vols. (Tokyo, 1984),
vol. 2, p. 620, cat. no. 290; S. A. Nash,
*Albright-Knox Art Gallery: Painting and
Sculpture from Antiquity to 1942* (New York,
1979), pp. 444-45.

career, when the artist enjoyed more commissions, the still
lifes, as Apollinaire noted, reveal "reserves of charm and
expression in the soul and hand of the old Douanier."[11]

Flowers in a Vase is typical of these compositions, which all
contain the same basic elements. It features a bouquet of cut
flowers held in a simple glass vase set on a table. The Buffalo
canvas is closely related to a still life painted in 1902 (New York,
Museum of Modern Art),[12] in which the vase is also separated
from the viewer by a strand of cut ivy. In the earlier version, the
ivy appears to be part of the fabric design; in the later Buffalo
version, it may be an actual plant set on the tablecloth.

The nucleus of the composition is the exuberant mass of
red and yellow tulips, pink peonies, daisies, mimosa, and blue
forget-me-nots positioned to reveal themselves most fully.
The individual elements are defined by their profiles rather
than by internal modeling, so that the composition has a flat,
collagelike appearance enhanced by the absence of shadows

and the crisp contours established by strict color contrasts.
The vertical striations on the vase and emerald green background serve as a foil for the bouquet, which is made up of
superimposed circular forms and unified by an internal rhythm
established by the curved contours and arcs of individual
leaves and petals. Though the flowers were painted with great
care and are easily identifiable, they are not naturalistic. They
are seen through the medium of Rousseau's imagination as
living, luminous, sculpted colors, which Charles Sterling aptly
described as "symbols of a lifetime of dreams."[13] The ivy, a
traditional symbol of fidelity and affection, adds to the sentimental richness of an image painted at a time when the artist
was suffering from the pangs of unrequited love.

American, 1859-1937

hough "entirely self-taught," Lathrop's dedication to art is suggested by the career of one of her daughters as a sculptor and of another as an illustrator.[1] The quality of this still life suggests that the elder Lathrop was more than a talented amateur.

Dessert Time is related to the tradition initiated by the simple breakfast pieces that first appeared in early seventeenth-century Holland.[2] Like its prototypes, it features the complement of objects associated with a specific meal. The dessert bowls and fruit are situated slightly below eye level, so that it appears as though the viewer is just settling down to enjoy this particular course.

Dominating the composition is a white ceramic bowl overflowing with plump grapes, a ripe peach, a pear, and some apples. Another pear and grapes have tumbled over the side, on the left. Their colors are reflected in the polished surface of the wooden table on which the still life is presented. The bowl rests on a fringed dessert doily, its diced red border reflected in the glossy undulations of the vessel. Further in the background, on the right, and partially hidden by the bowl and fruit, is a cream pitcher gaily decorated with a floral motif. The composition is illuminated from the left, and the light reflects off the slick interior of the pitcher's spout. The silver fruit knife leaning against the rim of the bowl serves as a counterpoint to the slight diagonal formed by the other objects in the composition. The textures of wood, cloth, ceramics, and the different fruit have been meticulously imitated. The subtle reflections and details such as the busy fringe of the napkin animate an otherwise static composition.

Although Lathrop was self-taught, she was not a naive painter. The sophisticated composition and the skill with which physical phenomena—such as the bloom on the grapes—are imitated in *Dessert Time* suggest a familiarity with the trompe l'oeil tradition of the 1880s. The pitcher, bowl, and napkin, which can be dated to this era, are portrayed in a manner concordant with the culinary customs of the age.[3] Given the absence of documentation, it is possible that *Dessert Time* exemplifies the widespread popularity of trompe l'oeil painting in that period. However, if, as is currently believed, *Dessert Time* was indeed painted in 1910, it must be seen as an expression of the tastes as well as the style of an earlier era and appreciated as an example of stylistic continuity sustained by an artist adhering to the trompe l'oeil tradition of her youth.

▲

Dessert Time,
1910
Oil on canvas, 10 3/8 x 14 5/8 in. (26.4 x 37.1 cm)
Inscribed, l.r.: *I. Pulis Lathrop*
Albany Institute of History and Art, 1987.6

PROVENANCE:
Corner House Antiques and Art, Manchester,
Vt.; Eden Galleries, Salem, N.Y.

American (born Norway), 1880-1940

hough once the subject of considerable critical attention, today Lie is largely forgotten.[1] During his lifetime, he was widely exhibited and respected especially for his landscapes, which dominated his work after about 1920. His reputation was established by paintings such as *Morning on the River* (ca. 1913; Memorial Art Gallery of the University of Rochester). Such harbor scenes were regarded by critics as "giving new poetry to modern urban life...and significance to latter-day industrial effort";[2] his expressive portrayals of monumental bridges were praised as "his paean to twentieth-century toil."[3] Lie's most famous work of this type is *The Conquerors* (1913; New York, Metropolitan Museum of Art), which celebrates the construction of the Panama Canal.

Lie was born in Norway. After his father's death in 1892, he studied painting for a year in Paris and then joined his family, which had emigrated to America. He worked days and studied nights at the Art Students League and National Academy of Design, becoming an Associate in 1912. In 1919, he helped organize the New Society of Artists in protest against the academy's refusal to accept as members some of the stylistically diverse painters known as The Eight. Lie maintained his ties with the academy, however, becoming a full Academician in 1925 and serving as president of the organization from 1934 to 1939.

Among the first to purchase Lie's pictures was the painter William Merritt Chase. Early success enabled Lie to visit Paris in 1906; there he was especially influenced by the sparkling light and brilliant color of Claude Monet (1840-1926). For Lie, color became "the chief medium through which we attain pictorial expression." He explained that color had to be used in an interpretive rather than an imitative fashion: "The actual, visual impression we derive from nature should be less forceful, less vivid, than the accompanying mental impression."[4]

The impact of Monet is evident in *The Black Teapot*, one of four works Lie chose to exhibit in the 1913 Armory Show (as no. 875). The painting features a brilliant array of autumn flowers—purple asters and vermilion nasturtiums—in a white bowl resting on a luminous white surface. Beside them is a glass vase containing lilies. The flowers are not depicted individually and with botanical precision, however, for Lie was concerned not with accurate representation but with the dazzling blaze of color and the *effect* produced by the bouquets within the spacious atmosphere of the painting. As Christian Brinton recognized in 1915, "Lie does not treat nature photographically or symbolically, but emotionally."[5] The drama of the floral mass is communicated by means of bold brush strokes of blazing color set against the white table and yellow background.

The glistening black teapot is the key to the painting. It is set boldly in the foreground, where it serves as a contrasting foil for the color and light that pervade the canvas. It also establishes the dynamics of the composition, first drawing our gaze into the expansive space from the direction indicated by its spout and then directing it along the diagonal leading to the blue plate set in the background. Lie's few still lifes clearly impressed critics, who admired their "virility and force." The reviewer who wrote that Lie's still lifes "are so powerfully painted, and have such breadth of style and handling, that one feels they might have been painted by giants"[6] could easily have been referring to *The Black Teapot*.

▲

The Black Teapot,
1911
Oil on canvas, 35 x 42 in. (87.9 x 106.7 cm)
Inscribed, l.l.: *Jonas Lie 1911*
Everson Museum of Art, 13.121

Plate 10

Provenance:
Purchased from the artist, 1913.

American, 1883-1965

I n an unpublished essay on the history of still life painting, Sheeler offers a personal interpretation of the tradition, describing its development up to the moment when he began his professional career. He identifies three major phases differentiated by the crucial innovations of Chardin and Cézanne. According to Sheeler, the earliest artists were concerned primarily with the associative value of objects. This attitude persisted during the Renaissance, when objects were used as illustrative adjuncts to portraiture, functioning as indicators of taste and social standing. The Dutch artists modified this habit, depicting objects of domestic utility which also had pictorial value. Implicit in this shift was the notion that still life might be an appropriate vehicle for the expression of aesthetic principles, an attitude that reached maturity in the work of Chardin. The Frenchman not only observed "the qualities peculiar to each object" but also developed his compositions "based upon a consideration of the assemblage of these qualities." This new attitude reached maturity in the work of the Post-Impressionist Cézanne, who freed still life from associative necessity: "It is true that objects of association continued to serve Cézanne…but their selection is based upon preferences in the matter of shapes, surfaces, and quantities related to a geometric structure." Cézanne, therefore, opened the way for the innovations of artists such as Picasso, who "sought still further to detach the object from the dictionary by stating it in terms of abstract form, thereby destroying its identity and associated memories and compelling the eye to observe its purely plastic relation to the complete design."[1] Implicit in this personal history of still life painting are the formal issues that preoccupied Sheeler throughout his career.

In 1912, when he painted *The Mandarin*, this understanding of the genre was unformed, and the artist was only beginning to assimilate a series of artistic experiences that influenced the formation of his personal style.[2] Sheeler's professional training had began nine years earlier, when he entered the Pennsylvania Academy of the Fine Arts and became a student of William Merritt Chase. Although he was never altogether comfortable with the emphasis Chase placed on spontaneity and bravura brushwork, Sheeler admired the vivacity and lush impasto of Velázquez, Hals, and Rembrandt, which he studied during European trips organized by his teacher. Sheeler's ideas began to solidify, however, when he traveled in 1908-09 to Italy and France with his family and his friend and colleague the painter and photographer Morton Schamberg (1881-1918).

Studying the works of the early Italian painters Giotto, Masaccio, and Piero della Francesca, Sheeler realized that

"design, in its larger sense, comprised the structure of a picture …[and] that forms must be placed with primary consideration for their relation to all other forms, as well as those adjacent, in the matter of their bulk, color, or direction of movement, if the picture as a conception is to achieve an architecture-like structure."[3] From Italy, Sheeler traveled to Paris, where he first saw the new paintings of Picasso, Matisse, Braque, van Gogh (1853-1890), Cézanne, and others. These "very strange pictures" initially bewildered Sheeler but also convinced him "that something profound was in the making."[4]

The Mandarin, one of the six paintings Sheeler exhibited in the 1913 Armory show (as no. 975), is among the few surviving pictures documenting the artist's struggle to understand the innovations of the Parisian avant-garde. The diminutive scale, thick impasto, and sense of immediacy reflect the continuing influence of Chase, but the brilliant Fauvist color and emphasis on geometrical structure reflect ideas encountered in Europe. Moreover, the simplicity of the composition is indicative of the experimental nature of this canvas.

In *The Mandarin*, Sheeler appears to have set himself specific formal problems that he sought to resolve in the terms provided by Cézanne and his immediate successors. All the elements of the picture have been placed with great deliberation. The "circle" suggested by the octagonal bowl within the rectangular canvas contrasts with two overlapping triangles described by the three fruits and the outline of the cloth, providing a dynamic geometric structure emphasized by the play of light over the forms. Eschewing traditional chiaroscuro techniques in rendering the spherical fruit and agitated drapery, Sheeler used thick strokes of saturated color to render the abstracted volumes.

Sheeler subsequently rejected the painterly style with which he experimented in *The Mandarin* in favor of the expressionless brushwork that made him a leader among the Precisionists. However, the effort "to convert the realistic presentation into a design of various contrasts of visual qualities based upon a geometric structure"[5] that is evident in this early picture defines the aesthetic purpose underlying the crystalline beauty of his later Precisionist work.

▲

The Mandarin,
1912
Oil on canvas, 10 1/8 x 13 11/16 in. (25.8 x 34.8 cm)
Inscribed, l.r.: *Sheeler 1912*
Munson-Williams-Proctor Institute Museum of Art, 63.90

PROVENANCE:
Purchased from the artist through Betty Parsons Gallery,
New York.

SELECTED BIBLIOGRAPHY:
M. Friedman, *Charles Sheeler* (New York, 1975), p. 20.

French, 1882-1963

raque acquired his ability to imitate surfaces and textures as an apprentice in a decorator's workshop. His formal education as a painter continued at the Ecole des Beaux-Arts, first in Le Havre and then in Paris. Influenced initially by the Post-Impressionists, he exhibited works at the 1906 Salon des Indépendants that were Fauvist in their brushwork and use of expressive color. Over the next couple of years, Braque became increasingly intrigued by the formal implications of Cézanne's paintings and aspirations. It was while preoccupied with these artistic problems that Braque was introduced to Picasso in 1907. Over the next five years, the two artists worked intensely and in close collaboration, trying, as Picasso glibly remarked, "to get rid of 'trompe-l'oeil' to find a 'trompe-l'esprit.'"[1] Together, they developed and refined the formal language that became known as Cubism.

Both artists were preoccupied with the problem of representing the three-dimensional volumes of nature on the two-dimensional picture surface. They rejected pictorial conventions that had dominated painting since the fifteenth century, and, treating the painting as an independent object rather than a window on nature, they invented an alternative language for representing forms and their position in space without imitating superficial appearances. The style they developed is representational but nonillusionistic and highly conceptual. Cubist paintings offer a two-dimensional interpretation of nature based on the fragmentation and analysis of objects rather than a "three-dimensional" illusion in which distance and depth are established by means of perspective and chiaroscuro.[2] The Cubists "analyzed" objects in terms of their constituent lines and planes seen from various viewpoints and represented these various viewpoints simultaneously. Each object is thus depicted in its totality by means of a purely pictorial language. In an interview given around 1908, Braque explains, "I…create a new sort of beauty, the beauty that appears to me in terms of volume, of line, of mass, of weight, and through that beauty interpret my subjective impression. Nature is a mere pretext for decorative composition, plus sentiment."[3]

Braque and Picasso studied objects, as Apollinaire wrote of Picasso, "as a surgeon dissects a corpse,"[4] finding in still life the most convenient laboratory in which to pursue their investigations. Daniel-Henry Kahnweiler, the patron and major dealer for these innovators, described the construction of a Cubist canvas:

Instead of beginning from a supposed foreground and going on from there to give an illusion of depth by means of perspective, the painter begins from a definite and clearly defined background. Starting from this background the

painter now works toward the front by a sort of scheme of forms in which each object's position is clearly indicated, both in relation to the…background and to other objects. Such an arrangement thus gives a clear and plastic view.[5]

Braque as well as Picasso integrated figure and ground by eliminating shadows or using them as component equivalents to mass, and they created planar units by linking the contours of objects with lines suggesting dimension or structure. This technique resulted in the distinctive faceted appearance of Cubist paintings. Underlying the process was the recognition that "a painting is a form of writing that creates signs. A woman on a canvas is not a woman—these are signs that I read as being a woman."[6]

Having developed this "analytical" method, the artists were able, beginning around 1911, to reverse the procedure and "synthesize" images from their constituent elements. They achieved this first by means of collage, which Braque invented in 1912, and later in paint, as in *Still Life with Pipe*. "When 'real details' are…introduced," Kahnweiler observed, "the result is a stimulus which carries with it memory images. Combining the "real" stimulus and the scheme of forms, these images construct the finished object in the mind."[7] Many of the attributes that characterize the "synthetic" phase of Cubism are present in the Rochester canvas. Its contents—the glass, cards, newspaper, and pipe—are likewise typical of Cubist still lifes, representing the world of the café that was integral to the artistic life of the period.

The composition is an oval. Braque and Picasso began to use this form in 1910 because it helped to establish the painting as an independent object and eliminated latent references to traditional perspective systems. We look directly down on the still life elements, which rest on a table, suggested by the wood-grained element in the lower left. Form is defined by line, which grounds the image firmly in reality. A glass is indicated by its profile and circular rim, a pipe is also indicated by its outline, and in the center, an open book is suggested by an abbreviated profile. A playing card is indicated by its sign, a spade; similarly, a newspaper is indicated by the letters *HO DE*, abstracted from the title *L'echo de Paris*. "As I still wanted to get as close as possible to reality," Braque explained, "in 1911 I introduced lettering into my paintings. They were shapes that could not be distorted since, as they were flat, the letters were outside space and their presence in the picture, by contrast, enabled the objects that were in space to be distinguished from objects outside space."[8]

Color, which Braque recognized as distinct from form,[9] has been reduced here to a simple monochrome, and the planes are defined by overlapping rectangles painted with a variety of marks that distinguish the textures of the various surfaces. These marks serve as well to establish a cohesive decorative and rhythmic pattern in the composition. In a related painting, *Still Life with Pipe* (1914; Paris, Musée Moderne de la Ville), sand was mixed with paint to emphasize these distinctions. Neither color nor texture has been used in a descriptive manner; rather, they too function as signs to suggest space and dimension. In both the Rochester and Paris paintings, the components of the composition—form, color, and substance—are treated separately, to be synthesized in the mind of the beholder.

▲

Still Life with Pipe,
1913-14
Oil on canvas, 16 1/4 x 13 in. (41.3 x 33 cm)(oval)
Inscribed, v.: G. *Braque*
Memorial Art Gallery of the University of Rochester, Marion Stratton Gould Fund, 54.12

PROVENANCE:
Galerie Kahnweiler, Paris (before 1914); private collection, Alsace; Perls Galleries, New York; Stanley Barbee, Los Angeles; Perls Galleries, New York.

SELECTED BIBLIOGRAPHY:
J. van der Marck et al., *In Quest of Excellence,* exh. cat. (Center for the Fine Arts, Miami, 1984), p. 190, no. 137; S. D. Peters, ed., *Memorial Art Gallery: An Introduction to the Collection* (Rochester, 1988), pp. 140-41; N. Worms de Romilly and J. Laude, *Braque: Le cubisme, fin 1907-1914* (Paris, 1982), p. 289, no. 236 (as "Playing Card and Pipe").

French, 1867-1947

onnard has been referred to as the last Impressionist, but this designation is based on superficial similarities and is inappropriate. The Impressionists worked directly from nature and attempted to transcribe with unprocessed immediacy every subtle nuance of directly perceived reality. Although his brushwork recalls their methods, Bonnard's purpose was conspicuously different. He sought to recall in his paintings the sensations first aroused by what he saw rather than the objects themselves. "It's not a matter of painting life," he wrote in 1946, "it's a matter of giving life to painting."[1] He therefore avoided working before his models, distancing himself from his subjects in order to recompose them from memory in the studio.[2] The painter Paul Signac (1863-1935) described his friend's creative process: "In the little sketchbook from which he is never separated, or better still in his memory, he jots down pell-mell all that life presents to him…. the eye of his dog, a ray of sunlight …the sponge in his bathtub. Then, wholly by instinct, without even attempting to give an appearance of reality to these often illegible objects, he expresses his love of life in magnificent pictures."[3] The resulting images are entirely subjective, a combination of the artist's feelings and memory expressed in forms and colors purposefully manipulated and heightened to suggest not only the beauty he saw but also the pleasure he felt in seeing it.

The delight expressed in Bonnard's paintings is the reflection of a man known for his "nonchalant gaiety" and wit.[4] The means by which these qualities are expressed— Bonnard's style—were distilled from a variety of early influences. He was born in comfortable circumstances and sent to Paris to study law. Instead, he found opportunity to indulge his natural inclination for art. He became fascinated with Japanese prints and enrolled in the Académie Julian. In 1888, he became friends with Edouard Vuillard (1868-1940), who introduced him to Paul Sérusier (1863-1935), Paul Ranson (1862-1909), and other young artists who subsequently formed the Nabis, or Prophets. Through Sérusier, they were influenced by Paul Gauguin's (1848-1903) belief that a painting should be a product of the artist's imagination rather than a mere copy of nature. They were impressed by Gauguin's radical style, in which forms were simplified, line was manipulated for expressive purposes, and pure, luminous colors were employed in a boldly subjective manner. In publicizing an exhibition he had organized for his friends in 1891, the actor and theatrical producer Alexandre Lugné-Poë wrote of the Nabis "disdain of vulgar naturalism" and their "love of poetic syntheses."[5]

Other members of the Nabis refined the lessons of Gauguin by creating evocative symbolic images, but Vuillard and Bonnard recognized the decorative potential of these ideas and adapted the formal principles to the representation of commonplace subjects. This can be seen to best advantage in Bonnard's screens, his work for the theater, and graphic work he produced for La revue blanche.[6] After about 1900, the two former Nabis developed related but individual styles. At Bonnard's 1910 exhibition, Apollinaire was charmed by the "fantasy and ingenuousness" of the artist's "cultivated and appealing manner." "I like Bonnard's painting very much," he wrote. "It is simple, sensual, witty…and, I do not know why, it invariably makes me think of a little girl with a sweet tooth."[7] What he was responding to was Bonnard's stated desire to "show nature when it's beautiful" or, to be more precise, to express in an affective manner his response to the beauty he perceived. To achieve this, Bonnard combined a variety of traditions into a personal, highly subjective style. Describing his method as "distortion for visibility's sake," he explained that "one can take all possible liberties of line, form, proportions, colors to make feeling intelligible and clearly visible."[8]

Wild Flowers belongs to a series of still lifes executed between 1915 and the early 1920s which shows Bonnard in the process of personalizing the Nabis aesthetic under the influence of Monet and August Renoir (1841-1919).[9] The cropped composition demonstrates the continuing impact of Japanese prints, while the heightened color scheme suggests the legacy of Gauguin and the Fauves. The spontaneous quality of the image—the impression that the composition is not composed but represents the suddenly apprehended beauty of a simple domestic arrangement noted in a passing glance— is the essence of Bonnard's accomplishment.

The curtain on the left and shutter on the right frame the doorway opening onto a balcony or porch surrounded by a wicker railing. The doorway is blocked by a circular table, and the view into the background is obscured by the undisciplined bouquet emerging from the conical vase and extending across the entire picture surface. Modeling by means of light and shade is minimal. The wicker pattern and the geometric motifs of the curtain, chair, and shutter further reduce the suggestion of three-dimensionality and emphasize the surface qualities of the design. The dull purple of the background serves as a harmonious foil for the russets, other purples, and oranges that unify the planes of the composition. The colors suggest a mood more than they describe physical facts. Although the flowers and vase occupy the physical center of the painting, the balance of tones prevents them from dominating the composition. Rather than offering a picture of specific objects in a specific setting, Bonnard has presented the visual and emotional impression produced by the scene in its totality. Only the more active brushwork of the flowers remains as an indication of what first captured his attention.

▲

Wild Flowers,
ca. 1915-20
Oil on canvas, 17 3/4 x 24 1/2 in. (45 x 62 cm)
Inscribed, l.r.: *Bonnard*
Albright-Knox Art Gallery, Charles Clifton Fund, 54.8

PROVENANCE:
Purchased from the artist by Bernheim-Jeune and
Co., Paris, 1920; Joseph Hessel, Paris; Knoedler and
Co., New York; Galeries Pétrides, Paris; Alex Reid
and Lefevre Gallery, London.

SELECTED BIBLIOGRAPHY:
J. and H. Dauberville, *Bonnard: Catalogue raisonné de
l'oeuvre peint,* 4 vols. (Paris, 1974), vol. 4, p. 355,
no. 02069 (as ca. 1915); S. A. Nash, *Albright-Knox
Art Gallery: Painting and Sculpture from Antiquity to 1942*
(New York, 1979), pp. 332-33.

painter of enigmas, de Chirico radically transformed his pictorial style in midcareer (cat. no. 30), making himself something of an enigma. His artistic inclinations had been encouraged by his parents. While in Greece, where his father, an engineer, designed railways, de Chirico took private drawing lessons and later studied at the Polytechnique Institute of Athens. After his father's death in 1905, de Chirico's artistic training continued at the Akademie der Bildenden Künste in Munich, where he was especially impressed by the idiosyncratic classicism of Arnold Böcklin (1827-1901), in whose work "the metaphysical power is released by the exactness and clarity of a definite apparition," achieving a "disconcerting surprise."[1] Equally influential were the visionary works of Max Klinger (1857-1920), who "extracts the romantic sense in its strangest and most profound aspects."[2]

In Munich, de Chirico was also introduced to a particular idealistic strain of German philosophy.[3] He admired Friedrich Neitzsche, who maintained in *The Birth of Tragedy* (1872) that "the beauteous appearance of…dream worlds…is the presupposition of all plastic art."[4] Through Nietzsche, the artist was introduced to the writings of Arthur Schopenhauer. De Chirico accepted Schopenhauer's belief that for original ideas to occur, it is necessary "to isolate oneself from the world…so completely that the most commonplace happenings appear to be new and unfamiliar."[5] According to Schopenhauer, the true essence of things was revealed through this experience. De Chirico described his paintings as "metaphysical" because of their dreamlike, revelatory character. His use of the term *metaphysical* derives from Schopenhauer's theory that the surfaces and appearances of everyday reality conceal an altogether different reality, a hidden spiritual world. Also influential were the theories of Otto Weininger regarding the emotive powers of simple geometric forms.

Working in Paris between 1911 and 1915, de Chirico saw himself as isolated. Whereas "the international set of 'Modern' painters" was "struggling stupidly amid exploited formulas and sterile systems," he believed that "the daemon in everything must be discovered."[6] What de Chirico discovered was a startlingly original pictorial language for describing "dream worlds." Depending on distorted perspective and the displacement and irrational juxtaposition of objects, his cityscapes, interiors, and still lifes are so cohesively structured and painted with such conviction that they make the unreal and inexplicable appear tangible and inevitable. Cryptic, mysterious, and ultimately ambiguous, they evoke, as their titles suggest, a sense of foreboding, solitude, stasis, and poignant melancholy—sensations that de Chirico associated with the metaphysical experience.[7]

During the First World War and until about 1918, de Chirico continued to produce "Metaphysical" paintings and formalized his theories. In his essay "On Metaphysical Art" (1919),[8] he suggests that everyone has moments in which they inexplicably apprehend "the mysterious aspects of objects" and that "art is the fatal net that catches these strange moments." This experience led de Chirico to assert that "every object has two aspects…one which we see nearly always…and the other which is spectral and metaphysical." Thus, "every profound work of art contains two solitudes." One is the "contemplative beatitude" arising from perfection of the formal composition. The second solitude is that "of signs, an eminently metaphysical solitude…which excludes every logical possibility."[9] Metaphysical paintings must appear serene but have the disturbing quality of suggesting the presence of a hidden unknown. Architectural motifs and other objects included in his paintings are "the signs of the metaphysical alphabet," and his precisely balanced use of their surfaces and volumes "constitutes the canon of metaphysical aesthetics."

The Regret belongs to a series of outdoor still lifes produced during de Chirico's convalescence in Ferrara. He offers a view down a narrow street, though the passage into the background is blocked by a flat surface. The ornamented horizontal at the top of this section suggests a frame for this picture or mirror, but it may equally be an architectural member attached to the overhanging marquee. The elements of the latter serve as brightly colored orthogonals. They recede precipitously into the background, coming to an abrupt halt at the illusory frame. A platform juts from the picture's surface into the background, and crowded into the space between it and the "dead end" of the street is a claustrophobic jumble of painting stretchers.

Dominating the composition is a flat, prussian blue triangular surface with truncated corners. The identity of this object is uncertain, but the frame around it suggests that it may be a peculiar trompe l'oeil painting. Its shape is clearly significant, however. "Symbols of a superior reality are often… seen in geometric forms. For example, the triangle has served from antiquity…as a mystical and magical symbol, and it certainly often awakens a sense of uneasiness and fear in the onlooker."[10] On the object's surface are six of the fancy biscuits de Chirico admired in Ferrara's Jewish quarter because

The Regret,
1916
Oil on canvas, 23 3/8 x 13 in.
(58.9 x 33 cm)
Inscribed, l.l.: *G. de Chirico / 1916*
Munson-Williams-Proctor Institute
Museum of Art, 54.150

Plate 11

PROVENANCE:
Roland Penrose, London; Sidney Janis
Gallery, New York.

SELECTED BIBLIOGRAPHY:
M. Fagiolo dell'Arco, *L'opera completa di
Giorgio di Chirico, 1908-1924* (Milan,
1984), no. 112; W. Rubin, ed., *De Chirico*,
exh. cat. (Museum of Modern Art, New
York, 1982), pl. 67; C. Bruni Sakraischik,
ed., *Catalogo generale Giorgio de Chirico*, 8
vols. (Milan, 1971-83), vol. 1, no. 31;
J. T. Soby, *Giorgio di Chirico*, 2d ed. (New
York, 1966), pp. 113-14.

of their "exceedingly strange and metaphysical shapes."[11] The biscuits are depicted with illusionistic precision; every bump and crevice on their surface is starkly visible in the crystalline light that also produces a maze of crisp shadows among the crowded angular forms.

De Chirico is often credited with having reintroduced classical perspective, but as William Rubin has demonstrated, he used it for anticlassical purposes.[12] The pictorial devices invented in the Renaissance are used conventionally to create a convincing image of the natural world. But in *The Regret*, they were used by de Chirico to create a convincing picture of a bizarre realm full of surprise. Rather than define a rational and measurable space, he subverted the logic of the system by creating a space that is shallow and ambiguous. He defeated reason, again, by employing perspective devices and illusionistic techniques to imbue the elements of the composition with an undeniable plausibility and presence. That there is no rational explanation either for the objects themselves or for their juxtaposition contributes to that sense of displacement and unease which de Chirico considered vital to the metaphysical experience.

Although *The Regret* was painted in 1916, it was first exhibited in Paul Guillaume's Parisian gallery in 1922. Early works such as this one were enthusiastically received by Apollinaire and the advanced artists in his circle; during the 1920s, they exerted a formative influence on the Surrealists. By the time it was exhibited, however, de Chirico had already become obsessed with technique and had abandoned the Metaphysical aesthetic in favor of a reactionary style decried by his former admirers.[13]

JUAN GRIS
29

Spanish, 1887-1927

ris, born into a large, well-to-do family, initially studied the sciences at the Escuela de Artes y Manufacturas, Madrid. Having had several art nouveau-style drawings published in prominent journals, he abandoned his technical studies in 1904 and entered the studio of the academic painter José Moreno Carbonero (1860-1942). Two years later, Gris emigrated to Paris. Almost immediately, he became friends with Picasso, who found him an adjacent studio in "Le Bateau Lavoir," and by 1911, Gris had assimilated the principles of Cubism. Over the next few years, he contributed significantly to the development of the style. He is usually credited with having initiated the shift from Analytic to Synthetic Cubism. The rigorous beauty of his compositions moved Gertrude Stein to observe, "Picasso created it [Cubism] and Juan Gris permeated it with his clarity and exaltations."[1]

In 1912, Gris participated in an exhibition by the Golden Section group, which emphasized the idea of pure, abstract proportions as the vital component in painting. Although this geometric relationship contributed to the harmony and balance of his compositions,[2] its presence was more intuitive than precise—as Gris explained to Amédée Ozenfant (1886-1960), "I had other methods of composition."[3] His paintings of this period are complex symphonies involving opulent color harmonies, the ingenious counterpoint of geometric forms, and elegant linear rhythms. These were followed in the early 1920s by less rigorously complex, more lyrical works and, finally, in the years immediately preceding Gris's untimely death, by paintings in which the formal qualities of his earlier work are reduced to their most basic and pristine components.[4]

At the time of his first retrospective in 1919, Gris explained: "Artists have thought to produce a poetic effect with beautiful models or beautiful subjects. We, on the other hand, believe we can produce it with beautiful elements."[5] For him, these "elements" were intellect and imagination, expressed through line and color: "I try to make concrete that which is abstract.... I mean I start with an abstraction in order to arrive at a true fact. Mine is an art of synthesis, deduction."[6] Rather than analyze the forms of things in order to represent them in a purely pictorial language, Gris—in theory at least—began with the manipulation of abstract colored shapes and adjusted them until objects could be discerned, although his paintings rarely had such pure origins.[7] "Cézanne turns a bottle into a cylinder, but I begin with a cylinder and...make a bottle—a particular bottle."[8]

In creating his paintings, Gris employed the classical armory of pictorial devices: "I think one can quite well take over Chardin's means without taking over either the appearance of his pictures or his conceptions of reality."[9] Interactions of line and plane, spatial ambiguities and visual metaphors, and color, which Gris used with exceptional originality and finesse, served as the lexicon in which he expressed a conceptual reality, which he termed "poetic" or "imaginary reality." The repertoire of devices discovered by Picasso and Braque served as his grammar. In the Utica *Still Life*, the bottle and glass are fragmented by overlapping transparent and opaque planes signifying the contiguous surfaces among which the objects are located. Broken and displaced by these planes, which pass under and over them, the contours merge elusively into other forms defined by different local colors. The deliberate multiplicity of form and dimension results in the ambiguity Winthrup Judkins has labeled "fluctuant representation."[10]

Volume and depth in this picture are implied by color contrasts and by the suggestion of chiaroscuro in the definition of the contours. However, our impulse to read these pictorial effects in terms of three-dimensional modeling is contradicted by the monochrome plane on which the bottle and glass are situated and by the absence of traditional modeling to define the spatial relationships between the planes. As a result, the elements of the composition are emphatically flattened in a collagelike manner against a picture plane, and this surface is energized by the interaction of the lines implied by the junctures of the planes. The larger pattern established by these tonal planes is echoed by their patterned surfaces. The three-dimensional bottle and glass and the space they occupy are thus fully integrated into the rhythmic two-dimensional surface pattern.

In 1925, Gris explained to the dealer Kahnweiler, "My aim is to create new objects which cannot be compared with any object in reality."[11] His purpose was to represent an object and the effect or emotion it produced, but not by mere imitation. "It will be," the critic Maurice Raynal explained, "to the objects it represents, what a word is to the object it signifies."[12] As Gris explained in a 1924 lecture:

> A picture with no representational purpose is to my mind always an incomplete exercise, for the only purpose of any picture is to achieve representation. Nor is painting which is merely the faithful copy of an object a picture... it still has no aesthetic...no selection of the elements of reality it expresses.... The essence of painting is the expression of certain relationships between the painter and the outside world.[13]

In the Utica painting, Gris synthesized from purely abstract shapes and colors a poetically vital bottle and glass, affirming the autonomy of art from nature and the elegance of his own vision.

▶

Still Life,
1917
Oil on panel, 18 1/8 x 10 5/8 in.
(46.1 x 27 cm)
Inscribed, l.l.: *Juan Gris / 9-17*
Munson-Williams-Proctor Institute
Museum of Art, 52.36

PROVENANCE:
Léonce Rosenberg, Paris (dealer); Galerie
Flechtheim, Berlin; Wally Streit, Hamburg;
his sale, Graupe, Berlin, June 3-8, 1931, lot
88; Mme Streit, Karoxbostel; H. M. Luther,
London; Reid and Lefevre, London; Sidney
Janis Gallery, New York.

SELECTED BIBLIOGRAPHY:
D. Cooper, *Juan Gris: Catalogue raisonné de
l'oeuvre peint...*, 2 vols. (Paris, 1977), vol. 1,
pp. 342-43, no. 233; M. Rosenthal, *Juan
Gris*, exh. cat. (University Art Museum,
University of California, Berkeley [New
York], 1983), pp. 89-90, no. 51.

Italian, 1888-1978

 n 1918, de Chirico's orientation began to shift away from the Metaphysical attitude and style he had begun to develop while in Paris in 1911 (cat. no. 28) and toward the classical ideals then being promoted by the journal *Valori plastici*. In the following year, he experienced a revelation while visiting the Galleria Borghese in Rome. As a result, he rejected his earlier accomplishments, declared himself to be a "classical" painter, and henceforth devoted his efforts toward utilizing the techniques of the old masters.[1] In 1922, he complained to the Surrealist theoretician André Breton about "those who say I am making museum art, that I have lost my road,"[2] and in general his new works were—and continue to be—poorly received. In his *Memoirs*, for example, de Chirico recalls one review of his 1923 exhibition: "In referring to some of my finest paintings of fruit [Emilio] Cecchi spoke of corpses, cemeteries and things in an advanced state of putrification."[3]

Florentine Still Life, which was included in the 1923 exhibition, exemplifies the artist's new classicism. Five apples, two bananas, a glass of red wine, and a few leaves are arranged on rumpled blue and white draperies set on a stone parapet. A swag of tan drapery at the upper left serves as a framing device, ornamenting the "window" that opens onto an expansive view of two buildings and a cloud-filled, brilliant blue sky. De Chirico achieved a naturalistic sense of atmosphere which enables our gaze to traverse comfortably the distance from foreground to background, although there is no horizon line or middle ground to aid us. De Chirico had experimented with the window-sill format during his Metaphysical period. In *The Transformed Dream* (1913; Saint Louis Art Museum) and *The Philosopher's Quest* (1914; Art Institute of Chicago), for example, a foreground still life introduces a panoramic landscape. In these paintings, however, the juxtapositions of bananas, pineapples, classical statuary, artichokes, and cannons are as paradoxical as Lautréamont's sewing machine and umbrella;[4] the crystalline light, breathless atmosphere, irrational spatial relationships, and vertiginous landscapes add to the impact of these perplexing images. In contrast, *Florentine Still Life* is painted in a manner that enables us to recognize its relationship to conventions established in the seventeenth century by Ambrosius Bosschaert the Elder and refined by de Heem. The window-sill motif may be seen, for example, in the underdrawing of Rochester's *Still Life* by the latter (cat. no. 3) and, more dramatically, in de Heem's *pronkstilleben* such as an example formerly in the Bergsten collection, Stockholm,[5] and one painted in 1640 that de Chirico may have admired in the Louvre. As in de Heem's paintings, the objects in *Florentine Still Life* exist in a luminous atmosphere that offers a clear sense of space and depth. Chiaroscuro has been used to model the fruits and suggest

volume and relief. Their surface details have been scrupulously imitated and the stone parapet rendered with almost illusionistic precision.

De Chirico described the paintings he exhibited in 1923 as "belonging to that period…which the historians of modern art call the romantic period."[6] The meaning of this statement is clarified in a 1925 essay on Gustave Courbet (1819-1877), a painter whose life and work de Chirico characterized as "romantic" and who evoked for him "a world of sad memories," "a tender vein of nostalgia," and "indefinite melancholy." Significantly, his descriptions of these emotions might well have served as titles for his Metaphysical paintings. De Chirico explained that "in each of Courbet's pictures, from the simplest still life to his largest compositions, we catch the refrain of a romantic melody," and he described the means by which the French painter achieved this effect: "Courbet placed the reality of a figure or an object in the foreground and bathed it in that warm summer twilight to which he could impart such pathos…. But behind the fruit and leaves…we see a distant sky with fleeting clouds."[7] Susan Peters recognized the significance of this passage and suggested that pictures Courbet produced while imprisoned in 1871-72, such as *Still Life with Apples* (Munich, Staatsgemäldesammlungen), were the immediate inspiration for the Rochester painting, though there are greater formal similarities with, for example, his *Still Life: Fruit* (Vermont, Shelburne Museum)[8] from the same period. De Chirico's interest in Courbet is especially significant because critics focusing on the formal aspects of his work have generally emphasized the radical division separating his Metaphysical from his later paintings. Only recently have they begun to acknowledge attributes common to both periods of the artist's creative life. The Rochester painting reveals melancholy and nostalgia as elements of continuity within de Chirico's disparate oeuvre.

De Chirico was not unique in reverting to a classical mode. Following two decades of radical experimentation and the trauma of the war, many artists responded to the ambience of retrenchment and struggled to reorient themselves by reviewing older traditions. In the context of 1923, therefore, *Florentine Still Life* may be seen not only as a product of de Chirico's new, personal enthusiasm but also as a particularly extreme (and prolonged) expression of the atavism then current among advanced European artists.[9] Nevertheless, the Surrealists viewed de Chirico's reaction as a betrayal and attacked him vociferously, tainting any understanding of his subsequent efforts.[10] *Florentine Still Life* indicates, however, that in the 1920s (and later) he could still produce works of substance and quality.

▲
Florentine Still Life,
1923
Oil on canvas, 18 3/4 x 25 in.
(49 x 64.5 cm)
Inscribed, l.r.: *g. de Chirico*
Memorial Art Gallery of the University of Rochester,
Gift of Helen C. Ellwanger in memory of
Gertrude Newell, 64.47

PROVENANCE:
Balzac Galleries, New York (by 1930); Gertrude Newell,
"Planterrose," Moumour (Basses Pyrénées), France;
Helen C. Ellwanger, Rochester.

SELECTED BIBLIOGRAPHY:
A. Lancellotti, *La seconda biennale romana d'arte* (Rome, 1923),
p. 26, no. 16; C. Bruni Sakraischik, ed., *Catalogo generale Giorgio
de Chirico*, 8 vols. (Milan, 1971-83), vol. 1, pt. 1: *Opera dal
1908-1930*, no. 53; *Giorgio de Chirico 1888-1978*, exh. cat.
(Galleria Nazionale d'Arte Moderna, Rome, 1982), p. 112, no.
43; S. D. Peters, ed., *Memorial Art Gallery: An Introduction to the
Collection* (Rochester, 1988), pp. 146-47.

French, 1881-1955

éger was deeply influenced by the major artistic movements of the twentieth century, but he consistently maintained his independence.[1] His paintings and, later, his ceramic pieces are the expression of his personal vision. Though he studied at the Ecole des Beaux-Arts under Gérôme, Léger's earliest surviving works reflect the influence of the Impressionists and especially Cézanne. He destroyed the majority of the paintings from his next phase, which was evidently tinctured by Fauvism, and achieved recognition in 1910 with his austere *Nudes in the Forest* (Otterlo, Rijksmuseum Kröller-Müller). Though this painting bore the imprint of Cubism, Léger's particular interest in form and volume found expression in the distinctive use of cylindrical forms, which caused a critic facetiously to christen his work "tubism."[2]

Léger rejected perspective but retained chiaroscuro, because—unlike the other Cubists, whose analytical method was designed to show objects simultaneously from different points of view—his vocabulary of geometric forms was designed to reconcile the physical reality he observed with the flatness of the canvas. In 1919, he told Kahnweiler, "I reacted against Impressionism...because of its lack of constructive form" and added, "Composition achieved by assembled surfaces, which is the characteristic of Cubist pictures, has never been my forte."[3] Although the subject is generally acknowledged in Léger's paintings, he focused on the manner of representation, because by 1913, he already believed that a painting was an independent, beautiful, and expressive object and not a copy of something else. As he said, "The realistic value of a work of art is completely independent of any imitative character." Defining realism not in terms of mimesis but in formal terms as "the simultaneous ordering of three great plastic components: Lines, Forms, and Colors," Léger freely manipulated these elements to achieve a satisfying rhythmic harmony within the frame.[4] Until he was mobilized in 1916, he continued to explore Cubist modalities but in terms of the theory of dynamic contrasts he had developed.

Léger refined these ideas after the First World War, finding corroboration and inspiration in the tenets of Purism.[5] This movement, announced by Amédée Ozenfant and Charles-Edouard Jeanneret (known as Le Corbusier; 1887-1966) in their manifesto, *Après le cubisme* (1918), was subsequently promoted through their journal, *L'esprit nouveau* (1920-25), to which Léger contributed.[6] Taking science as their ideal and the machine as their model, the Purists assumed the inherent value of precision, simplicity, and proportional harmony. "A work of art," they declared, "should provoke a sensation of mathematical order"; paintings were defined as "machines

to move one's emotions."[7] Assuming that specific combinations of form, line, and color provoked consistent responses, they believed that a properly designed painting would produce predictable reactions in spectators. In effect, as Christopher Green observed, "the Purist painting becomes a more or less complex organization of surfaces over a basic armature of harmonious proportion."[8]

Although Léger's adherence to Purism was not dogmatic, he painted a series of still lifes during the 1920s that demonstrate his affinity for its principles. "My goal is to achieve a maximum of pictorial efficiency by contrasts of all the plastic means," he said.[9] He acknowledged the artist's job to be the creation of beauty, which was for him exclusively a matter of formal qualities, "completely independent from sentimental, descriptive, and imitative values."

Therefore, natural and man-made objects were equally raw material for the artist because "a machine or a machine-made object [could] be beautiful when the relationship of lines describing its volumes" was properly balanced and ordered.[10]

In a letter published in 1924, Léger declares, "I can take a subject from anywhere. I like the forms necessitated by modern industry and I use them." His still lifes of the 1920s represent an affirmation of the modern urban and industrial environment: "The contemporary environment is clearly the manufactured and 'mechanical' object: this is slowly subjugating the breasts and curves of women, fruit, the soft landscape—inspiration of painters since art began."[11] His preference for bold industrial colors and machine-made, mass-produced objects acknowledged the beauty unconsciously incorporated in these utilitarian products. Thirty years after painting the Rochester canvas, Léger recalled, "In 1923 and 1924 I produced paintings with as their main theme 'objects' isolated from space and without anything in common between them. I felt that the object which had been neglected, overlooked, could replace the subject."[12]

Léger described his inventive process as a search "for a state of plastically organized intensity," which he achieved by the application of the "law of contrasts": "Instead of opposing comic and tragic characters...I organize the opposition of contrasting values, lines, and curves. I oppose curves to straight lines, flat surfaces to molded forms, pure local colors to nuances of gray."[13] These principles were clearly applied in the construction of *Still Life with Glass* and other paintings of this period—for example, *The Siphon* (Buffalo, Albright-Knox Art Museum). At first glance, *Still Life with Glass* appears to be a

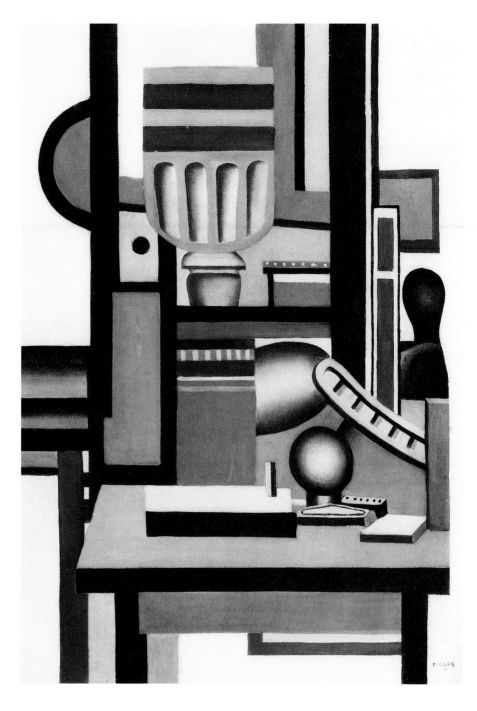

▶

Still Life with Glass,
1924
Oil on canvas, 25 1/4 x 18 in.
(64.1 x 45.7 cm)
Inscribed, l.r.: *F. LEGER / 24*; v., u.l.:
NATURE - MORTE. / 24 / F LEGER
Memorial Art Gallery of the University of
Rochester, Marion Stratton Gould Fund,
46.11

PROVENANCE:
Galerie Simon, Paris;
Léonce Rosenberg, Paris
(dealer); private collection;
Nierendorf Gallery, New York.

precisely ordered grid of similarly proportioned rectangles and curved shapes that lie flat against the picture plane. Strong, contrasting tints isolated in adjacent blocks add a dynamic quality to the design. The slight angle at the lower left, however, serves as a rudimentary perspective device, establishing the beige trapezoid in the lower portion of the composition as a table. Resting on the table, and integrated within the architectural armature, are, perhaps, a book, an electric light, a domino, and other items, all described in terms of their basic geometric forms. Extending from the right into the center of the picture is an adjustable lamp, and on the shelf above is a footed glass.[14] The still life items have been treated not as "subjects" but as "objects" integrated in a precisely calculated composition. They have not been used symbolically, as in seventeenth-century Dutch paintings, nor have they been used for their quotidian connotations, as in nineteenth-century American or even Cubist still lifes. Rather, they

were selected for the formal qualities of their machine-made shapes. The curved surfaces of the pressed glass and other manufactured objects are indicated in a schematic manner that establishes a contrast with the adjacent flat, colored areas, but this abstracted modeling does not contravene the basic planar structure of the composition. This structure has the effect of isolating the objects and emphasizing the geometric qualities Léger identified as beautiful.

Eliminating from the area near the lamp and the glass the second dark rectangle, the decorative "dentils," and the circle while making other minor adjustments, Léger simplified this composition in a somewhat larger version (1924; Basel, Galerie Beyeler).[15]

French, 1876-1936

ufresne worked for several years as a commercial artist before enrolling in the Ecole des Beaux-Arts, where he worked with the medalist Hubert Ponscarme (1827-1903). He subsequently supported himself by working in the studio of the sculptor Alexandre Charpentier (1856-1909). Dufresne first achieved public recognition for pastels exhibited around 1906, two years before he exhibited oil paintings at the Salon des Indépendants. In 1910, he won the Prix de l'Afrique du Nord and spent two years in Algeria. After being gassed during the First World War, Dufresne served in the camouflaging unit commanded by his friend André Dunoyer de Segonzac (1884-1974), who introduced him to the ideas of the Cubists. Their influence is most evident in the rather somber compositions he painted in the immediate aftermath of the war. As the artist sought a personal style during the 1920s, his palette lightened, and he became increasingly involved in decorative projects. Tapestries he designed were included in the influential 1925 Exposition des Arts Décoratifs, and later Dufresne become tapestry designer for the Paris Opéra.

Beginning around 1918, Dufresne produced a series of still lifes dominated by the influence of Cézanne.[1] Unlike the Cubists, who had responded to the implications of Cézanne's innovations, Dufresne, like other artists of his generation, responded to Cézanne's mannerisms as expressions of a personal style. A mature example of this exploratory phase, the Buffalo canvas incorporates techniques, motifs, and colors familiar from such paintings as Cézanne's Still Life with Plaster Cast (fig. 17; Stockholm, Nationalmuseum), one of a series of still lifes that served as a sort of palimpsest for the next generation of painters. In Plaster Torso, Bouquet of Flowers (1919; Museu de Arte de São Paolo),[2] Matisse translated Cézanne's composition into his own decorative idiom, exaggerating the contrapposto of a plaster torso by outlining its solid forms and contrasting its fluid grace with flat fields of luminous color.

Painted a decade later, Dufresne's Still Life reflected contemporary critical attitudes regarding Cézanne.[3] As in his paintings, the still life subject is carefully positioned on a table seen from above. Cézanne, however, usually set his objects on a corner, so that the angle of the table functioned as an orthogonal, establishing an illusion of depth to complement the sensation of atmosphere and volume it was his goal to achieve. This feature is absent from Dufresne's composition. The edges of the table are cropped by the frame, and as a result, the objects have been pushed closer to the picture plane. The frontality of the classical torso and flat patterning of the background augment the planar quality of the composition.

Dufresne emulated Cézanne's techniques—his use of color to suggest spatial depth and of thick brush strokes to build up tonal patches that define volumes and establish the solidity of forms. But Dufresne's brush strokes overlap and merge to create volume in a much more conventional manner. Whereas color and light become synonymous in Cézanne's paintings, Dufresne's use of light approximates traditional chiaroscuro, defining contour and volume and serving to clarify spatial relationships. In Still Life, the muted tonality of the sculpture clearly establishes its intermediate position in the composition. Its chalky surface is not highlighted with the same intensity as the white rumpled cloth or the white cup resting on the lacquered tray. These brilliant whites serve to pull the foreground elements forward, clarifying the distance, for example, between the cup and the pot of geraniums. As in Cézanne's related compositions, the most vibrant colors have been reserved for the fruit in the foreground. This area receives the brightest illumination, which reveals with great intensity the saturated black of the lacquer and vivid yellow, red, and green of the fruit. Dufresne may have known Plaster Torso, Bouquet of Flowers, and Matisse's subsidiary influence can be detected in the subject matter and the use of patterned surfaces as a design element. The arabesques of the rosy fabric in Still Life serve as an effective foil for the smooth, fully rounded surfaces of the torso.

Dufresne rejected the abstractions of Cubism in favor of a more representational mode of expression, and the traditional subject matter of this painting is coincident with this aesthetic choice. In his search for a more pliant style, he turned to Cézanne, the master in whose work the Impressionist experiment culminated and who served as inspiration for the innovations of the School of Paris. Although Dufresne studied the techniques and compositional formulas developed by Cézanne, he failed in this painting to achieve fully the harmony, balance, and cohesive power that make the latter's still lifes so riveting. What he succeeded in doing was to "correct" those elements in Cézanne that critics of the 1920s objected to as unfinished and idiosyncratic. The revisionist nature of the Buffalo Still Life is characteristic of the dominant conservatism that followed World War I; it also indicates Cézanne's looming but modified stature among the Parisian avant-garde.

▶

Still Life,
ca. 1928
Oil on canvas, 31 7/8 x 22 1/8 in.
(81 x 56 cm)
Inscribed, l.l.: *dufresne*
Albright-Knox Art Gallery,
Bequest of A. Conger Goodyear, 66.9.5

PROVENANCE:
Alexander Reid and Lefebvre, Ltd.,
London; A. Conger Goodyear (1929).

SELECTED BIBLIOGRAPHY:
 S. A. Nash, *Albright-Knox Art Gallery:
Painting and Sculpture from Antiquity to
1942* (New York, 1979), p. 475.

French, 1882-1963

rom 1908 until 1915, Braque worked in close collaboration with Picasso as the two artists invented the formal language of Cubism seen in *Still Life with Pipe* (cat. no. 26). After the First World War, this intimate relationship was not resumed, and the remainder of Braque's career may be seen as an independent and concentrated effort to refine and develop the implications of the artists' joint innovations.

During the 1920s, Braque produced several small paintings in which the complexities of Cubism were simplified in treating the glasses, bowls, and fruit that constitute the traditional components of still life. In the Buffalo composition, a glass, a pear, and a bowl containing almost transparent grapes are set on a wooden pedestal table. The claustrophobic overlapping of Cubism has been relaxed, and each geometric form is clearly defined in space. Braque's early training as a decorator is evident in his ornamental treatment of the background wall, the *faux* marble, and the table's surface. The center of the composition is activated by the intensely green pear. Sharp tonal contrasts have been used to suggest the volumes of each object, although the objects themselves have been described in linear terms that establish a rigid grid of horizontals and verticals as the dominant structural component.

In describing the development of Cubism, Daniel-Henry Kahnweiler asserted that the new style addressed representational and structural questions, "representational in that it tries to reproduce the formal beauty of things; structural in its attempt to grasp the meaning of this formal beauty."[1] At the time *Glass, Grapes, and Pear* was painted, Braque was preoccupied by questions of structure. In this painting, he was less interested in the objects themselves than in the relationship among the various elements of the composition: "The space between seems to me to be as essential an element as what they call the object. The subject matter consists precisely of the relationship between these objects and between the object and the intervening spaces."[2] In contrast to the "modern" subject matter of his rigorously Cubist *Still Life with Pipe*, Braque reverted to more traditional still life subjects as he grappled with pictorial problems resolved in the magnificent Pedestal Table series he painted in the 1920s.

▲

Glass, Grapes, and Pear,
1929
Oil on canvas, 9 3/4 x 16 3/8 in. (24 x 41 cm)
Inscribed, l.r.: G *Braque* / *29*
Albright-Knox Art Gallery,
Room of Contemporary Art Fund, 41.9

PROVENANCE:
Paul Rosenberg, Paris; Rosenberg and Helft,
London; Bucholz Gallery, New York.

SELECTED BIBLIOGRAPHY:
C. Morice, "Georges Braque," *Cahiers d'art* 8,
nos. 1-2 (1930), p. 5; S. A. Nash,
*Albright-Knox Art Gallery: Painting and Sculpture from
Antiquity to 1942* (New York, 1979), p. 470;
N.-S. Worms de Romilly, *Catalogue raisonné de l'oeuvre
de Georges Braque,* 7 vols. (Paris, 1959-73), vol. 4
(1928-35), no. 27.

Keeffe is among the most original, powerful, independent painters of the first generation of American modernists.[1] She received some initial training at the Chatham Episcopal Institute but began her formal studies in 1905 under John Vanderpoel (1857-1911) at the Art Institute of Chicago. In 1907, she moved to New York and, like so many of her colleagues, studied with William Merritt Chase at the Art Students League, winning a first prize in one of his still life classes. It was at this time that she experienced her first brush with modernism, visiting the 1908 Rodin exhibition at Alfred Stieglitz's Little Galleries of the Photo-Secession, the premier American avant-garde gallery later known as "291."

A crisis in confidence caused O'Keeffe to turn to commercial work, but her interest in painting was reawakened at the University of Virginia by Alon Bement, who taught the principles formulated by the influential theorist Arthur Wesley Dow (1857-1922). In 1914, she moved to New York to study with Dow himself. Combining ideas derived from his contact with Gauguin at Pont-Aven and from the study of oriental art, Dow taught that effective art depends not on subject matter but on the rhythmic manipulation of color, line, and mass, and he praised the flat patterning, economy of line, and use of negative space found in oriental painting.[2]

While teaching in Columbia, South Carolina, O'Keeffe sent a friend some charcoal drawings. They were shown to Stieglitz (1864-1946), who was so impressed that he immediately included them in a group show that opened in 1916. In the following year, he lauded O'Keeffe in a solo exhibition and offered to support her so that she might devote herself entirely to painting. Stieglitz's patronage extended to passion, and, after his divorce in 1924, the couple was married. In addition to his other qualities, Stieglitz was an effective publicist, and once she was launched by him, O'Keeffe enjoyed continuously increasing success. He continued to show her work in his Anderson Gallery exhibitions and at An American Place, where *Jawbone and Fungus* was first exhibited in 1932. It was praised by the anonymous *Art News* critic as "one of her most elegant designs."[3]

Stieglitz's circle included Charles Demuth, Arthur G. Dove, Marsden Hartley, John Marin, Paul Strand, and O'Keeffe, and his galleries were a crucible for American modernism. Throughout her long career, O'Keeffe's work encompassed the interest in expressive abstraction and economy of means shared by other members of the "Seven Americans." In addition to purely abstract compositions, she painted landscapes, though she is probably most admired for her still lifes, among which the flower series of the 1920s and the bone series of the 1930s and early 1940s are the most fascinating.

The bone paintings are based on objects the artist collected in the New Mexico dessert. They exhibit a tendency toward monumentality that recalls the earlier flower paintings.[4] In both large and small canvases, this effect is achieved by either of two methods. In some cases, the object is set before a barren landscape and depicted from a low, frontal viewpoint. This has the effect of eliminating the middle ground that would ordinarily provide markers for judging scale. In other instances, such as *Jawbone and Fungus*, the subject is isolated so that it occupies most of the picture surface. In the Rochester painting, scale is distorted by the cropping of the composition and by the absence of context. Painted in the studio (as suggested by the simplified shadow cast by the fungus), the donkey's jawbone is balanced on a plain surface that could function as a surrogate landscape overshadowed by billowing storm clouds. Both the bone and the fungus are illuminated by a clear, direct light that simplifies their forms. Surface details have been suppressed, and the objects have been rendered in flat patches of thickly applied paint contained within strict contours. As Lloyd Goodrich observed, by isolating objects from "ordinary reality" and magnifying them, O'Keeffe achieved a type of abstraction that imbues her subjects with new significance.[5]

As in many of O'Keeffe's paintings, the intrinsic interest of the objects has been subordinated here to their functions as vehicles for a decorative and emotional effect. The drama of *Jawbone and Fungus* derives from the contrast between jagged and curving forms and from the counterpoint of black, white, and gray. The impact of Dow's teaching is evident in the way O'Keeffe transformed the objects into an evocative abstract design within a rectilinear frame.

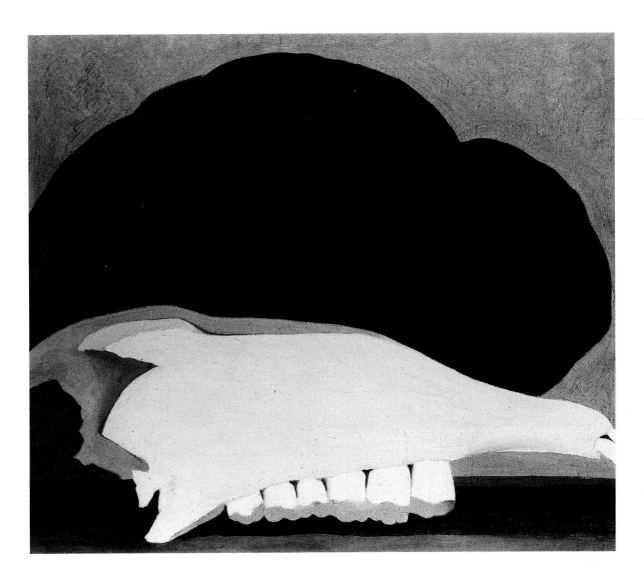

▲

Jawbone and Fungus,
1930
Oil on canvas, 17 x 20 in. (43.2 x 50.8 cm)
Inscribed, v.: *Jawbone and Fungus / 1930 / Georgia O'Keeffe*
Memorial Art Gallery of the University of Rochester,
Marion Stratton Gould Fund, 51.11

PROVENANCE:
Senator William Benton; Encyclopaedia Britannica Collection
of Contemporary American Painting.

SELECTED BIBLIOGRAPHY:
Anonymous review, "Georgia O'Keeffe. An American Place,"
Art News 30, no. 14 (January 2, 1932), p. 9; G. Pagano, *The
Encyclopaedia Britannica Collection of Contemporary American
Painting,* 2d ed. (Chicago, 1946), p. 89 (incorrectly dated 1933);
R. G. Pisano, *An American Place,* exh. cat. (Parrish Art
Museum, Southampton, N.Y., 1981), no. 41; *Order and Enigma:
American Art between the Wars,* exh. cat. (Munson-Williams-
Proctor Institute Museum of Art, Utica, 1984), pp. 64-65;
C. Schwartz, *Nevelson and O'Keeffe: Independents of the
Twentieth Century,* exh. cat. (Nassau County Museum of Fine
Art, Roslyn Harbor, N.Y., 1983), p. 35.

American, 1882-1952

ith his long beard and a career marred by alcoholism and marked by struggle, Carles is in many ways a romantic figure, a paradigmatic and somewhat tragic bohemian. His studio was notoriously chaotic and the production of each painting an ordeal, causing him to work and rework canvases, often over prolonged periods of time. "The use of the medium," he explained, "is like some element of nature.... I have no theories. I do not know when I begin to paint what will appear on the finished canvas.... I paint to see what the idea will look like in reality."[1] Able to maintain long-lasting friendships with artists and patrons, Carles was an effective and generous teacher, but his drinking and inability to play the game of departmental politics obliged him to leave his post at the Pennsylvania Academy of the Fine Arts, Philadelphia, in 1925. Though he received awards and occasional critical praise, his disdain for commercial enterprise (signaled by his refusal to sign or date his paintings) limited his success. The constant features of Carles's career were his unremitting intensity and his infatuation with color.

Carles studied at the Pennsylvania Academy of the Fine Arts and mastered the Impressionist-tinged bravura style of his teacher, William Merritt Chase. In 1907, he traveled to Paris, where he mingled with Gertrude and Leo Stein, Picasso, and Matisse, and with Alfred Maurer (1868-1932) and other young American painters influenced by the innovations of the European avant-garde. He became friends with Edward Steichen (1879-1973), who secured for Carles a position in the stable of artists exhibited at "291," Alfred Stieglitz's aggressively avant-garde New York gallery. During subsequent European visits, Carles formed friendships with Léger (cat. no. 31) and Constantin Brancusi (1876-1957) and in this context gradually abandoned the tradition in which he had been trained and began to experiment under the influence of a diversity of modernist impulses.

Experimentation, in a sense, was the essence of his art. His early Fauvist style became increasingly complex and recondite, evolving in his late works into free geometric and "biomorphic" compositions that appear to presage Abstract Expressionism. This evolution accorded with Carles's belief that "those who look to painting to find subject matter are not in need of paintings. They should go to the theater." Although his paintings have been called abstract, the artist himself rejected this term: "I think that when a painting gets so concrete, that it looks so much like itself that it doesn't look like anything else, 'abstract' is a hell of a name for it."[2]

Still Life with Flowers dates from the middle of Carles's career, when he was most fascinated by the innovations of the Cubists and the chromatic explorations of the Synchromists. Like them, he made many of his most daring experiments using still life, which "has no story to tell, other than the story of line, form and color, and always this is the painter's real story."[3] In this painting, a small, flaring vase is located on a rumpled cloth set on a table angled so that its top is clearly visible. Stabilizing the dynamic rhythm of the composition, a straight-backed chair stands on a patterned floor to the right. Characteristically, Carles selected organic forms as his primary subject. Filling the upper two-thirds of the canvas, a profusion of flowers is depicted as twisting forms and colored shapes fragmented and illuminated by bright prisms of light. Black and white have been used to delimit form, while resonant color contrasts create a sense of plastic structure, replacing conventional modeling by means of light and shadow. The result is a picture of great energy and sensuous appeal.

▶

Still Life with Flowers,
ca. 1933-35
Oil on canvas, 49 x 36 in. (124.5 x 91.4 cm)
Albright-Knox Art Gallery, Edward Hayes
and Elisabeth H. Gates Fund, 69.6

PROVENANCE:
S. Beryl Lush, Chestnut Hill, Pa.; Graham
Gallery, New York (by 1967).

SELECTED BIBLIOGRAPHY:
S. A. Nash, *Albright-Knox Art Gallery:
Painting and Sculpture from Antiquity to 1942*
(New York, 1979), pp. 502-3.

Spanish, 1881-1973

man of prodigious and protean talent, Picasso was among the most prolific and influential artists of the twentieth century. He studied first with his father and then at the Escuela de Bellas Artes, Barcelona, and the Real Academie de Bellas Artes de San Fernande, Madrid. In 1904, he moved to Paris, where his work evolved through several distinct phases.

In 1907, Guillaume Apollinaire introduced Picasso to Georges Braque (cat. nos. 26, 33). The two artists collaborated closely in developing both Analytical and Synthetic Cubism, the style which preoccupied Picasso until about 1916. His work assumed a significantly more classical cast in the aftermath of the First World War, reflecting the conservative impulse referred to as the "call to order" by the poet Jean Cocteau.[1] In the mid-1920s, Picasso became intrigued by the Surrealists and assimilated elements of their artistic philosophy, but in a characteristically personal fashion.[2] The calligraphic fancy evident in much of this work was translated into a language of horrific seriousness in his monumental *Guernica* (1937; Madrid, Buen Retiro) and related paintings and prints. Following the Second World War, Picasso's work became more personal and perhaps more decorative. The accomplishments of his previous fifty years provided the artist with a repertoire of motifs and styles which he manipulated with astonishing dexterity.

Glass, Vase and Fruits is one of a series of intimate, brightly colored still lifes that Picasso painted between April 19 and 30, 1937.[3] Such creative bursts were characteristic of the artist, who developed comprehensively the implications of any theme that fascinated him. In its component parts—fruits and containers on a table—the Buffalo still life is clearly related to the tradition that can be traced from Jan de Heem to Rubens Peale and Antoine Vollon (cat. nos. 3, 12, 17). The Spaniard's intuitive command of Cubism enabled him to use its devices in a deft and free manner, so there is a sense of spontaneity in his imaginative translation of this venerable motif into a modern idiom.

What seems to have interested Picasso most on this occasion was the fundamentally decorative character of the traditional still life. He treated the forms with reductive simplicity, combining flattened shapes in a crisp, collagelike manner to form a balanced geometric ensemble. An abbreviated system of faceting was used to suggest volumes; shadows have been reduced to geometric schemata. Using thick impasto and transparent washes, the brushwork varies in accordance with the nature of the surfaces depicted. The fanciful shape of the pitcher and the bright blues and luminous terra-cottas contribute to the picture's playful and decorative appearance. Painted only a few days before the Germans obliterated the town of Guernica, the sharp angularity that adds a spritely quality to *Glass, Vase and Fruits* would become an instrument for expressing anguish and horror at this brutal incident.

▲

Glass, Vase and Fruits,
1937
Oil on canvas, 15 x 24 in. (38 x 61 cm)
Inscribed, u.l.: *21 Av 37 / Picasso*
Albright-Knox Art Gallery,
Gift of the Seymour H. Knox Foundation, 69.10

PROVENANCE:
Paul Rosenberg, Paris (1937); Paul Rosenberg and
Co., New York; Seymour H. Knox, Buffalo (1955).

SELECTED BIBLIOGRAPHY:
S. A. Nash, *Albright-Knox Art Gallery: Painting and
Sculpture from Antiquity to 1942* (New York, 1979),
pp. 436-37; C. Zervos, *Pablo Picasso*, 33 vols. (Paris,
1932-78), vol. 8 (1957), no. 364.

uhn began drawing at the age of eight and steadfastly pursued an artistic career, producing a multitude of still lifes and landscapes that brought him considerable renown. He remains best known for his portraits, among which his bold and somewhat melancholy circus performers are the most memorable.[1] Kuhn's early career was somewhat unusual. After a brief period of study at the Brooklyn Polytechnic Institute, he traveled to San Francisco, where he worked as a cartoonist. Between 1901 and 1903, he honed his natural abilities at the Académie Colarossi, Paris, and the Akademie der Bildenden Künste, Munich.

After returning to New York, the young artist's interest in the accomplishments of the Parisian avant-garde matured in the company of friends, among whom the painter Arthur B. Davies (1862-1928) and Kuhn's first patron, the prescient collector John Quinn, were the most notable. Eventually, these men helped form the Association of American Painters and Sculptors, the organization responsible for the Armory Show. As executive secretary, Kuhn traveled to Europe and visited the *Second Post-Impressionist Exhibition* at Roger Fry's Grafton Gallery in London. Together with Davies, Kuhn attended the *International Kunstausstellung* in Cologne, which became the model the New York artists sought to surpass. In Paris, they met the critic Walter Pach, who shepherded them to galleries and studios, helping them select the European works that would make the 1913 exhibition such a formative event in the history of American art.[2]

While on this European expedition, Kuhn's admiration for Cézanne increased. On November 6, 1912, he wrote to his wife that the Cubists were "intensely interesting now that I have had a chance to study them—mostly literary and lacking in that passion of sex evidence which is absolutely necessary for me. However they have helped me understand Cézanne. He's growing every day with me."[3] This fascination persisted. Shortly before his death thirty-seven years later, Kuhn observed, "Artists all took little sections out of Cézanne.... They got decoration instead of penetration. I've tried to get the whole

Cézanne and give it a new flavor."[4] The solidity and substantiality he admired in Cézanne (fig. 17) are evident in his powerfully composed and boldly colored *Chair with Apples*, a "banal subject...painted with tuning-fork adjustment of tone" which the artist characterized as "the arbitrary carried...to the highest refinement."[5]

Built upon Kuhn's favorite color combination, green and orange, the painting is a successful exercise in pure composition using a motif made famous by van Gogh. In the absence of the biographical and symbolic allusions that inform *Van Gogh's Chair* (1888/89; London, Tate Gallery), for example, *Chair with Apples* represents Kuhn's vision of architectonic perfection. The unpretentious chair is the primary subject, dominating the canvas by virtue of its mass, central location, and glaring color. The circular platter and spherical apples emphasize the chair's sturdy form, which has been modeled with thick brush strokes that conform to the blocky structures they represent. The chair is painted a vivid, saturated orange that contrasts wildly with the green wall and brown floor, causing it to stand out against the background. The strident color contrast enhances the illusion of three-dimensionality emphasized by the angle at which the chair is situated in relation to the viewer.

In painting this still life, Kuhn was not concerned with representing a chair or apples but with these objects as color-supporting forms appropriate for expressing specific aesthetic ideas. This was recognized by Aline Louchlin when the painting was first exhibited in 1946:

> You are struck by the rightness which controls the daring color dissonance (the almost vulgar orange of the chair, the forest-green walls, and the pale, cool green of the apples...) and transforms it into an affirmation of chromatic strength. You are arrested by the justice of tonal progressions, which move like the stirring chords of a Bach chorale. And you are aware at once of the coherence and logic.[6]

▶

Chair with Apples,
1940
Oil on canvas, 40 1/2 x 30 in.
(102.9 x 76.2 cm)
Inscribed, l.c.: *Walt Kuhn / 1940*
Munson-Williams-Proctor Institute
Museum of Art, 60.1

PROVENANCE:
Fred. L. Palmer, New York.

SELECTED BIBLIOGRAPHY:
P. R. Adams, *Walt Kuhn, Painter: His Life and Work* (Columbus, Oh., 1978), p. 192, no. 398; P. Bird, *Fifty Paintings by Walt Kuhn* (Studio, N.Y., 1940), p. 50.

American, 1885-1965

orn in upstate New York, Avery moved in 1898 to Hartford, Connecticut, where he was obliged to find employment to help support his family. Nevertheless, he also began to study at the Connecticut League of Art Students in 1905 and six years later identified himself as a professional artist. He worked nights so that he could transfer to the School of the Art Society of Hartford. Only after moving to New York in 1925 (and with the aid of his beloved wife) was Avery able to devote himself wholly to painting.[1]

In addition to his conventional training, Avery gained familiarity with the most advanced tendencies in European and American painting through friends, journals, and regular visits to museums and galleries. In its quotidian subject matter, optimistic tone, lyrical design, and arbitrary color, his work may be most closely related to the aesthetic of Matisse, but Avery's mature style is nonetheless wholly individual and only tangentially related to the dominant artistic trends of his day. With their emphasis on the simplification of form and subjective, expressive coloring, Avery's paintings proved influential for the development of Abstract Expressionism. Mark Rothko (1903-1970), who admired the "gripping lyricism" of Avery's pictures, characterized his colleague as "a great poet-inventor who invented sonorities never seen…before."[2]

Pink Tablecloth was painted in 1944, the artist's most productive year, during which he also enjoyed a peak of popularity and his first solo museum exhibition. It exemplifies Avery's achievement of a personal style in which the simplification of shapes and the expressive potential of color harmonies became dominant concerns. As Robert Hobbs pointed out, the Utica painting is related to Avery's 1928 *Red Tablecloth* (Milton Avery Trust). In the earlier painting, the dark tonalities of Braque (cat. no. 26, 33) and brilliant color contrasts and staccato brushwork of Matisse are dominant, but in the 1944

canvas these elements have been recast in Avery's personal idiom.[3] The color contrasts have been moderated; the broad expanses of orange wall, pink tablecloth, and brown floor harmonize in a unique chromatic equilibrium.

Although *Pink Tablecloth* contains the full complement of objects associated with a conventional breakfast still life, the bread, knife, and coffeepot are not objectively represented. They have been transformed, as Barbara Haskell has observed, "for the sake of formal relationships."[4] The illusion of space is only minimally indicated by the diagonal lines of the table and by the cursory modeling of forms. For example, the cylindrical volumes of the table legs are indicated by simple lines scratched through to the canvas, and the mass of the two-handled pitcher is only suggested by textured zigzags incised in the thick pigment. The description of nature has not been abandoned, however, and the individual objects are clearly delineated, but as simplified, flattened chromatic masses that function as abstract equivalents to the objects themselves. The positive and negative spaces defined by purposeful outlines are balanced, and this balance is correlative to the equilibrium by which the colors are harmonized. This balance is not mathematical but aesthetic, for the picture is not about the objects depicted but precisely about relationships between form and color. Just as he formed a precarious concord between arbitrary shapes and artificial hues, Avery also maintained in his work a precarious balance between the traditions of representation and the complete abstraction that emerged among the generation of American artists which followed his own.

▲
Pink Tablecloth,
1944
Oil on canvas, 32 1/8 x 48 1/8 in. (81.6 x 122.3 cm)
Inscribed, l.c.: *Milton Avery / 1944*
Munson-Williams-Proctor Institute Museum of Art,
Gift of Mr. and Mrs. Roy R. Neuberger, 53.439

SELECTED BIBLIOGRAPHY:
B. Haskell, *Milton Avery*, exh. cat. (Whitney Museum
of Art, New York, 1982), pp. 77-92; R. Hobbs, *Milton Avery*
(New York, 1990), pp. 128-29; P. D. Schweizer, ed.,
*Masterworks of American Art from the Munson-Williams-Proctor
Institute* (New York, 1989), pp. 166-67.

American (born Canada), 1907-1967

hreaded by a piece of twine, elements including a lemon, a potato, a hollow ceramic pipe, an onion, a piece of bread (or stone?), and a fragment of wood are suspended motionless before a luminous, indeterminate surface. Mysteriously illuminated, they exist in isolation. The rationale for their juxtaposition is intentionally enigmatic, the narrow confines of the canvas strictly limiting any contextual analysis. Although such objects are usually disregarded as mundane, the artist has transformed these items by the most painterly of means into objects of wonder: they glow softly in a radiant void, engaging our attention. This metamorphosis constitutes the essence of Murch's unique artistry: "I leave no room for the observer to think about the subject within the world of the picture, but the picture area becomes the subject."[1]

Murch studied at the Ontario School of Art, Toronto, before emigrating in 1927 to New York, where he evolved a unique and intensely personal style. At the Grand Central School, he studied with Arshile Gorky (1904-1948), a pivotal figure in the evolution of abstract art. Gorky's belief in painting as independent from nature and his emphasis on the importance of organic fantasy profoundly influenced Murch, who was simultaneously fascinated by the Surrealists, especially after visiting the 1936 Museum of Modern Art exhibition *Dada, Fantastic Art and Surrealism*. Murch was particularly impressed by the visionary works of Pierre Roy (1880-1950), in whose clinically cool paintings organic and mechanical objects are combined in a disturbing and evocative fashion. Among the old masters at the Metropolitan Museum of Art, Murch also discovered particular qualities that were especially congenial:

the impasto technique and chiaroscuro of Rembrandt, the play of light in Jan Vermeer (1632-1675), and especially the quiescent, almost reverential aura which constitutes the magic of Chardin. These diverse influences were combined in accordance with Murch's desire to achieve a "peculiar beauty" that would "strike a chord inside...a chord that is inexplicable."[2] In character and mood, his pictures are most closely akin to the hermetic little worlds created from found objects by his friend Joseph Cornell (1903-1972).

In this example, fruits and vegetables remain identifiable, but by the painter's controlled use of light and color, they have been transmuted from comestibles into objects of fascination. The strangely glittering background recalls Murch's early experience in a stained-glass shop. Details that might particularize the objects have been stripped away to reveal their "poetic" essence. Their volumes persist, but their distinctly textured surfaces have become luminous and friable, as though subject to some sort of decay. The ghostlike evanescence of the forms casts an elegiac mood over the composition. These formal devices were the means by which Murch shared his discovery of the spiritual beauty in the most mundane objects: "To reduce the subject to the way it is reduced in an abstract painting permits the artist to emphasize the poetry. To force out poetry, this is my job."[3]

▸
Objects,
1954
Oil on canvas, 24 3/8 x 12 1/4 in.
(61.9 x 31.1 cm)
Inscribed, l.r.: *Walter Murch*
Munson-Williams-Proctor Institute
Museum of Art, 57.32

PROVENANCE:
Purchased from the artist through
Betty Parsons Gallery, New York.

SELECTED BIBLIOGRAPHY:
J. Collischan van Wagner, "Walter Murch
(Catalogue Raisonné)," unpub. Ph.D. diss.,
University of Iowa, 1972, p. 171, no. 124.

American, 1930-1987

ike Oscar Wilde and Marcel Duchamp (1887-1968), Warhol's mythic persona was as significant a part of his artistic activity as any object he created. A shy, quiet youth, he transformed himself into a dominant celebrity, experiencing far more than the fifteen minutes of fame he predicted for everyone. In his various roles as filmmaker, rock-and-roll producer, photographer, publisher, author, television show host, and—most of all—through the trenchant paintings he produced as an art entrepreneur, he became, in a manner of speaking, the pictorial chronicler of his age. His works mirror with seeming impassivity the glitter, horror, and superficiality of the decades during which he was a shining art star. "If you want to know all about Andy Warhol," he explained in a 1967 interview, "just look at the surface: of my paintings and films and me, and there I am. There is nothing behind it."[1]

A laconic man of considerable wit, Warhol possessed a distinct graphic talent that brought him early success as a commercial artist. His later notoriety in the art world depended largely on his ability to combine this talent with his unerring instinct for the banal. Like other Pop artists, Warhol depicted things "that anybody walking down Broadway could recognize in a split second."[2] But from the welter of media images and commercial products, the objects he selected inevitably possess a particular and powerful social and emotional resonance. Moreover, he viewed these emblems of modernity not as an iconoclast but as an "iconophile" cognizant of their of symbolic power.

The power inherent in the images Warhol selected is augmented by the manner in which he manipulated them. Stopping-out details that suggested specificity, cows, poppies, Coca Cola bottles, and movie stars are depicted as two-dimensional icons. Isolating them from their tabloid or commercial contexts, Warhol intervened in numerous other ways as well. He determined the frame size and number of times the image might be multiplied, he adjusted contours, and he emblazoned the forms with dramatic and often garish colors. Although he explained that the reason he was "painting this way is that I want to be a machine,"[3] his was not a passive, mechanical art. He oversaw the production of his images but cherished accidents: "My paintings never turn out the way I expect them to, but I'm never surprised."[4] Because he used preprocessed imagery, it might also be said that, strictly speaking, his pictures of photographs, money, and newspaper illustrations are still lifes in the tradition represented, for example, by Haberle's *Torn in Transit* (cat. no. 19). With his more conventional still lifes of containers, skulls, or hammers and sickles, Warhol's pictures of pictures share in the allusive richness of the still life tradition.[5]

In 1980, Warhol declared, "I like boring things, but that doesn't mean I'm not bored with them." This paradox may offer a clue to the images he selected and replicated, for he added (with a certain irony, I believe): "The more you look at the same exact thing the more the meaning goes away, and the better and emptier you feel."[6] *Big Electric Chair* is a case in point. It is related thematically to the artist's 1962-63 "Disasters," which depict car wrecks, airplane accidents, suicides, and poisonings. They originated in response to catastrophe: "I guess it was the big plane crash picture, the front page of a newspaper: 129 DIE. I was also painting the Marilyns. I realized that everything I was doing must have been Death. It was...a holiday...and every time you turned on the radio they said something like '4 million are going to die.' That started it."[7] The images Warhol selected are horrific not merely because of their content but also because of the purposelessness they represent and their anonymity: "My death series was divided into two parts, the first one famous deaths and the second one people nobody every heard of.... It's not that I feel sorry for them, it's just that people go by and that it doesn't really matter to them that someone unknown was killed."[8] Warhol responded by making such events even more abstract; as he put it, "When you see a gruesome picture over and over again, it doesn't really have any effect."[9]

The "Disasters" are especially unnerving because of the reversals involved in these "plebeian catastrophes."[10] Automobiles, airplanes, packaged foods, and hospitals that are viewed generally in a positive sense, as conveniences, are converted by incomprehensible circumstances into sites of meaningless death. In *Big Electric Chair*, a benign domestic object has become an instrument of socially sanctioned violence. Although Warhol claimed that "there was no profound reason for doing a death series...just a surface reason,"[11] this surface reason was extraordinarily potent at a time when capital punishment was the subject of acrimonious public debate.[12] Warhol introduced the subject in 1963, when the electric chair in Sing Sing State Penitentiary, New York, performed the state's last executions.

It is not known whether the photograph Warhol used depicts the chair at Sing Sing. Nonetheless, he used the same anonymous documentary image in the versions of the subject produced in 1963, 1965, and 1967.[13] As in other versions, he manipulated the image in Utica's *Big Electric Chair* to maximize the grim significance of this terribly simple device. In contrast to the aesthetic and intellectual appeal made by Kuhn's *Chair with Apples* (cat. No. 37), everything about Warhol's picture is designed to augment its emotional impact. We peer at the chair through a gritty light, and the pigmented surface retains stains and accidents from its production that enhance the sordid quality of the image. The chair is isolated within its stark chamber, situated at a point distant enough to permit safe viewing but near enough to provoke anxiety. Midway

between the bleached area on the right and the obscuring darkness on the left, it dominates the composition, though its form appears almost fragile in the corrosive intensity of the flashbulb chiaroscuro. For this 1967 version,[14] Warhol employed two screens and either accidently or intentionally failed to achieve proper registration between the dark purple and black.[15] This disjunction adds a disquieting vibrating quality to the image, as though it is charged with electricity.

Warhol's manipulation of a newspaper photograph suggests that his reaction and intention were not passive. The chair is presented factually, but not objectively, and its effect may be numbing. In Warhol's terms, that it is ultimately a boring subject in no way detracts from its compelling quality. *Big Electric Chair* is not just a chair. It is the ultimate still life.

▲

Big Electric Chair,
1967
Acrylic and silkscreened enamel on canvas, 54 x 74 in.
(137.2 x 188 cm)
Munson-Williams-Proctor Institute Museum of Art,
86.56 (© 1991 The Estate and Foundation of Andy Warhol/
ARS, New York)

PROVENANCE:
Leo Castelli, New York; Gian Enzo Sperone, Turin; Blum Helman Gallery, New York; Robert and Jane Meyerhoff, Baltimore; sale Christie's, New York, May 6, 1986, lot 45.

SELECTED BIBLIOGRAPHY:
N. Sundell, *The Robert and Jane Meyerhoff Collection* (privately printed, 1980), pp. 74-75; P. D. Schweizer, ed., *Masterworks of American Art from the Munson-Williams-Proctor Institute* (New York, 1989), pp. 206-7.

American, born 1938

oncurrent with the appearance of Pop art in the 1960s, another group of "realist" artists emerged. Less socially engaged, perhaps, than their colleagues, and clearly less enthralled by media imagery, these artists' work reveals a common acuteness of observation. Their predominantly formal concerns link them closely with the Abstract Expressionists.[1] A painter of nudes, Philip Pearlstein (born 1924), has declared, for example, "I'm interested in abstraction—subject matter never interests me."[2] Janet Fish has explained that "realism, so-called, is a matter of painting what you choose to see. I look for a complex interaction of color, and that is what I find. So I paint that."[3]

The technical and representational strategies employed by these artists were as diverse as the themes they favored, rousing considerable controversy among critics seeking to define the movement.[4] Recognizing that no representation is capable of either transmitting perceived data in its totality or being objectively "true," critics seem only to agree that the New Realism is characterized by unidealized representation of meticulously observed subjects. Although this is not the context in which to discuss the debate regarding the significance of these representations, Donald Kuspit has made an important point regarding the relationship between form and content. He has stressed that in the most compelling of the New Realist paintings, meaning is related directly to the appropriation by the artists of traditional iconographic and formal conventions.[5]

Janet Fish studied at Smith College and Yale University and began her career working in an Abstract Expressionist style. In the 1960s, she began to paint in a more representational manner, establishing a significant reputation during the 1970s with geometrically structured pictures of bottles and glasses. "I would keep on arranging them until I had a very strong feeling about the set-up. When I felt it was right I would start painting it."[6] Later compositions, such as *After Leslie Left*, are more diverse in their contents and less rigidly structured. "I pick things for a still life in order to set up a situation—a strong visual situation. Those objects are not necessarily logical together.... What matters is the relationships between colors and forms."[7]

After Leslie Left offers a bird's-eye view of the objects left behind by Leslie and Chuck Close when Fish purchased their SoHo loft. A domestic narrative is implied by the insignificant detritus, and—as in Dutch still lifes in which a human presence is suggested by cut fruit or a smoking pipe—the keys and half-finished cup of coffee evoke the presence of the recent tenants. In such works, Fish told Carter Ratcliff, "there may be hints of narrative, yet the important point is that all those messages are coming across at the level of gesture and color."[8]

The pink feather-duster, shopping coupons, glossy *House and Garden* magazine, bowl of bananas, green Depression-glass creamer, begonias, billowing curtains, dried sponge, plastic bag, and Windex bottle[9] represented for the artist a challenging variety of shapes and colors. The disparate objects are arranged in a dynamic spiral unified by the swirl of bright commercial pastels and by the reflected and refracted light ricocheting off the sleek and transparent surfaces. Activated by the play of crystalline light over the entire surface of the canvas, the composition is integrated by the artist's fluid brushwork, which suggests rather than imitates the various textures. As she explained in 1980,

> My primary subject is light, the manner in which it transforms appearances, altering color and atmosphere, shattering and reordering forms.
> My approach is also determined by a love for the sensual properties of the medium, the sense of a painted surface, the play of form, scale, and color. I like working with complex structures, the excitement of orchestrating the whole and the surprise at what I can find in the process.[10]

After Leslie Left is not about the things themselves, and Fish made no attempt to render either their bulk, density, or tactile qualities. The brushwork is descriptive, but instead of substance, it describes light and the interaction of colors within a contrived, complex environment: "The energy is in the color, the mark-making, the bounce of the light. That is the content."[11] The glittering luminosity of *After Leslie Left* suggests that the artist's focus on the most fleeting of surface effects represents an appropriation of the Impressionist enterprise to enrich the contemporary domestic context.

▲

After Leslie Left,
1983-84
Oil on canvas, 48 x 62 in. (121.9 x 157.4 cm)
Inscribed, l.r.: *JANET FISH* ©
Albright-Knox Art Gallery, Norman E. Boasberg,
George Cary, and Charles W. Goodyear Funds, 1984.2

PLATE 12

PROVENANCE:
Robert Miller Gallery, New York.

SELECTED BIBLIOGRAPHY:
G. Henry, *Janet Fish* (Geneva, 1987), fig. 70;
S. Krane et al., *Albright-Knox Art Gallery:*
The Painting and Sculpture Collection:
Acquisitions since 1972 (New York, 1987), p. 130.

Cat. No. 1

1. Copy of letter to Mortimer Brandt, November 7, 1964, Frick Art Reference Library, New York.

2. Letter to B. Barryte, May 2, 1991, Memorial Art Gallery archives.

3. B. de Dominici, *Vite de' pittori, scultori e architetti napoletani*, 3 vols. (Naples, 1742-45), vol. 3, pp. 577-78. See also L. Salerno, *La natura morta italiana* (Rome, 1984), pp. 84-89; idem, *New Studies on Italian Still Life Painting* (Rome, 1989), pp. 246-48; F. Zeri and F. Porzio, eds., *La natura morta in Italia*, 2 vols. (Milan, 1989), vol. 2, pp. 954-56, with bibliog. On the Neapolitan still life tradition, see N. Spinosa, "La natura morta in Napoli," in ibid., pp. 852-71.

4. See Salerno (note 3), pp. 130-33; Zeri and Porzio (note 3), vol. 1, pp. 455-59, with bibliog. On the still life tradition in central Italy, see A. C. Ferretti, "La natura morta a Bologna e in Romagna," in ibid., pp. 438-47.

5. For the Italian still life tradition, see Zeri and Porzio (note 3). The most accessible surveys in English are Salerno (note 3), which is bilingual; C. Sterling, *Still Life Painting from Antiquity to the Twentieth Century*, 2d rev. ed. (New York, 1981), pp. 80-92; and the well-illustrated volume by J. T. Spike, *Italian Still Life Paintings from Three Centuries*, exh. cat. (National Academy of Design [New York], Florence, 1983).

6. With its broad band of landscape and twisted bicolored handles, the vase most closely resembles Talavera de la Reina wares produced in Toledo, Spain, during the second half of the seventeenth century (letter from José G. Moya Valgañón [Museo Nacional de Artes Decorativas, Madrid] to B. Barryte, June 26, 1989, Memorial Art Gallery archives).

Cat. No. 2

1. Smith's 1836 entry accurately describes the Ithaca painting: "The composition consists of two partridges and a teal, suspended on separate nails against a wall. Upon a table under them is laid an antique cross-bow. This study from nature is painted in the artist's most vigorous style and possesses extraordinary effect."

2. A. Houbraken, *De Groote Schouburgh der Nederlantsche Konstschilders en Schilderessen...* (1718-20), 2d ed. (The Hague, 1753), vol. 3, p. 206; J. von Sandrart, *Academie der Bau-, Bild- und Mahlerey-Künste* (1675), ed. A. R. Peltzer (Munich, 1925), p. 203, cited in *Corpus of Rembrandt Paintings, III (1635-1642)*, pp. 12-13 (hereafter cited as *Corpus*).

3. Werner Sumowski rejects Bol, Lambert Doomer, Carel Fabritius, Samuel van Hoogstraten, Nicholas Maes, H. Dullaert, and Godefried Kneller as possible authors (letter, May 31, 1988, Herbert F. Johnson Museum archives). In his note on the painting, Sullivan (1984) suggests a possible attribution to Bol, but he has subsequently rejected this possibility (letter to B. Barryte, February 19, 1991).

4. *Corpus*, p. 38.

5. The history of the genre is described in Sullivan (1984).

6. Hofstede de Groot (1916) identified the birds as two woodcocks (snipes) and a coot. Following Smith, the authors of *Corpus* identify them as two partridges and a teal.

7. Sullivan (letter, note 3) indicated that crossbows appear rarely in game pieces.

8. Those privileged to hunt often commissioned game pieces to celebrate the sport. Beyond this obvious function, their use and precise social significance is disputed. Sullivan (1984, p. 79) suggested that the prestige associated with hunting caused game pieces to become popular household ornaments expressing the social pretensions (or aspirations) of those not legally able to hunt. With reference to Rembrandt's Dresden painting, which is usually seen as a self-portrait, the authors of *Corpus* refuted the argument that the painting is an expression of Rembrandt's social ambitions, explaining (p. 38, n. 106) that the idea of social ambition as an iconographic theme is an anachronistic misconception. While this may be true, it does not contradict Sullivan's argument that *possession* of a game piece was a device for signaling social position. See also S. A. Sullivan, "Rembrandt's *Self-Portrait with a Dead Bittern*," *Art Bulletin* 42 (1980), pp. 236-43.

9. J. van Beverwijck, *Schat der Gezontheyt* (Utrecht 1651), p. 131, cited in E. de Jongh et al., *Still-Life in the Age of Rembrandt*, exh. cat. (Auckland City Art Gallery, 1982), p. 140.

10. On partridges and lust, see B. Rowland, *Birds with Human Souls* (Knoxville, 1978), pp. 123-27. See also M. Friedmann, *A Bestiary for Saint Jerome: Animal Symbolism in European Religious Art* (Washington, D.C., 1980), pp. 282-82, with bibliog.

11. Sullivan (1984), pp. 74-75; E. de Jongh, "The Interpretation of Still-Life Paintings: Possibilities and Limits," in de Jongh et al. (note 9), pp. 32, 34.

Cat. No. 3

1. On de Heem's career, see S. Segal, *Jan Davidsz. de Heem en zijn Kring*, exh. cat. (Centraal Museum, Utrecht, 1991).

2. Ibid., p. 57.

3. On the early phase of his career, see I. Bergström, "De Heem's Painting of His First Dutch Period, *Oud Holland* 71, no. 4 (1956), pp. 173-83; idem, "Another Look at De Heem's Early Dutch Period, 1626-1635," *Mercury* 7 (1988), pp. 37-50; F. G. Meijer, "Jan Davidsz. de Heem's Earliest Paintings," *Mercury* 7 (1988), pp. 26-36.

4. J. von Sandrart, *L'Academia todesca della architectura, scultura & pittura...*, 3 vols. (Nuremberg, 1675-79), vol. 3, pp. 211-376, cited in B. Haak, *The Golden Age: Dutch Painters of the Seventeenth Century*, trans. E. Willems-Treeman (New York, 1984), p. 402.

5. I. Bergström, *Dutch Still-Life Painting in the Seventeenth Century*, trans. C. Hedström and G. Taylor (New York, 1956), pp. 195-214.

6. Segal (note 1), p. 163. The possibility that the outlines describe a niche rather than a window frame is diminished by the absence of any internal lines. It is possible, of course, that this element relates to an entirely different, rejected composition.

7. S. Segal, *A Fruitful Past*, exh. cat. (Gallery P. de Boer, Amsterdam, 1983), pp. 29, 31.

8. Ibid., pp. 36-37.

9. Ibid., p. 56; L. de Girolami Cheney, "The Oyster in Dutch Genre Paintings: Moral and Erotic Symbolism," *Artibus et historiae* 15 (1987), pp. 135-58.

10. Segal (note 7), p. 57.

11. S. van Hoogstraten, *Hooge Schoole der Schilderkonst* (1678), cited in E. de Jongh et al., *Still-Life in the Age of Rembrandt*, exh. cat. (Auckland City Art Gallery, 1982), pp. 85-86.

12. The partially abraded signature appears within the outlines of the stone window embrasure. This element, never completed, was evidently painted over. On the basis of a photograph, however, Sam Segal questions the authorship of the painting (letter to B. Barryte, July 20, 1991, Memorial Art Gallery, archives).

Cat. No. 4

1. Literature on Bailly is limited, but see J. Bruyn, "David Bailly, 'fort bon peintre en pourtraicts et en vie coye,'" *Oud Holland* 66, no. 3 (1951), pp. 148-64; no. 4 (1951), pp. 212-27, esp. pp. 156-63. On his *vanitas* portraits, see N. Popper-Voskuil, "Self Portraiture and *Vanitas* Still-life Painting in 17th-century Holland in Reference to David Bailly's *Vanitas* Oeuvre," *Pantheon* 31 (1973), pp. 58-74. On portraits in still lifes, see C. Brusati, "Stilled Lives: Self-Portraiture and Self-Reflection in Seventeenth-Century Netherlandish Still-Life Painting," *Simiolus* 20, nos. 2/3 (1990/91), pp.168-82, with additional biblio.

2. Bruyn (note 1), p. 151. More recently, Onno ter Kuile asserted that Bailly studied with de Gheyn II, while the elder artist was in Leiden ca. 1595-98 (*Seventeenth-Century North Netherlandish Still Lives* [The Hague, 1985], p. 35).

3. See B. A. Heezen-Stoll, "Ein *Vanitas* stilleven van Jacques de Gheyn II uit 1621: Afspiegeling van Neostoïsche Denkbeelden," *Oud Holland* 93 (1979), pp. 217-50; M. Morford, *Stoics and Neostoics: Rubens and the Circle of Lipsius* (Princeton, N.J., 1991).

4. Bruyn (note 1), pp. 161-62, fig. 8.

5. See Popper-Voskuil (note 1), esp. p. 72, n. 1, for bibliography regarding Bailly's reputation. It should be noted that three of Bailly's pupils, Pieter Potter and Bailly's own nephews Harmen and Peiter van Steenwijck, specialized in *vanitas* still lives.

6. See, for example, K. Boström, "David Baillys Stilleben," *Konsthistorisk Tidskrift* 18, no. 4 (1949), pp. 99-110, fig. 2 (*Vanitas Still Life* [location unknown]); E. de Jongh et al., *Still-Life in the Age of Rembrandt*, exh. cat. (Auckland City Art Gallery, 1982), no. 38 (*Still Life with Sculpture and Books* [Saint Gilgen, F. C. Butôt collection]).

7. The painting is ascribed to de Gheyn III (1595-1641) in *Ijdelheid der Ijdelheden* (1970), where marks on the edge of the book under the putto's upraised arm are interpreted as *gem...de gijn..CXXIX*. The attribution to de Gheyn II is rejected by the authors on stylistic grounds. The alternative attributions are also cited.

8. On the development of the genre, see R. B. Sonnema, "The Early Dutch Vanitas Still-Life," unpub. master's thesis, California State University, Fullerton, 1980; I. Bergström, *Dutch Still-Life Painting in the Seventeenth Century*, trans. C. Hedström and G. Taylor (New York, 1959), pp. 154-90; D. O. Merrill, "The '*Vanitas*' of Jacques de Gheyn," *Yale University Art Gallery Bulletin* 25, no. 3 (March 1960), pp. 4-29; H. Rudolph, "'Vanitas ,' die Bedeutung mittelalterlicher und humanistischer Bildenhalt in der niederländischen Malerie des 17. Jhr.," *Festschrift Wilhelm Pinder* (Leipzig, 1938), pp. 405-33. In 1660, for example, the Spanish artist Valdés Leal painted *Vanitas* (Hartford, Wadsworth Atheneum), which incorporated in its imagery ideas derived from Saint Ignatius of Loyola (see E. du Gué Tapier, *Valdés Leal: Baroque Concept of Death and Suffering in His Paintings* [New York, 1956], pp. 22-30; F. Nordström, "The Crown of Life and the Crowns of Vanity," *Figura*, n.s., 1 [1959], pp. 127-37). On the proliferation of the theme throughout Europe, see *Les vanités dans la peinture au XVIIe siècle*, exh. cat. (Musée des Beaux-Arts, Caen, 1990); A. Veca, *Vanitas: simbolismo del tempo*, exh. cat. (Galleria Lorenzelli, Bergamo, 1981).

9. The print, Hollstein 36, is illustrated in ter Kuile (note 2), fig. 12, which is also the source for the translation (p. 34). On Matham's print, see also P. Fischer, *Music in Paintings of the Low Countries in the 16th and 17th Centuries* (Amsterdam, 1975), pp. 63-64.

10. In *Ijdelheid de Ijdelheden* (1970), it is suggested that the miniature is a portrait of Maurits Huygens on the basis of its resemblance to his likeness by Rembrandt (Hamburg, Kunsthalle).

11. Bergström (note 8), fig. 134d.

12. Ibid., fig. 134a. For the iconography of smoking, see de Jongh et al. (note 6), pp. 101-5. For the importance of tobacco in contemporary Dutch society, see S. Schama, *The Embarrassment of Riches* (Berkeley, 1988), pp. 193-215, with bibliog.

13. Schama (note 12), pp. 350-56, figs. 134b-c. On "tulipomania," see also W. Blunt, *Tulipomania* (London, 1950); N. W. Posthumus, "The Tulip Mania in Holland in the Years 1636 and 1637," *Journal of Economic and Business History* 1, no. 4 (August 1929), pp. 434-66. On shell still lifes, see S. Segal, *A Prosperous Past: The Sumptuous Still Life in the Netherlands 1600-1700*, ed. W. B. Jordan, exh. cat. (Kimbell Art Museum [Fort Worth], The Hague, 1988), pp. 77-92.

14. On musical instruments as a *vanitas* motif, see Fischer (note 9), pp. 45-72.

15. H. Janson, "The Putto with the Death's Head," *Art Bulletin* 19 (1937), pp. 423-49.

16. I. Bergström, "De Gheyn as a *vanitas* Painter," *Oud Holland* 85, no. 3 (1970), pp. 143-57.

17. W. Strauss, ed., *Hendrik Goltzius: Commentary, Illustrated Bartsch*, vol. 3 (New York, 1982), pp. 158-61. On this motif, see Sonnema (note 8), pp. 24-26; W. Stechow, "Homo Bulla," *Art Bulletin* 20 (1938), pp. 227-28; I. Bergström, "Homo Bulla," in *Les vanités* (note 8), pp. 49-54; Schama (note 12), pp. 512-15; M. F. Durantini, *The Child in Seventeenth-Century Dutch Painting* (Ann Arbor, Mich., 1983), pp. 191-204.

Cat. No. 5

1. On the genre, see S. Segal, *Flowers and Nature: Netherlandish Flower Painting of Four Centuries*, exh. cat. (Nabio Museum of Art [Japan], The Hague, 1990), pp. 59-64.

2. A. Houbraken, *De Groot Schouburg*, 3 vols. (Amsterdam, 1718-21), vol. 1, pp. 154, 230, 295, 297, 325. Other contemporary sources include S. van Hoogstraten, *Inleyding tot de Hooge Schoole der Schilderkonst* (Rotterdam, 1678), p. 169; B. de Monconys, *Journal des voyages* (Lyons, 1666), vol. 2, p. 161; J. C. Weyerman, *De Levens-beschryvingen der Nederlandsche Konstschilders en Konst-schilderessen*, 4 vols. (The Hague, 1729-69), vol. 2, pp. 102-3. Modern literature includes A. D. de Vries, "Otto Marseus," *Oud Holland* 1 (1883), pp. 166-68; F. F. Guelfi, "Otto Marseus van Schrieck a Firenze: Contributo all storia dei rapporti fra scienza e arte figurative nel seicento Toscano," *Antichità viva* 16, no. 2 (1977), pp. 15-26; no. 4 (1977), pp. 13-21. L. Bol, "Schilders van Flora en Fauna en Bos en Struweel," in *Goede Onbekenden* (Utrecht, 1982), pp. 97-105, discusses Marseus as well as his followers. On Marseus and the Bentvogels, see G. J. Hoogewerff, *De Bentvueghels* (The Hague, 1952), p. 139. On the character of the "Bent," see also D. A. Levine, "The Bentvueghels: 'Bande Académique,'" in *IL 60: Essays Honoring Irving Lavin on His Sixtieth Birthday*, ed. M. A. Lavin (New York, 1990), pp. 207-19.

3. Bol (note 3), figs. 1-5.

4. See Segal (note 1), pp. 228-29.

5. M. J. Curley, trans., *Physiologus* (Austin, 1979), p. 16. See also H. Friedmann, *A Bestiary for Saint Jerome: Animal Symbolism in European Religious Art* (Washington, D.C., 1980), pp. 293-96.

6. *Physiologus* (note 5), pp. 66-7; Friedmann (note 5), pp. 268-69.

7. Friedmann (note 5), pp. 291-93, with bibliog.

8. G. Ferguson, *Signs and Symbols in Christian Art*, New York, 1961, pp. 19-20; see also the present catalogue, no. 7.

9. V. C. Habicht, "Ein vergessener Phantast der holländischen Malerei," *Oud Holland* 41 (1923-24), pp. 31-37.

10. I. Bergström, "Marseus, peintre des fleurs, papillons et serpents," *L'oeil* 233 (December 1974), pp. 24-29, 65.

Cat. No. 6

1. The most recent survey of the genre is S. Segal, *Flowers and Nature: Netherlandish Still Life Painting of Four Centuries*, exh. cat. (Nabio Museum of Art [Japan], The Hague, 1990), pp. 13-72, with bibliog.

2. Ibid., p. 50.

3. Letter to Paul Schweizer, October 23, 1989, Munson-Williams-Proctor Institute Museum of Art archives. Kuretsky identifies a similar painting in P. Mitchell, *European Flower Painters* (Schiedam, 1981), p. 245. A painting signed by both Ruysch and Stuven is in the Národní Galerie, Prague (Segal [note 1], p. 237, n. 5).

4. P. Gammelbo, *Dutch Still Life Paintings from the 16th to the 18th Centuries in Danish Collections* (Leigh-on-Sea, 1960), no. 153.

5. On the history of the Proctor collection, see P. Schweizer, ed., *Masterworks of American Art from the Munson-Williams-Proctor Institute Museum of Art* (New York, 1989), p. 7.

Cat. No. 7

1. On Frederick Ruysch, see G. A. Lindeboom, *Dutch Medical Dictionary: A Biographical Dictionary of Dutch Physicians and Surgeons 1475-1975* (Amsterdam, 1984), pp. 1700-4. He is depicted performing an autopsy on an infant in the portrait by Jan van Neck, *The Anatomy Lesson of Dr. Frederick Ruysch* (1638; Amsterdam, Historisches Museum).

2. Much of our information on Ruysch's life is based on the account by Johan van Gool, who visited the artist when she was eighty-four and still painting (*De Nieuwe Schouburgh de Nederlantsche Kunstschilders en Schilderessen*, 2 vols. [The Hague, 1750-51], vol. 1, pp. 210-33).

3. Berardi (1987-88); S. Segal, *Jan Davidsz. de Heem en zijn Kring*, exh. cat. (Centraal Museum, Utrecht, 1991), pp. 160-64, with illustrations of the Vaduz and Bamberg paintings. On the Rotterdam canvas, see also F. Meijer, *Still Life Paintings from the Golden Age*, exh. cat. (Museum Boymans-van Beuningen, Rotterdam, 1989), p. 102-3; S. Segal, *Flowers and Nature: Netherlandish Flower Painting of Four Centuries*, exh. cat. (Nabio Museum of Art [Japan], The Hague, 1990), no. 65.
4. Segal, *Flowers and Nature* (note 3), pp. 177-79, 199-200; idem, *A Prosperous Past: The Sumptuous Still Life in the Netherlands 1600-1700*, ed. W. B. Jordan, exh. cat. (Kimbell Art Museum [Fort Worth], The Hague, 1988), p. 214, nos. 12, 15.
5. See Berardi (1987-88), pp. 10-12.

Cat. No. 8
1. I am grateful to Joan Baden for identifying the flowers.
2. On the history of this collection, see P. D. Schweizer, *Masterworks of American Art from the Munson-Williams-Proctor Institute Museum of Art* (New York, 1989), p. 7.

Cat. No. 9
1. Number 697 is described in the Salon catalogue as follows: "Un vase d'albâtre de differentes fleurs, posé sur un socle où se trouvent quelques fruits dans un plat de cristal et au bas un autre vase rempli de différentes fleurs" (An alabaster vase with different flowers, set on a base on which there are some fruits in a crystal plate and at the base of which there is another vase with different flowers). To account for the difference in size, Boven and Segal (1980) suggested that the frame may have been included in the Salon dimensions. Much of the biographical information in this entry is taken from E. Hardouin-Figier and E. Grafe, *French Flower Painters of the Nineteenth Century* (London, 1989), pp. 363-64.
2. On the history of the genre, see I. Bergström, *Dutch Still-Life Painting in the Seventeenth Century*, trans. C. Hedström and G. Taylor (New York, 1956), pp. 42-97; S. Segal, *A Flowery Past—A Survey of Dutch and Flemish Flower Painting from 1600 to the Present*, exh. cat. (Gallery P. de Boer, Amsterdam, 1983); idem, *A Prosperous Past: The Sumptuous Still Life in the Netherlands 1600-1700*, ed. W. B. Jordan, exh. cat. (Kimbell Art Museum [Fort Worth], The Hague, 1988), pp. 93-120; idem, *Flowers and Nature: Netherlandish Flower Painting of Four Centuries*, exh. cat. (Nabio Museum of Art [Japan], The Hague, 1990), pp. 13-72. See also E. B. Macdougall, "Flower Importation and Dutch Flower Painting 1600-1700," in *Still Lifes of the Golden Age*, ed. A. K. Wheelock, Jr., exh. cat. (National Gallery of Art, Washington, D.C., 1989), pp. 27-34; J. G. van Gelder, "Van Blompot en Blomglas," *Elsevier's Geïllustreerd Maandschrift* 46 (1936), pp. 73-82, 155-66.
3. Its design resembles, for example, Gerard van Spaendonck's *Flowers in an Alabaster Vase and in a Basket, with Bird's Nest* (private collection), illustrated in Segal, *Flowers and Nature* (note 2), no. 70.
4. Boven and Segal (1980), p. 202.
5. Bergström (note 2), p. 14.
6. G. de Lairesse, *Het Groot Schilderboek* (Amsterdam, 1707), pp. 259-98, 355-58 (on flower painting), cited in A. Gasten, "Dutch Still-Life Painting: Judgements and Appreciation," in E. de Jongh et al., *Still-Life in the Age of Rembrandt*, exh. cat. (Auckland City Art Gallery, 1982), p. 17.
7. E. de Jongh, "Grape Symbolism in Paintings of the 16th and 17th Centuries," *Simiolus* 7, no. 4 (1974), p. 166.

Cat. No. 10
1. L. Karr, "Painting on Velvet," *Antiques* 20 (September 1931), p. 162. The following information and quotations are from this article (pp. 162-65). Karr's discussion of technique is largely based on *Art Recreations*, published by Tilton and Company, Boston, in 1860. On theorem painting in the American tradition, see also W. Born, *Still-Life Painting in America* (New York, 1947), pp. 19-20.
2. Emily S. Penfield, the artist's granddaughter and the donor, cut the theorem to its present oval shape because the edges of the pillow had been damaged.

Cat. No. 11
1. It may be significant that in the 1840s still life briefly flourished in Charleston, when Thomas and William Wightman were active (W. H. Gerdts and R. Burke, *American Still Life Painting* [New York, 1971], p. 60).
2. Copy of B. Hasbrouck to Vose Galleries, May 25, 1983, Albany Institute of History and Art.
3. Copy of William Gerdts to Vose Galleries, May 7, 1982, Albany Institute of History and Art.
4. I am grateful to Patricia Tice for this information.
5. W. H. Gerdts, *Painters of the Humble Truth: Masterpieces of American Still Life 1801-1939*, exh. cat. (Philbrook Art Center [Tulsa], Columbia, Mo., 1981), pp. 81-84.
6. John F. Francis employs a similar format in his 1860 *Strawberries and Cakes* (New York, James Ricau collection), illustrated in Gerdts (note 5), fig. 5.6. An open-air setting is found earlier in *Still Life with Parrot and Vase* (1841; New York, Coe Kerr Gallery) by the Philadelphia painter Joseph Biays Ord (Gerdts and Burke [note 1], fig. 5.3).

Cat. No. 12
1. On this portrait, see J. Wilmerding, "America's Young Masters Raphaelle, Rembrandt, and Rubens" in N. Cikovsky, *Raphaelle Peale Still Lifes*, exh. cat. (National Gallery of Art, Washington, D.C., 1988), pp. 73-91, with bibliog.
2. R. Peale, "Journal of Woodland Farm," Archives of American Art, Washington, D.C., microfilm D10:1881-2259, journal pp. 115, 186, cited in Anderson (1983), pp. 32, 35.
3. Pliny the Elder, *Natural History*, 35:112; see C. Sterling, *Still Life Painting from Antiquity to the Twentieth Century*, 2d rev. ed. (New York, 1981), pp. 25-33.
4. On paintings by Jacob van Hulsdonck (1582-1647) and other early seventeenth-century Dutch still life painters whose works were accessible in America, see J. I. H. Baur, "The Peales and the Development of American Still Life," *Art Quarterly* 3 (Winter 1940), pp. 82-84. On the Dutch tradition, see I. Bergström, *Dutch Still-Life Painting in the Seventeenth Century*, trans. C. Hedström and G. Taylor (New York, 1956), esp. pp. 68-74 on Balthasar van der Ast, whose works are similarly austere; N. R. A. Vroom, *A Modest Message as Intimated by the Painters of the "Monochrome Banketje,"* rev. ed., 2 vols. (Scheidam, 1980).
5. Anderson (1983), p. 35, fig. 2. The painting was sold from the Arthur J. Sessel Estate, Parke-Bernet Galleries, New York, October 23-25, 1958, lot 528. The basket also appears in Rubens's *Silver Basket with Fruit* (ca. 1815; location unknown); see J. A. H. Sweeney, "Paintings from the Sewell C. Biggs Collection," *Antiques* 119 (April 1981), p. 893, pl. 5.
6. Cikovsky (note 1), frontis., fig. 80.
7. On Raphaelle's still lifes, see ibid. Jules Prown offers a particularly sensitive reading of Raphaelle's *Fruit in a Silver Basket* (Detroit, Manoogian collection) in *American Paintings from the Manoogian Collection*, exh. cat. (National Gallery of Art, Washington, D.C., 1989), pp. 98-100.

Cat. Nos. 13, 14
1. The most important literature on Roesen includes W. Gerdts, *Painters of the Humble Truth: Masterpieces of American Still Life*, exh. cat. (Philbrook Art Center [Tulsa], Columbia, Mo., 1981), pp. 84-88; L. G. Marcus, *Severin Roesen: A Chronology* (Williamsport, 1976); M. A. Mook, "Severin Roesen, the Williamsport Painter," *Lycoming College Magazine* 25, no. 6 (June 1972), pp. 33-40; R. B. Stone, "'Not Quite Forgotten': A Study of the Williamsport Painter, S. Roesen," *Lycoming Historical Society Proceedings and Papers* 9 (November 1951), pp. 3-40. For information on these paintings, I am grateful to Judith O'Toole, whose catalogue raisonné on Roesen is forthcoming.
2. Gerdts (note 1), p. 87; Lois Marcus to Paul Schweizer, March 8, 1983, Munson-Williams-Proctor Institute Museum of Art archives.
3. Gerdts (note 1).

Cat. No. 15
1. I am grateful to Thayer C. Tolles for many suggestions and factual details incorporated in this entry.
2. W. H. Gerdts and R. Burke, *American Still Life Painting* (New York, 1971), p. 134.
3. See, for example, D. Bolger, "'Cards and Letters from His Friends': Mr. Hulings' Rack Picture by William Michael Harnett," *American Art Journal* 22, no. 2 (1990), pp. 4-32; W. H. Gerdts, "The Bric-a-Brac Still Life," *Antiques* 81 (November 1971), pp. 744-88; B. S. Groseclose, "Vanity and the Artist: Some Still-Life Paintings by William Michael Harnett," *American Art Journal* 19, no. 1 (1987), pp. 51-59; C. Mandeles, "William Michael Harnett's *The Old Cupboard Door* and the Tradition of *Vanitas*," *American Art Journal* 18, no. 3 (1986), pp. 52-62. Much new information is anticipated from the retrospective exhibition being organized by the Amon Carter Museum, Fine Arts Museums of San Francisco, and Metropolitan Museum of Art.
4. Biographical information is derived primarily from a newspaper interview, "Painted Like Real Things," originally published in the *New York News* ca. 1889-90, and reprinted in Williams (1943), pp. 260-62.
5. W. G. Constable, *Art Collecting in the United States of America* (London, 1964), pp. 91-133.
6. On the tradition of this motif, see S. Schwarz, *Das Bücherstilleben in der Malerei des 17. Jahrhunderts* (Weisbaden, 1987); J. Becker, "Das Buch in Stilleben—Das Stilleben in Buch," in *Stilleben in Europa*, exh. cat. (Westfälisches Landesmuseum für Kunst und Kulturgeschichte, Münster, 1979), pp. 447-78, 589-94.
7. J. Wilmerding, *Important Information Inside: The Art of John Peto and the Idea of Still-Life Painting in Nineteenth-Century America*, exh. cat. (National Gallery of Art, Washington, D.C., 1983), pp. 111-13.
8. Harnett's statements in this and the following paragraph are recorded in "Painted Like Real Things" (note 4). The flute mentioned was his own. Harnett was an amateur flautist, and the instrument was listed in the catalogue of his 1893 estate sale.

Cat. No. 16
1. Frankenstein's suggestion (1969, p. 187), "J. M. Scherrah," was based on his reading of an infrared photograph taken by the conservator Sheldon Keck.
2. Ibid., nos. 18, 28.

Cat. No. 17
1. See, for example, E. Hardouin-Fugier and E. Grafe, *The Lyon School of Flower Painters* (Leigh-on-Sea, 1978).
2. R. Muther, *The History of Modern Painting*, 2d ed., 4 vols. (New York, 1907), vol. 2, pp. 550-52; A. E. Bye, *Pots and Pans, or Studies in Still-Life Painting* (Princeton, N.J., 1921), p. 127. There is little recent literature on Vollon, but of these few sources the most useful is G. Weisberg, "A Still Life by Antoine Vollon, Painter of Two Traditions," *Bulletin of the Detroit Institute of Arts* 56, no. 4 (1978), pp. 222-29. I am grateful to Carol Tabler, who is currently completing a dissertation on Vollon, for information and references incorporated into this entry.
3. K. Cox, "Antoine Vollon, A Painter's Painter," *Manhattan Magazine* 2 (1883), p. 558.
4. Preface, Barroilhet sale catalogue, March 10, 1856, cited in P. Rosenberg, *Chardin 1699-1779*, exh. cat. (Cleveland Museum of Art, 1980), p. 87. On the reappraisal of Chardin, see J. W. McCoubrey, "The Revival of Chardin in French Still-Life Painting, 1850-1870," *Art Bulletin* 46, no. 1 (March 1964), pp. 39-53.
5. C. Sterling, *Still Life Painting from Antiquity to the Twentieth Century*, 2d ed. (New York, 1981), p. 118. See also Cox (note 3), p. 559: "In criticisms upon Vollon one constantly finds him compared to Chardin."
6. Cox (note 3), p. 560.
7. J. Clarétie, *Peintres et sculpteurs contemporains* (Paris, 1884), p. 206.

8. Rosenberg (note 4), pp. 305-7.
9. See N. Bryson, *Looking at the Overlooked: Four Essays on Still Life Painting* (Cambridge, Mass., 1990), pp. 13-15.
10. E. Zola, *Mon Salon—Manet, Ecrits sur l'art* (Paris, 1866), p. 76.
11. C. Cook, *Art and Artists of Our Time*, 3 vols. (New York, 1888), vol. 1, p. 183.
12. Other related works in public collections include *Eggs on a Plate* (Melbourne, National Gallery of Victoria); *Still Life with Copper Jug* (Rotterdam, Museum Boymans-van Beuningen); and *Eggs* (Lyons, Musée des Beaux-Arts). A reinterpretation of the Buffalo composition was recently sold at Sotheby's, Amsterdam, November 21, 1988, lot 161.
13. M. Faré, *La nature morte en France* (Geneva, 1962), pp. 259-60, cited in Weisberg (note 2), p. 226.

Cat. No. 18
1. Clipping, Edward Weiburn and Richard LaBarre Goodwin papers (lent by Clairbell Goodwin), microfilm reel N60-1, frame 188, Archives of American Art, Washington, D.C.
2. The first version of Harnett's *After the Hunt* (Columbus Museum of Art) was painted in Munich in 1883. The fourth version (fig. 13; Fine Arts Museums of San Francisco), painted in 1885, was exhibited in the Paris Salon. It was sold to Theodore Stewart, who contributed to the vogue for large-scale trompe l'oeil pictures by hanging it in his famous New York saloon (Frankenstein [1969], p. 66; W. Gerdts and R. Burke, *American Still Life Painting* [New York, 1971], p. 142).
3. See, for example, Weenix's *Dead Partridge* (The Hague, Mauritshuis) and Hondecoeter's *Dead Cock* (Brussels, Musées Royaux des Beaux-Arts) (S. A. Sullivan, *The Dutch Gamepiece* [Totowa, N.J., 1984], figs. 138, 150).
4. Archives of American Art, Washington, D.C.
5. Mirrored views constitute a leitmotif in trophy pictures. The earliest example with which I am familiar is a nature study by Lucas Cranach the Elder, *Two Dead Waxwings* (Dresden, Staatliche Kunstsammlungen, Kupferstichkabinett [see Sullivan (note 3), p. 6, fig. 2]).

Cat. No. 19
1. Haberle's oeuvre is surveyed in Sill (1985).
2. One other package picture belongs to the Brandywine River Museum (ca. 1892); see Sill (1985), no. 27, pl. 8. The other known example belongs to Berry-Hill Gallery, New York (*American Paintings V*, exh. cat. [Berry-Hill Gallery, New York, 1988], no. 78). I am grateful to Bruce Weber for this information. A letter from Vera Haberle Demmer (August 31, 1965) dates the Rochester painting to 1888-89. Referring perhaps to additional package pictures, another letter (August 22, 1966) mentions "five John Haberle 'Trompe l'oeil' drawings of scenes—done in the 1880s." (Memorial Art Gallery archives).
3. The subject is discussed most concisely in M. Milman, *Trompe-l'Oeil Painting* (Geneva, 1982), pp. 54-81. See also M. L. d'Orange Mastai, *Illusion in Art: Trompe l'Oeil, A History of Pictorial Illusionism* (New York, 1975), pp. 176-83, 207-12. On early American examples, see W. H. Gerdts, "A *Deception* Unmasked; An Artist Discovered," *American Art Journal* 18, no. 2 (1986), pp. 4-23.

Cat. No. 20
1. On the early appearance of this genre in America, see W. H. Gerdts, "A *Deception* Unmasked; An Artist Uncovered," *American Art Journal* 18, no. 2 (1986), pp. 4-23, with bibliog.
2. See Frankenstein (1969); idem, "Harnett, True and False," *Art Bulletin* 31, no. 1 (March 1949), pp. 38-56.
3. L. Goodrich, "Harnett and Peto: A Note on Style," *Art Bulletin* 31, no. 1 (March 1949), pp. 57-59.

4. Frankenstein (1969), pp. 79-81. Leemans's painting is illustrated in O. ter Kuile, *Seventeenth-Century North Netherlandish Still Lifes* (The Hague, 1985), no. 34. An example by Johannes's brother Anthonie Leemans, *Hunting Still Life* (Cologne, Wallraf-Richartz Museum), is illustrated in S. A. Sullivan, *The Dutch Gamepiece* (Totowa, N.J., 1984), fig. A164. Two examples by Gijsbrechts are in the Danish royal collection at Rosenborg (P. Gammelbo, *Dutch Still Life Paintings in Danish Collections* [Leigh-on-Sea, 1960], nos. 246-47). On the Netherlandish tradition, see Sullivan, pp. 68-72.
5. Copy of letter to Knoedler and Co., March 26, 1965, Munson-Williams-Proctor Institute Museum of Art archives. Other versions are in the Dallas Museum of Fine Art and a New York private collection (Wilmerding [1983], p. 180, n. 16).
6. Wilmerding (1983), p. 220.

Cat. No. 21
1. D. Perez-Tibi, *Dufy*, trans. S. Whiteside (New York, 1989), p. 8.
2. G. Stein, "Raoul Dufy" (1946), in *Reflections on the Atomic Bomb, Previously Uncollected Writings*, vol. 1, ed. R. B. Haas (Los Angeles, 1973), pp. 72-73.
3. Cited in Perez-Tibi (note 1), pp. 19-20.
4. Ibid., p. 22 (citing *Notebook*, No. 3, p. 13, Musée National d'Art Moderne, Paris, A.M. 36-66-D).
5. Ibid.
6. Cited in J. Lassaigne, *Dufy*, trans. J. Emmons (Geneva, 1954), p. 106. Unfortunately, the sheer mass of the artist's output and the very effectiveness of his invention have proved detrimental to our understanding of its significance. The superficial characteristics of Dufy's style reappear in works by an endless number of imitators—especially sports illustrators and wallpaper designers. Their formulaic adaptation, bastardization, and repetition of his techniques and motifs impede our ability to appreciate the charm and originality of his accomplishment.
7. See, for example, Laffaille (1972), vol. 1, nos. 280-82.
8. On this phase of Dufy's career, see Perez-Tibi (note 1), pp. 39-48, which serves as the basis for the following discussion.
9. For other examples, see (note 7).

Cat. No. 22
1. "Henri Rousseau," *Transition* 3 (1948), pp. 30-31.
2. On Rousseau's personality, see, for example, the reminiscences of A. Basler, "Recollections of Henri Rousseau," *Arts* 11, no. 6 (June 1927), pp. 313-19; W. Udhe, "Henri Rousseau," in *Five Primitive Masters*, trans. R. Thompson (New York, 1949); and the biographical sketch by G. Apollinaire, "The Douanier" (1914), in L. C. Breunig, ed., *Apollinaire on Art: Essays and Reviews 1902-1918*, trans. S. Suleiman (New York, 1972), pp. 339-54. For an analysis of Rousseau's relationship to the beaux-arts tradition, see R. Goldwater, *Primitivism in Modern Art*, rev. ed. (New York, 1967), pp. 178-91.
3. Udhe (note 2), p. 21.
4. G. Apollinaire, "Salon des Indépendants," *La revue des lettres et des arts*, May 1, 1908, cited in Breunig (note 2), p. 45.
5. G. Apollinaire, "Watch Out for the Paint! Salon des Indépendants...," *L'intransigeant*, March 19, 1910, cited in Breunig (note 2), p. 68.
6. G. Apollinaire, "Folk Painting," *Paris-Journal*, July 24, 1914, cited in Breunig (note 2), p. 426.
7. H. Rousseau, "Autobiographical Note," in *Henri Rousseau*, exh. cat. (Museum of Modern Art, New York, 1985), p. 256.
8. Cited in M. Hoog, "Rousseau in His Time," in ibid., p. 63.
9. Cited in Breunig (note 2), p. 349.
10. Ibid., p. 350. On Rousseau's influence, see C. Lachner and W. Rubin, "Henri Rousseau and Modernism," in *Henri Rousseau* (note 7), pp. 35-89.
11. Breunig (note 2), p. 351.
12. Certigny (1984), no. 186.
13. C. Sterling, *Still Life Painting from Antiquity to the Twentieth Century*, rev. ed. (New York, 1981), p. 143.

Cat. No. 23
1. "Foreword" to anonymous, unpaginated exhibition checklist, "Paintings and Drawings by I. Pulis Lathrop, Gertrude K. Lathrop, Dorothy P. Lathrop," October 1-25, 1937, Albany Institute of History and Art.
2. On this tradition, see especially N. R. A. Vroom, *A Modest Message as Intimated by the Painters of the "Monochrome Banketje,"* 2 vols. (Schiedam, 1980).
3. I am indebted to Patricia Tice for information regarding the objects and their social context.

Cat. No. 24
1. See, for example, F. N. Price, "Jonas Lie, Painter of Light," *International Studio* 82 (November 1925), pp. 102-07; C. Brinton, "Jonas Lie: A Study in Temperament," *American-Scandinavian Review* 3, no. 4 (July-August 1915), pp. 196-207; anonymous, "Jonas Lie of Norway and America: A Painter Who Has Found the Secret of Suggesting on Canvas Nature's Manifold Moods," *Craftsman* 13, no. 2 (November 1907), pp. 135-39; R. V. S. Berry, "Jonas Lie: The Man and His Art," *American Magazine of Art* 16, no. 2 (February 1925), pp. 59-66. I am grateful to Ruth Pasquine for information on the artist and on *The Black Teapot*.
2. Brinton (note 1), p. 205.
3. Berry (note 1), p. 64.
4. Brinton (note 1), p. 205.
5. Ibid., p. 202.
6. M. F. B., review of a Boston Art Club exhibition, *Evening Transcript*, March 22, 1920 (clipping, American Academy of Design, New York, archives). I am grateful to Barbara Krulik for access to the academy's file on Lie.

Cat. No. 25
1. Unpub. and undated typescript, Watson Forbes Papers, microfilm D56.1092-1094, Archives of American Art, Washington, D.C.
2. On Sheeler's development as an artist, see C. Troyen, "'From the Eyes Inward': Paintings and Drawings by Charles Sheeler," in C. Troyen and E. E. Hirshler, *Charles Sheeler: Paintings and Drawings*, exh. cat. (Museum of Fine Arts, Boston, 1987), pp. 2-43.
3. Charles Sheeler Papers, microfilm Nshl: 27-34, Archives of American Art, Washington, D.C. These reminiscences, originally solicited by a New York publisher, became the basis for Constance Rourke's biography, *Charles Sheeler, Artist in the American Tradition* (New York, 1938).
4. Sheeler Papers (note 3), Nshl: 62-64.
5. Sheeler typescript (note 1), D56.1094.

Cat. No. 26
1. F. Gilot and C. Lake, *Life with Picasso* (London, 1965), p. 70. This phrase has also been attributed to the writer Jean Cocteau.
2. The literature on Cubism is vast. For succinct discussions, see E. Fry, *Cubism* (New York, 1966), pp. 9-41; J. Golding, "Cubism," in *Concepts of Modern Art*, ed. A. Richardson and N. Stangos (New York, 1974), pp. 53-81; D.-H. Kahnweiler, *The Rise of Cubism*, trans. H. Aronson (New York, 1949).
3. Interview with G. Burgess, "The Wild Men of Paris," in *Architectural Record* (May 1910), p. 405, cited in Fry (note 2), p. 53.
4. G. Apollinaire, "On the Subject in Modern Painting," *Les soirées de Paris*, February 1, 1912, cited in L. C. Breunig, ed., *Apollinaire on Art: Essays and Reviews 1902-1918*, trans. S. Suleiman (New York, 1972), p. 198.
5. Kahnweiler (note 2), p. 11.
6. D.-H. Kahnweiler, *Mes galeries et mes peintres*, 2d ed. (Paris, 1982), cited in B. Zurcher, *Georges Braque: Life and Work*, trans. S. Nye (New York, 1988), p. 76.
7. Kahnweiler (note 2), pp. 11-12.
8. D. Vallier, "Braque, la peinture et nous," *Cahiers d'art*, no. 1 (October 1954), cited in Zurcher (note 6), pp. 75-76.
9. "Light becomes color when it hits an object" (letter to D.-H. Kahnweiler, October 1919, cited in Zurcher [note 6], p. 135).

Cat. No. 27

1. Cited in A. Terrasse, "Bonnard's Notes," in *Bonnard: The Late Paintings*, exh. cat. (Phillips Collection, Washington, D.C., 1984), p. 70.
2. J. Clair, "'The Adventures of the Optic Nerve,'" in *Bonnard: The Late Paintings* (note 1), p. 30.
3. P. Signac, "Les besoins individuels et la peinture," *Encyclopédie française*, vol. 16 (Paris, 1935), chap. 2, cited in J. Rewald, *Pierre Bonnard*, exh. cat. (Museum of Modern Art, New York, 1948), p. 40.
4. A. Lugné-Poë, *La parade I, Le sot du tremplin* (Paris, 1930), p. 195, cited in Rewald (note 3), p. 18.
5. The article, published originally in *Art et critique* and reprinted in *La parade I* (note 4), pp. 213-14, is cited in Rewald (note 3), p. 18.
6. See B. Waller and G. Seiberling, *Artists of "La revue blanche,"* exh. cat. (Memorial Art Gallery, Rochester, 1984).
7. G. Apollinaire, "The Bonnard Exhibition," *L'intransigeant*, March 10, 1910, in L. C. Breunig, ed., *Apollinaire on Art: Essays and Reviews 1902-1918*, trans. S. Suleiman (New York, 1972), p. 61.
8. P. Bonnard, *Notebooks*, February 16, 1932; January 1 and 15, 1943, cited in *Bonnard: The Late Paintings* (note 1), p. 69.
9. For related examples, see Dauberville and Dauberville (1974), nos. 776, 777, 783-85; no. 1031 includes a similar vase in the background.

Cat. No. 28

1. G. de Chirico, "Arnold Böcklin," *Il convegno* (May 1920), reprinted in M. Carrà, *Metaphysical Art*, trans. C. Tisdall (London, 1971), p. 138.
2. G. de Chirico, "Max Klinger," *Il convegno* (May 1921), reprinted in Carrà (note 1), p. 100.
3. On de Chirico's philosophical influences, see Soby (1966), pp. 15-42; M. W. Martin, "Reflections on De Chirico and *Arte metaphysica*," *Art Bulletin* 60, no. 2 (June 1978), pp. 342-52; I. Davies, "Giorgio de Chirico: The Sources of Metaphysical Painting, Schopenhauer and Nietzsche," *Art International* 26, no. 2 (January-March 1983), pp. 53-60.
4. F. Neitzsche, *The Birth of Tragedy*, in *The Complete Works of Friedrich Nietzsche*, ed. O. Levy (London, 1909), pp. 28-29, cited in Soby (1966), p. 27.
5. De Chirico cites passages from Schopenhauer (*Parerga and Paralipomena*, trans. I. B. Saunders, 2 vols. [Berlin, 1851], pp. 465, 531) in his unpublished manuscript "Meditations of a Painter" (Soby [1966], p. 28).
6. G. de Chirico, "Zeuxis the Explorer," *Valori plastici* (November 15, 1918), reprinted in Carrà (note 1), p. 154.
7. A. Soffici, "De Chirico e Savinio," *Lacerba* (July 1, 1914), cited in J. M. Lukach, "De Chirico and Italian Art Theory, 1915-1920," in Rubin (1982), p. 37.
8. The quotations that follow are from the translation in Carrà (note 1), pp. 87-91.
9. On de Chirico's notion of "solitudes," see W. Bohn, "Giorgio de Chirico and the Solitude of the Sign," *Gazette des Beaux-Arts* 117 (April 1991), pp. 169-71.
10. De Chirico, "On Metaphysical Art," reprinted in Carrà (note 1), p. 91.
11. G. de Chirico, *Memoirs*, trans. M. Crosland (Coral Gables, Fla., 1971), p. 80.
12. W. Rubin, "De Chirico and Modernism," in Rubin (1982), pp. 58-61.
13. Ibid., pp. 55-79. Following Soby, Rubin emphasized that in later years, de Chirico produced numerous facsimiles and variants of his Metaphysical paintings. For example, Rubin reproduces (as fig. 28) eighteen versions of *The Disquieting Muses* (1917; private collection) which de Chirico painted between 1945 and 1962.

Cat. No. 29

1. G. Stein, *The Autobiography of Alice B. Toklas* (New York, 1933), p. 111.
2. W. M. Camfield, "Juan Gris and the Golden Section," *Art Bulletin* 46, no. 1 (March 1969), pp. 128-34.
3. Letter, March 25, 1921, in *Letters of Juan Gris*, trans. D. Cooper (London, 1956), p. 105. See Rosenthal (1983), p. 29.
4. Like other members of the avant-garde in the postwar period, Gris responded to the general reaction against the intense experimentation that had characterized the prewar period: see K. E. Silver, *Esprit de Corps: The Art*

of the Parisian Avant-Garde and the First World War, 1914-1925 (Princeton, N.J., 1989), esp. pp. 156-65, 235-37.
5. Statement in *Valori plastici* (February-March, 1919), p. 2, cited in D.-H. Kahnweiler, *Juan Gris: His Life and Work*, trans. D. Cooper, 2d ed. (New York, 1969), p. 191.
6. Gris, *L'esprit nouveau*, no. 5 (1921), pp. 533-34, cited in Kahnweiler (note 5), p. 193.
7. C. Green, "Synthesis and the 'Synthetic Process' in the Painting of Juan Gris 1915-19," *Art History* 5, no. 1 (March 1982), pp. 87-104.
8. Gris, cited in Kahnweiler (note 5), p. 193.
9. Letter to D.-H. Kahnweiler, August 25, 1919, in ibid., p. 65.
10. W. Judkins, *Fluctuant Representation in Synthetic Cubism: Picasso, Braque, Gris, 1910-1920* (New York, 1976), pp. 21-23.
11. Kahnweiler (note 5), p. 144.
12. M. Raynal, *Quelques intentions du cubisme* (1919), cited in E. F. Fry, *Cubism* (New York, 1966), p. 153.
13. Gris, cited in Kahnweiler (note 5), pp. 200-201.

Cat. No. 30

1. On the context in which de Chirico's metamorphosis occurred, see P. Fossati, "Intorno al 1920," *Prospettiva*, nos. 57-60 (April 1989-October 1990) ("Scritti in ricordo di Giovanni Previtali," vol. 2), pp. 468-84; M. Fagiolo dell'Arco, "'Classicismo Pittorico': Valori plastici, Magic Realism and Novecento," and P. Vivarelli, "Classicism and Tradition in Italian Art of the 1920s" in E. Cowling and J. Mundy, *On Classic Ground: Picasso, Léger, de Chirico and the New Classicism 1910-1930*, exh. cat. (Tate Gallery, London, 1990), pp. 359-82.
2. Cited in J. T. Soby, *Giorgio de Chirico*, 2d ed. (New York, 1966), p. 158.
3. *The Memoirs of Giorgio de Chirico*, trans. M. Crosland (Coral Gables, Fla., 1971), p. 112.
4. The reference is to comte de Lautréamont (Isidore Ducasse), who described the hero of his book *Les chantes de Maldoror* (Paris, 1874) as being "as handsome...as the fortuitous encounter on a dissecting table of a sewing machine and an umbrella." This simile was adopted by the Surrealists as a sort of credo, expressing their belief in imaginative disequilibrium.
5. Sold Christie's, New York, January 15, 1988, lot 107.
6. *Memoirs* (note 3), p. 112.
7. G. de Chirico, "Gustave Courbet," in *The Painter's Object*, ed. M. Evans (London, 1937), pp. 127, 130. De Chirico's interest in Courbet was evidently quite fashionable. On December 2, 1919, Juan Gris wrote to Daniel-Henry Kahnweiler: "Courbet is much in vogue this year. Somebody is trying to put him across and send up the prices and the painters are following like a lot of sheep. Courbet is their only god" (cited in D.-H. Kahnweiler, *Juan Gris: His Life and Work*, trans. D. Cooper [New York, 1969], p. 32).
8. R. Fernier, *La vie et l'oeuvre de Gustave Courbet: Catalogue raisonné*, 2 vols. (Lausanne, 1977), vol. 2, no. 776; see S. Faunce and L. Nochlin, *Courbet Reconsidered*, exh. cat. (Brooklyn Museum, New Haven, Conn., 1988), no. 80. Courbet's parapet still life appears to have influenced other compositions by de Chirico, for example, his *Still Life with Castle* (1959; Milan, private collection) and his *Fruits in a Village* (1960; private collection), illustrated in Sakraischik (1971-83), vol. 8, nos. 82, 1109. After his conversion in 1919, de Chirico repeatedly referred to Courbet, quoting, for example, the latter's *Woman in the Waves* (1866; New York, Metropolitan Museum of Art) in his *Nymphs Bathing* (1948; Rome, private collection), on which see Fernier, vol. 2, no. 628; Faunce and Nochlin, no. 68; Sakraischik (1971-83), vol. 5, pt. 2, no. 422.
9. See K. E. Silver, *Esprit de Corps: The Art of the Parisian Avant-Garde and the First World War, 1914-1925* (Princeton, N. J., 1989).
10. For recent efforts at reappraising de Chirico's later works, see C. B. Sakraischik, *Giorgio de Chirico*, trans. H. Barnes, exh. cat. (Gallerie La Medusa, Rome, 1976), p. 9; M. di Carlo et al., *Giorgio de Chirico 1920-1950*, exh. cat. (Palais du Gouvernement [Monaco], Milan, 1989).

Cat. No. 31
1. Léger's career is most succinctly described in D. Cooper, *Fernand Léger et le nouvel espace* (Geneva, 1949). See also P. de Francia, *Fernand Léger* (New Haven, 1983), esp. pp. 68-106.
2. L. Vauxcelles, in *Gil Blas*, September 30, 1911, cited in D.-H. Kahnweiler, "Fernand Léger," *Burlington Magazine* 92 (March 1950), p. 63. Vauxcelles had a definite knack for naming styles, since he christened Fauvism (after seeing a sculpture by Aristide Maillol in the same gallery as one of Rousseau's jungle scenes) as well as Cubism (after overhearing a jibe made by Matisse about one of Braque's early cubistic landscapes).
3. Vauxcelles (note 2), p. 64.
4. F. Léger, "The Origins of Painting and Its Representational Value" (1913), in *The Functions of Painting*, trans. A. Anderson (New York, 1973), pp. 3-4; see B. J. Nickels, "Fernand Léger: Paintings and Drawings, 1905-1930," unpub. Ph.D. diss., Indiana University, 1966, p. 193.
5. See R. Rosenblum, *Cubism and Twentieth-Century Art*, rev. ed. (New York, 1976), pp. 133-56. On the emergence of this movement and its intellectual context, see K. E. Silver, *Esprit de Corps: The Art of the Parisian Avant-Garde and the First World War, 1914-1925* (Princeton, N.J., 1989), esp. pp. 362-99.
6. Léger was also influenced by the similarly idealistic contemporary Dutch movement De Stijl, and by Piet Mondrian's "Neo-plasticism."
7. Quotations from *Après le cubisme* (1918); "Le purisme," *L'esprit nouveau*, no. 4, January 1921; and *Le peinture moderne* (1925) are cited in J. Golding, "Léger and the Heroism of Modern Life," in *Léger and Purist Paris*, exh. cat. (Tate Gallery, London, 1970), p. 18. For a summary of Purist philosophy, see C. Green, "Purism," in *Concepts of Modern Art*, ed. T. Richardson and N. Stangos (New York, 1974), pp. 82-87; Silver (note 5).
8. C. Green, "Léger and L'Esprit Nouveau 1912-1928," in *Léger and Purist Paris* (note 7), p. 49.
9. F. Léger, *Pensées*, cited in Nickels (note 4), p. 351; see also pp. 282-98.
10. F. Léger, "The Machine Aesthetic: The Manufactured Object, the Artisan, and the Artist" (1924), in *Functions of Painting* (note 4), pp. 52-53, 60. Léger's admiration for the beauty of machines and mechanical objects is curiously reminiscent of a contemporaneous statement by the American painter Robert Henri: "I love the tools made for mechanics....They are so beautiful...and straight to their meaning. There is no 'Art' about them, they have not been made beautiful, they are beautiful" (*The Art Spirit* [Philadelphia, 1923], pp. 48-49).
11. The letter, dated 1922, was published in *Bulletin de l'esprit nouveau*, no. 4 (April 1924) (translated in *Léger and Purist Paris* [note 7], p. 86).
12. Cited in Golding (note 7), p. 21.
13. F. Léger, "Notes on Contemporary Plastic Life" (1923), in *Functions of Painting* (note 4), p. 25.
14. Referring to the larger version of this composition (see below), C. Green identified the "glass" as a coffee-percolator (*Léger and the Avant-Garde* [New Haven, 1976], p. 270). That it is indeed a glass is indicated by the appearance of a similar object in Braque's *Glass, Grapes, and Pear* (cat. no. 343) and, more clearly perhaps, in Picasso's construction, *Glass, Knife, and Sandwich on a Table* (1914; London, Tate Gallery), illustrated in D. Cooper and G. Tintrow, *The Essential Cubism: Braque, Picasso, and Their Friends*, exh. cat. (Tate Gallery, London, 1983), pp. 368-69, no. 194.
15. De Francia (note 1), pl. 30.

Cat. No. 32
1. For another example, see F. Fosca, *Charles Dufresne* (Paris, 1958), pl. xiv.
2. E. Cowling and J. Mundy, *On Classic Ground: Picasso, Léger, de Chirico and the New Classicism 1910-1930*, exh. cat. (Tate Gallery, London, 1990), cat. no. 118.
3. On Cézanne's critical fortune during the postwar period, see K. E. Silver, *Esprit de Corps: The Art of the Parisian Avant Garde and the First World War, 1914-1925* (Princeton, N.J., 1989), pp. 325-32.

Cat. No. 33
1. D.-H. Kahnweiler, *The Rise of Cubism*, trans. H. Aronson (New York, 1949), p. 1.
2. G. Charbonnier, *Le monologue du peintre: Entretien avec Georges Braque* (Paris, 1959), pp. 10-11, cited in B. Zurcher, *Georges Braque: Life and Work*, trans. S. Nye (New York, 1988), p. 154.

Cat. No. 34
1. On O'Keeffe's career, see J. G. Castro, *The Art and Life of Georgia O'Keeffe* (New York, 1985); C. C. Eldredge, *Georgia O'Keeffe* (New York, 1991); L. Goodrich and D. Bry, *Georgia O'Keeffe*, exh. cat. (Whitney Museum of American Art, New York, 1970).
2. On Dow, see F. C. Moffatt, *Arthur Wesley Dow (1857-1922)*, exh. cat. (National Collection of Fine Arts, Smithsonian Institution, Washington, D.C., 1977); N. E. Green, *Arthur Wesley Dow and His Influence*, exh. cat. (Herbert F. Johnson Museum of Art, Ithaca, N.Y., 1990).
3. "Georgia O'Keeffe. An American Place" (1932), p. 9.
4. On the series, see esp. Eldredge (note 1), pp. 119-41.
5. Goodrich and Bry (note 1), pp. 17-18.

Cat. No. 35
1. A. de Haas, "Academy Art Exhibition Closes," *Public Ledger* (March 30, 1924), p. 16, cited in B. A. Wolanin, *Arthur B. Carles (1882-1952): Painting with Color*, exh. cat. (Pennsylvania Academy of the Fine Arts, Philadelphia; 1983), p. 15. On Carles's life and career, see also H. G. Gardiner, "Arthur B. Carles: A Critical and Biographical Study," *Philadelphia Museum of Art Bulletin* 64, nos. 302-3 (January-June 1970), pp. 139-84.
2. Carles to Hugh Breckenridge, 1052:268, Archives of American Art, Washington, D.C., cited in Wolanin (note 1), p. 96.
3. Quoted by Hugh Breckenridge in G. L. Carr, "Hugh Henry Breckenridge, Philadelphia Modernist," *American Art Review* 4 (May 1978), p. 98, cited in Wolanin (note 1), p. 139.

Cat. No. 36
1. K. E. Silver, *Esprit de Corps: The Art of the Parisian Avant-Garde and the First World War, 1914-1925* (Princeton, N.J., 1989), esp. pp. 278-80.
2. W. Boeck and J. Sabartés, *Picasso* (New York, 1955), pp. 193-205.
3. Zervos, vol. 8 (1957), nos. 358, 359, 367-69.

Cat. No. 37
1. Adams (1978), pp. 238-78, includes 570 oils in his catalogue raisonné, but the artist's graphic production remains uncatalogued. In addition, Kuhn is known to have destroyed numerous works throughout his career.
2. See M. W. Brown, *The Story of the Armory Show* (New York, 1988).
3. Cited in Adams (1978), p. 50.
4. Cited in B. B. Perlman, *Walt Kuhn 1877-1949*, exh. cat. (Midtown Galleries, New York, 1989), p. 11.
5. Bird (1940), p. 50.
6. A. Louchlin, "Kuhn," *Art News* 45 (November 1946), p. 39.

Cat. No. 38
1. On Avery's career, see A. Breeskin, Introduction, in *Milton Avery*, exh. cat. (National Collection of Fine Arts [Washington, D.C.], Greenwich, Conn., 1969); C. Greenberg, "Milton Avery," *Arts* 32 (December 1957), pp. 40-45.
2. Memorial address delivered January 7, 1965, cited in Haskell (1982), p. 181.
3. Hobbs (1990), pp. 47, 128-29.
4. Haskell (1982), p. 108.

Cat. No. 39

1. Cited in C. Gray, "Walter Murch, Modern Alchemist," *Art in America* 51, no. 3 (June 1963), pp. 83; see also E. W. Watson, "Walter Murch, Painter of the Impossible," *American Artist* 19 (October 1955), pp. 23-27, 62-63.
2. W. Murch, undated note and autobiography, Murch Papers, Archives of American Art, Washington, D.C. (cited in J. Collischan van Wagner, *Walter Murch: Paintings and Drawings*, exh. cat. [Hillwood Art Gallery, Greenvale, N.Y., 1986], p. 7). I am grateful to Dr. van Wagner for information on this painting.
3. Cited in Gray (note 1), p. 84.

Cat. No. 40

1. G. Berg, "Andy: My True Story," *Los Angeles Free Press*, March 17, 1967, p. 3, cited in K. McShine, ed., *Andy Warhol: A Retrospective*, exh. cat. (Museum of Modern Art, New York, 1989), p. 457. In the same catalogue, R. Rosenblum, "Warhol as Art History," pp. 25-37, offers a rich appraisal of Warhol's artistic significance.
2. A. Warhol and P. Hackett, *POPism: The Warhol '60s* (New York, 1980), p. 39. For a succinct description of this movement in New York, see L. R. Lippard, *Pop Art* (New York, 1966), pp. 69-138.
3. G. R. Swenson, "What is Pop Art?: Answers from 8 Painters, I," *Artnews* 62 (November 1963), p. 26.
4. Warhol, cited in McShine (note 1), p. 459.
5. Warhol's works are briefly treated in a still life context in L. L. Cathcart, *American Still Life 1945-1983*, exh. cat. (Contemporary Arts Museum [Houston], New York, 1983), p. 21.
6. Warhol, cited in McShine (note 1), p. 50.
7. Swenson (note 3), p. 60.
8. Quoted in P. Gidal, *Andy Warhol: Films and Paintings* (London, 1971), p. 38, cited in McShine (note 1), p. 53.
9. Swenson (note 3), p. 60. On the series generally, see N. Printz, "Painting Death in America," in *Andy Warhol: Death and Disasters*, exh. cat. (Menil Collection, Houston, 1988), pp. 11-22; R. Crone, *Andy Warhol* (New York, 1970), pp. 29, 55.
10. P. Schjeldahl, "Warhol and Class Content," *Art in America* 75 (May 1987), p. 118.
11. Berg, cited in McShine (note 1), p. 460.
12. On Warhol's "Disasters" as emotional responses to social circumstances, see T. Crow, "Saturday Disasters: Trace and Reference in Early Warhol," *Art in America* 85, no. 5 (May 1987), pp. 129-36.
13. *Andy Warhol: Death and Disasters* (note 9), p. 82.
14. In some early versions (1963), more of the death chamber is visible, including a door on the left and a lighted sign invoking silence. A series of screenprints was also published in 1971 (F. Feldman and J. Schellmann, *Andy Warhol Prints: A Catalogue Raisonné* [New York, 1985], pp. 50-51).
15. On Warhol's technique, see M. Livingston, "Do It Yourself: Notes on Warhol's Techniques," in McShine (note 1), pp. 70-73.

Cat. No. 41

1. The history of the movement is summarized in A. Martin, "Modern Realism is Really Real Modernism: Contemporary Realism in Context," in *Real, Really Real, Superreal*, exh. cat. (San Antonio Museum of Art, 1981), pp. 15-22.
2. Cited in F. Goodyear, "Contemporary Realism: The Challenge of Definition," *American Art Review* 4 (November 1978), p. 55.
3. Interview with C. Ratcliff, in *Janet Fish*, exh. cat. (Robert Miller Gallery, Inc., New York, 1985), no pagination.

4. The varieties of "new realism" are conveniently described by L. Nochlin, "The Flowering of American Realism," in *Real, Really Real, Superreal* (note 1), pp. 25-35.
5. D. Kuspit, "What's Real in Realism," *Art in America* 69 (September 1981), pp. 84-95.
6. Interview with C. Nemser, "Conversation with Janet Fish," *Feminist Art Journal* 5, no. 3 (Fall 1976), p. 6.
7. Ratcliff interview (note 3).
8. Ibid.
9. Fish painted Windex bottles in her earlier serial works "because I thought they were the most obnoxious blue I had ever seen" (Nemser interview [note 6], p. 9). She also noted that "they're made in the shape of women, like so many cleaning products. You always grab them around the waist and squeeze" (Henry [1987], p. 22).
10. *Real, Really Real, Superreal* (note 1), p. 72.
11. Quoted in Krane et al. (1987), p. 130.

LIST OF ARTISTS

Anonymous (Dutch [?], seventeenth century), 56

Anonymous (Dutch [?], eighteenth century), 60

Anonymous (Italian, seventeenth-early
  eighteenth century), 44

Avery, Milton, 120

Bailly, David, 50

Bonnard, Pierre, 98

Braque, Georges, 96, 110

Carles, Arthur B., 114

Chirico, Giorgio de, 100, 104

Dufresne, Charles, 108

Dufy, Raoul, 86

Fish, Janet, 126

Goodwin, Richard La Barre, 80

Gris, Juan, 102

Haberle, John, 82

Harnett, William, 72

Heem, Jan Davidsz. de, 48

Kuhn, Walt, 118

Lathrop, Ida Pulis, 90

Léger, Fernand, 106

Lie, Jonas, 92

Murch, Walter, 122

O'Keeffe, Georgia, 112

Peale, Rubens, 68

Peto, John Frederick, 84

Picasso, Pablo, 116

Pitkin, Elizabeth, 64

Rijn, Rembrandt Harmandsz. van
  (school of), 46

Roesen, Severin, 70

Rousseau, Henri (called Le Douanier), 88

Ruysch, Rachel, 58

Schmidt(?), J. M., 76

Schriek, Otto Marseus van, 54

Sheeler, Charles, 94

Spaendonck, Cornelis van, 62

Vanderlyn, John, Jr,. 66

Vollon, Antoine, 78

Warhol, Andy, 124